WESTMAR COLLEG

Class and Society in Early America

INTERDISCIPLINARY APPROACHES TO HISTORY SERIES
Gerald E. Stearn, editor

Class and Society in Early America

GARY B. NASH
University of California, Los Angeles

PRENTICE-HALL, INC., Englewood Cliffs, New Jersey

C-13-135111-7   P-13-135103-6

Library of Congress Catalog Card Number 71-110436

Printed in the United States of America

Current printing (last number):
10 9 8 7 6 5 4 3 2 1

PRENTICE-HALL INTERNATIONAL, INC., London
PRENTICE-HALL OF AUSTRALIA, PTY. LTD., Sydney
PRENTICE-HALL OF CANADA, LTD., Toronto
PRENTICE-HALL OF INDIA, PRIVATE LIMITED, New Delhi
PRENTICE-HALL OF JAPAN, INC., Tokyo

contents

1

Social Structure and the Interpretation of Colonial American History 1

2

Historical Background 15

3

Traditional Sources and Traditional Interpretations 21

A. SOURCES

1. CADWALLADER COLDEN
   "State of the Province of New York" (1765)   22

2. *American Husbandry* (1775)   23

3. MICHEL-GUILLAUME JEAN DE CRÈVECOEUR
   Letters from an American Farmer (1782)   25

B. INTERPRETATIONS

4. JAMES TRUSLOW ADAMS
   Provincial Society, 1690–1763   27

4

A. SOURCES

Tax Records   51

5. *Tax List, Philadelphia County, Pa.* (1693)   53

6. *Assessor's Return, Chester County, Pa.* (1759)   55

Land Records   57

7. *First Purchasers of Pennsylvania List* (1682)   58

8. *Rent Roll, Sussex County, Del.* (1689)   61

9. *Deed of Property, Philadelphia, Pa.* (1688)   62

Probate Records   63

10. *Will of David Reece, Chester County, Pa.* (1705)   64

11. *Inventory of Estate, Jonathan Dickinson,*
    Philadelphia, Pa. (1723)   65

Census Records   73

12. *Census Report, Suffolk County, Mass.* (1765)   74

B. INTERPRETATIONS

13. BERNARD BARBER
    "Social Stratification"   75

14. NORMAN H. DAWES
    "Titles as Symbols of Prestige in Seventeenth-Century
    New England"   89

15. JACKSON T. MAIN
    "The Economic Class Structure of the North"   100

16. AUBREY C. LAND
    "Economic Base and Social Structure: The Northern
    Chesapeake in the Eighteenth Century"   117

17. JAMES A. HENRETTA
"Economic Development and Social Structure
in Colonial Boston"   133

18. KENNETH LOCKRIDGE
"Land, Population, and the Evolution of New England
Society, 1630–1790"   149

19. JAMES T. LEMON AND GARY B. NASH
"The Distribution of Wealth in Eighteenth-Century
America: A Century of Change in Chester County,
Pennsylvania, 1693–1802"   166

5

Unsolved Problems and New Directions 189

6

Suggestions for Further Reading 195

Index 201

preface

Interdisciplinary Approaches to History is the long title for a new series based on a simple notion: How ideas are transmitted from one discipline (or category of scholarship) to another. Historians, although students of change, are reluctant to experiment with new techniques. And scholars who arrive at fresh conclusions by using new methods on familiar data are often suspect. The new series asks: Does this intellectual commingling seriously change our image of the past, and if not, why not?

Professor Gary Nash's book, *Class and Society in Early America,* is a demonstration in the new techniques of historical inquiry. His Introduction (I. Social Structure and the Interpretation of Colonial American History) indicates the change in tone which new concepts impose upon the familiar past. The basic change, Professor Nash tells us, is in "the study of social rather than institutional questions: the accumulation and distribution of wealth, the extent and rate of vertical and horizontal mobility, the degree of stratification, the social origins of elites . . . the effect of slavery on class structure and consciousness." Vertical mobility, degree of stratification, social origins of elites, class consciousness—new terms not available to traditional historians who relied on "literary" evidence in making "literary" conclusions (III. Traditional Sources and Traditional Interpretations). Voltaire's description of 18th-century English society—like a mug of ale it held "froth at the top and dregs at the bottom, but [was] sound and bright and strong in the middle"— while charming, is inadequate for a new generation of scholars impatient with the benign countenance of inherited historical images.

Polished phrases, known epigrams, discursive memoirs, and boring homilies have proved unpersuasive to a new generation of scholars more deeply involved than many of their predecessors in the issues of their day. Neglected sources—for example, tax, land, probate, and census records—are cataloged and exploited for the first time (IV. A. New Sources and New Interpretations). These new materials or "data" must be assembled and strained through the filter of disciplines already at work on similar, though contemporary, problems. If sociologists have investigated income distribution and the sources of power within a community of our time, the generalizations derived should hold true even if we vary the data. Thus the definitions of "social stratification" of a noted sociologist, Bernard Barber (IV. A. 13), are quoted at length and "borrowed" to shape new facts (IV. A. 5–12). Then, using case studies in class and society in colonial America (IV. B. 14–19), we can observe the *applied* transmission of ideas. "The problem," Professor Nash tells us, "is in making this mass of data, most of it subjective and often contradictory, yield to analysis." After bringing us along, from old certainties to new, though troublesome, directions, Professor Nash summarizes the state of current problems (V) adding a lucid and helpful primer on further reading (VI).

Additional books are forthcoming in the series. They, too, will use the techniques of other disciplines—e.g., psychology, economics, political science, anthropology—and they too will follow the structure so brilliantly implemented here by Professor Nash. Hopefully, the series will realize its purpose by showing the rich fertility of a hybrid imagination.

Gerald Emanuel Stearn

SERIES EDITOR

Class and Society in Early America

1

social structure and the interpretation of colonial american history

All societies, even the oldest and most primitive, have been stratified to some degree. Many sociologists and historians regard this as
proof that social gradations are inevitable. Others argue that societies structure themselves because it is functional to do so. Occupational roles of varying degrees of difficulty and skill must be filled,
and unequal rewards and evaluations accomplish this most effec-
tively. Whether social stratification is inevitable is a question best
left to the sociologist, the cultural anthropologist, or the philosopher. Historians are concerned with understanding *how* and *to
what degree* societies structure themselves and the *effects* of this
layering process on the political, social, economic, and cultural life
of a people. The historian's focus is on change—or process. The
structure of society commands his attention because it is one important variable among many that, properly understood, will help
to explain the meaning of the past and the subtle forces which
transform societies from their past to their present forms.

All students of social structure, whether sociologists or historians,
quickly learn that societies differ in their needs, values, and organi-

zation, and thus evaluate social roles differently. For example, societies involved in extended warfare or temporarily threatened internally or externally may place military men at the top of the social pyramid. During periods of war our national heroes have been military leaders. Other societies, with different needs, confer the greatest prestige and power upon religious leaders, businessmen, politicians, or even intellectuals. John Cotton, a Puritan minister, enjoyed an elevated status in the Massachusetts Bay colony in the 1630's because he served a primary need in a community where men were as much concerned with the disposition of their souls as with the disposition of their land. But in early Virginia, military figures like John Smith and Thomas Dale enjoyed the greatest esteem because the settlers recognized, grudgingly at times, that martial leadership was indispensable to the colony struggling for survival against Indians, wilderness, and internal faction.

The evaluation of social roles, then, varies with time and place. Moreover, once established, status hierarchies rarely remain fixed. Men are continually redefining the worth and importance of roles as the needs of their society change under the impact of technological innovation, economic development, demographic trends, war, ideological movements, and other factors. We know, for example, that in New England the merchant began to displace the clergyman as the central figure in the community in the second half of the seventeenth century. Puritan ministers were still entitled to great respect, and their voices remained resonant in community affairs; but power and prestige gravitated slowly toward men whose commercial activities and accumulating wealth made them increasingly visible and functional in a society with changing needs and aspirations. The status hierarchy also changed in seventeenth-century Virginia. As the wilderness receded and the fight for survival was won, the tobacco planter replaced the military leader at the top of the social scale. The ownership of land and slaves gradually became the criterion of social prominence. Much later, great fortunes would be founded on finance and industry rather than on land. When that occurred, those who had occupied a place near the top of the social ladder in an agricultural society found themselves "merely respectable," displaced by men who had seized upon new and more profitable fields of economic activity. Students of history have become familiar with the concepts of "status decline" and "status anxiety," terms indicative of the amorphous and ever changing nature of social hierarchies.

Thus, though rarely static, social stratification always concerns the rank ordering of individuals according to their social roles. But more is involved than this. The distribution of wealth and power is equally important in the structuring of societies and also varies with time, place, and circumstances. To some degree the hierarchies of wealth, power, and prestige overlap, but each has its own dynamics and each exists semi-independently of the others. Thus, the wealthiest man of the community is not necessarily the most powerful or prestigious. Nor is the social group with the greatest power always the richest. Men like Alexander Hamilton and James Madison enjoyed unusual power and prestige in the early years of American nationhood, but like many other officeholders and political thinkers, they were not notable for their wealth. Similarly, New England clergymen once commanded great respect though their economic leverage was extremely limited. Tavern keepers, on the other hand, often possessed considerable wealth but limited status. And every town had its "gentlemen" whose inherited rank could not disguise their precarious economic position. Nonetheless, a general, if not an absolute, relationship exists between wealth, power, and prestige, especially in small or pre-industrialized societies.

In recent years the study of social structure has commanded more and more attention among historians because of the growing awareness that changes in the social profile of a society often reflect important economic shifts, and often precede and are causally linked to political movements. Social structure has assumed such a significant role in historical analysis that it is no longer possible to write political history, for example, without analyzing the operative social forces silently at work beneath the surface of events. English and European historians have been far more responsive to the interrelationships of social structure and politics than their American counterparts. More than twenty years ago, one prominent English historian, Lawrence Stone, argued that a shift in the distribution of income among the different classes of English society "was the basic cause of the [political] upheavals of the mid-17th century."[1]

[1] "The Anatomy of the Elizabethan Aristocracy," *Economic History Review*, Ser. 1, 18 (1948), 1–53.

Historians have argued vehemently and fruitfully about this proposition ever since; but it is significant that the controversy has not
concerned the *relevance* of changes in the social structure to the
origins of the English Civil War, but rather the precise *nature* of
these social alterations. Similarly, French historians have been
employing demographic and quantitative analyses to show how
changes in the structure of society during the Old Regime created
chronic tensions which eventually found political expression in
the French Revolution. In both English and French history, the
emphasis has been on the linkages between reallocations of socio-
economic power and political change.

American historians have generally been more cautious and less
imaginative in illuminating political history with social analysis.
Nowhere is this more evident than in our thinking about the nature
of eighteenth-century American society and the origins of the
American Revolution. We know that the colonies experienced
impressive population growth and economic development in the
half-century before the Revolution. Between 1713 and 1763 the
population of the five largest colonial towns almost tripled, while
the population of all the colonies expanded fivefold. Never in
American history was the influx of non-English people—in this
case, mostly African, German, and Scotch-Irish—so proportionately
large. During this period imports from England increased in value
from about £300,000 to £2,000,000. The population of African
slaves, another index of economic development in the eighteenth
century, rose from 40,000 to 150,000. Family size and structure also
changed. Unfortunately, we know almost nothing about the effects
of these demographic and economic changes on the structure of
colonial society or the role which this restructuring may have
played in transforming attitudes and values, reshaping political
life, or creating conditions ripe for revolution. Colonial historians
have worked prodigiously to show the impact of England's new
imperial policy during and after the Seven Years' War (1756–1763)
on certain colonial interest groups such as merchants, southern
planters, and New England farmers. Likewise, they have scrutinized
the growth of representative legislative bodies in each of the provinces and have traced the maturation of political leadership and
political ideology. But only in recent years has a new generation of
historians, more acutely attuned to the conceptual models of so-

ciologists and economists, begun to identify the inner sources of
social change by studying social rather than institutional questions:
the accumulation and distribution of wealth, the extent and rate of
vertical and horizontal mobility, the degree of stratification, the
social origins of elites, the changing locus of political and economic
power, the effect of slavery on class structure and consciousness.

That this new mode of analysis has been slow in developing is
mildly surprising because historians have not been inattentive to
class consciousness in the colonial period. Students of American
society have long been aware that Englishmen in the New World
gave close attention to rank, status, and social roles, and that
colonial society, modeling itself on the mother country, was roughly
divided into social and economic groups if not classes. It has often
been pointed out that the theme of social control, which depended
upon a careful differentiation of roles as well as the disciplined
organization of society, permeates early colonial thinking. In Massachusetts, for instance, John Winthrop's plans for social unity and
political stability flowed from his premise that "in all times some
must be rich, some poore, some highe and eminent in power and
dignitie; others meane and in subjeccion."[2] Similarly, in drawing
up plans for his "holy experiment" in Pennsylvania, William Penn
stressed orderly patterns of taking up land, economic regulation,
and firm lines of authority—all of which he assumed would be promoted by the traditional arrangement of social classes. And the
Carolina proprietors planned a highly stylized, almost feudal, pro-
gram of land settlement and government in their attempts to in-
troduce structure and order to their colony. This determination
to combat the disintegrative effects of the New World wilderness
and the individualistic tendencies of land-hungry Englishmen, who
even in the mother country had been threatening to upset the "just
relations among men" in their headlong scramble for wealth and
position, is reflected prominently in the thinking of almost all the
early colonial promoters and planners.

Historians have also agreed that colonial leaders believed that a
system of social gradations and internal subordination was not
only sanctioned by God but was essential to the maintenance of
order, stability, and cohesion, especially in the undisciplined wil-

[2] "A Modell of Christian Charity," 1630, in *Collections of the Massachusetts
Historical Society*, 3rd Ser., 7 (Boston, 1838), 33.

derness of North America. In this sense, the English colonists, particularly in the first stages of settlement, appear at least as status conscious as their contemporaries at home. The care taken to differentiate individuals by dress, by titles, in social etiquette, and even in justice is evidence of this. Puritans in early New England, for example, did not file into church on Sunday mornings and occupy the pews in random fashion. Rather, each was assigned a seat according to his rank in the community. "Dooming the seats," as it was aptly called, was the responsibility of a church committee which used every available yardstick of social respectability—age, parentage, social position, service to the community, and wealth—in drawing up a seating plan for the congregation. A Puritan never entered his church without being reminded where he and each of his fellow worshippers stood in the ranks of the community.

Similarly, the early colonists attached great importance to proper dress. When an individual of low birth or dubious social position garbed himself in apparel associated with the middle or upper class, he not only was accused of "putting on airs," but also was rewarded for his presumptiousness by the wrath of the local magistrates. Several colonies took the trouble to pass laws warning against the wearing of "excess apparel" by common folk. A Massachusetts Act of 1651 declared, "our utter detestation and dislike that men and women of meane Condition should take upon themselves the garb of gentlemen, by wearing gold or silver, lace or buttons, or points at their knees or to walk in bootes or women of the same rancke to weare silke or tiffany horlles or scarfes, which though allowable to persons of greater estates, or more liberal education, yet we cannot but judge it intollerable in persons of such like condition."[3]

Social status was also carefully defined at the earliest colonial colleges where upon entrance each student was given a class rank which defined his social position within the group. Even in justice the seventeenth-century colonist was attentive to the niceties of social ordering. Whipping, the most common punishment meted out by the courts for minor offenses, was not permitted for men of rank in many colonies, though the stripping away of the right to

---

[3] Quoted in Marcus W. Jernegan, *The American Colonies, 1492–1750: A Study of Their Political, Economic, and Social Development* (New York, 1929), pp. 179–80.

use "Mister" before one's name, or "Gentleman" after it, may have been more painful than the lash. If capital punishment were one's fate, he would die according to social rank in several colonies, including Maryland where the law allowed women to be burned at the stake, men of "ordinary rank" to be hanged, drawn, and quartered, and "Lords of the manor" to be beheaded with dignity.

Thus, it is relatively easy to find evidence of traditional English concepts of rank and order crossing the Atlantic with the first settlers. But it is also possible to find evidence that the early settlers rubbed elbows so frequently and faced equally such abrasive conditions in the wilds of British America that they gradually shucked off inherited notions of social hierarchy. In struggling for survival, an aristocratic pedigree often had little practical value. "In Virginia," wrote John Smith, a leader of the first settlement on the Chesapeake Bay, "a plaine Souldier that can use a Pickaxe and spade, is better than five Knights."[4] Evidence supporting the view that attitudes changed markedly in response to the new environment can also be found in the insistent pleas of colonial leaders that men keep their places and hew to traditional social values, supposedly requisite for a stable, well-ordered society. The perceptive student will not search the documentary record very long before realizing that clergymen and political leaders expended a remarkable amount of energy exhorting the people to maintain inherited social customs, ordained by God and proven by the record of civilization. Historians have cited the anxious tone of these colonial jeremiads as strong evidence that many colonists, especially those not at the top of the colonial pyramid, found the old hierarchical notions out of place and out of time. By the same reasoning, one might conclude that the General Court of Massachusetts would not have found it necessary to declare their "utter detestation" at the wearing of gold and silver and silks by the socially inconspicuous if such individuals had not been violating the traditional social code.

Faced with contrary evidence concerning the evolution of early American society, historians have recognized the importance of determining the actual structure of society in its formative years so as to provide a baseline from which to measure the extent and significance of subsequent changes. It will never be possible to re-

---

4 Quoted in Sigmund Diamond, "From Organization to Society: Virginia in the Seventeenth Century," *American Journal of Sociology*, 63 (1958), 457–75.

construct precisely the structure of the earliest American settlements, of course, because data on the social origins and wealth of
their inhabitants is fragmentary at best. But a number of recent
studies of colonial communities provide evidence that only a small
percentage of immigrants were drawn from either the top or the
bottom layers of English society. Though men of the nobility often
invested money in colonizing schemes, they rarely traded the com-
forts of the genteel life in England for the rigors of the "howling
wilderness" in North America. Neither did the abjectly poor or
the criminal come in significant numbers, because years, and often
generations, of poverty had snuffed out the fires of ambition in
these individuals. Those who came were overwhelmingly from the
middle stratum of English society. Farmers, artisans, and small
tradesmen predominated, and the best estimates indicate that at
least half of the early immigrants came as indentured servants
(though this does not mean they were unskilled or unambitious).
If Voltaire's comparison of English society and English ale was
accurate—"froth at the top and dregs at the bottom, but sound and
bright and strong in the middle"[5]—then American colonial society
was fortunate in its initial composition. Further studies of the social
origins of the early settlers will be required before we can lay this
point to rest.

Understanding something of the social composition of early
colonial society, we can ask how life in seventeenth-century British
America affected community structure and the age-old European
concepts of the "natural degrees among men." How did population
growth, economic development, and the "colonial experience" alter
the structure of the immigrant society? One might suspect that
significant changes in social structure and social attitudes occurred
during the years spanning the planting of the first permanent
English settlement at Jamestown in 1607 and the outbreak of the
American Revolution more than 150 years later. Did frontier conditions erode older notions of social arrangement and continue the
leveling process implicit in the recruitment of largely middle-class
immigrants? Or did attitudes ingrained through centuries of ac-
ceptance persist with modifications and find support in trans-
planted institutions and in a trend toward greater stratification

[5] Quoted in Dixon Wecter, *The Saga of American Society* (New York, 1937),
p. 12.

caused by population growth and economic development? Or did the social structure, initially compressed, gradually become more elaborate until the Revolution introduced a new period of social leveling?

Insofar as historians have approached this basic problem, they have disagreed on the extent of change, the quality of change, the timing involved, and most of all on the effect of these changes on institutions, thought, and behavior. Though most colonial historians agree that American society experienced a gradual modification of inherited social beliefs in the early stages of settlement because of the primitive quality of life, the elasticity within classes, and the mobility between them, there is little agreement as to how far this equalizing process advanced and when, if ever, it was reversed. Some historians claim that the leveling of society and a corresponding rise of egalitarian attitudes continued throughout the colonial period, accelerated during the Revolutionary era, and culminated in the Age of Jackson. With land widely available and a shortage of labor guaranteeing high wages to every ambitious man, America quickly nurtured—and maintained—a "middle class" character. Born on the frontier, America assumed a frontier social structure and a corresponding frontier ethos that emphasized mobility, equality, opportunity, and an abiding suspicion of class structures.

Other historians disagree. They point out that while the recruitment of the immigrant population and the crudity of the new environment ensured a rough equality in the early decades of settlement, colonial society began to crystallize after several generations. As population, wealth, and commercial activity increased, society became more layered and men placed greater emphasis upon social gradations. Growth widened the gap between the base and the summit of society, they argue, and promoted the emergence of a genuinely superior class of individuals who assumed a commanding position in social, economic, and political affairs. This emerging elite has sometimes been called a "native aristocracy," although the term is employed without the sociological or legal precision used to describe the upper stratum of contemporary European society. Those who see this "Europeanization" of society admit that colonial America retained a fluidity unmatched in Europe and developed no pervasive class consciousness like that found on the continent. But it is argued that as society matured, social gradations became more pronounced. There emerged a truly wealthy class of planters and merchants whose members aped the English gentry in their political forms and mannerisms, just as they copied them in cultivating the arts and pursuing symbols of respectability—libraries, coaches with liveried servants, powdered wigs, race horses, and the like. Inevitably class consciousness increased with this advancing stratification. This line of argument was strongly advanced by the so-called Progressive school of historians, writing in the first three decades of the twentieth century, and it has been re-argued in the last decade.

Both those who argue that colonial society was characteristically "middle class" on the eve of the Revolution and those who see a movement towards its stratification along European lines imply that social structure and social attitudes are interrelated, moving along parallel paths. Although the connection between structure and values is rarely discussed explicitly, it is commonly assumed that a relatively undifferentiated society produces democratic social values, while a society with a firm system of social gradations perpetuates class consciousness. The possibility that social attitudes can become more equalitarian while the structure of society becomes less so has rarely been considered by historians. Sociologists call this a dysfunctional situation because social attitudes and social structure presumably are operating at cross-purposes rather than in mutual support of each other. It is possible that in extreme cases this kind of dysfunctionalism creates revolutionary tensions. For example, in a society embracing equalitarian values, a hardening of class lines leads to the concentration of social, economic, and political power, and thus stifles ambition and spawns widespread unrest. The social and political instability in the American colonies at the end of the seventeenth century can be explained in these terms. As "room at the top" disappeared, channels of upward mobility became clogged, and ambitious men found themselves checked. It is not surprising that this development of "stasis" in a previously open and dynamic society produced such revolutionary figures as Nathaniel Bacon in Virginia, John Coode in Maryland, Jacob Leisler in New York, and John Culpeper in North Carolina. The insurrections they led in the 1670's and 1680's can be best understood, perhaps, as political expressions of growing frustration with a society becoming less mobile, closing doors to wealth and power once open. Is it possible that these thoroughly middle-class leaders of the late seventeenth century are related in a sociologic sense to middle-class aspirants like John Adams, Patrick Henry, James Otis, and Alexander Hamilton, who three-quarters of a century later found a solution to career problems in a larger revolutionary movement? Several colonial historians have attempted to show that the revolutionary vanguard was composed primarily of members of the colonial middle class, which was strikingly successful in the first half of the eighteenth century, but hard hit by the depression of the 1760's. Carl Bridenbaugh, for example, has written that the economic and social dislocation after the end of the Seven Years' War "stirred up an ominous restlessness, not only concerning the mother country's restrictive attitudes but even more about the gentry who held them in credit bondage and enjoyed all the privileges in society." During the decade preceding the Revolution, it was this broad, ambitious, and now frustrated middle class "that listened to the siren call of a liberty it thought by right it ought to possess."[6]

The extent of disagreement among American historians over the social contours and attitudes of colonial society can be dramatized by inspecting a single colony—Virginia—and comparing the conclusions of three recent scholars who have studied its colonial past. David A. Williams, who has studied political alignments in the eighteenth century, finds that Virginia "exploited slave labor, nearly destroyed its yeoman farmer class, and turned over its government to a planter gentry. Landownership was a prerequisite for voting and essential for political advancement and social prestige, and though many were landowners, government remained a monopoly of the wealthy and well born."[7] Robert E. and B. Katherine Brown, who have pioneered in colonial social analysis by delving deeply into tax lists, wills, deeds, and other local records, reach a different conclusion. In their view, Virginia enjoyed "an open, mobile class structure" before the Revolution. While all men were not of the same status, "social mobility made easy advancement possible for

6 *Cities in Revolt: Urban Life in America, 1743–1776* (New York, 1955), p. 291.
7 "The Virginia Gentry and the Democratic Myth," in Howard H. Quint, Dean Albertson, and Milton Cantor, *Main Problems in American History* (Homewood, Ill., 1968), I, 25.

men with ability and ambition" and "except for slavery and British influence, what now passes in this country as middle-class representative democracy was well-entrenched in the Old Dominion long before the American Revolution."[8] Still another scholar, Gordon R. Wood, has suggested that while there were no clear-cut class or sectional conflicts in Virginia, the gentry class, that ruled politics, was beset by a social crisis that arose from economic difficulties. In a state of incipient decline, perhaps resulting from changes in the structure of the international tobacco trade, the gentry of the Chesapeake colony found in the Revolutionary movement a solution to social strain *within* their class.[9]

Thus modern scholarship has not narrowed the area of disagreement on the structure and values of colonial American society and may, in fact, have broadened it. Certainly the problem is not one of insufficient data. Whether writing fifty years ago or today, historians have always found in personal correspondence, travel accounts, and other documents ample evidence upon which to build an interpretation of colonial society. The problem is in making this mass of data, most of it subjective and often contradictory, yield to analysis. For every Nathaniel Bacon complaining about monopolies of political and economic power, one can find a Governor Berkeley to deny the charges. For every John Adams who saw an aristocratic in-group blocking the way of talented young lawyers like himself, there is a Thomas Hutchinson who saw order and stability threatened in Massachusetts by an excess of social fluidity. Depending upon what evidence is chosen, Philadelphia in the 1750's can be seen as a replica of English society, with a native-grown aristocracy copying English fashions and culture, or as a provincial capital where, as one contemporary writer put it, "the people . . . are generally of the middling Sort, and at present pretty much upon a Level. . . ."[10]

With a gamut of facts and opinions available, each historian has been free to select at will; thus a variety of hypotheses about early American society have been persuasively advanced. As a

[8] *Virginia, 1705–1786: Democracy or Aristocracy?* (East Lansing, Michigan, 1964), pp. 307–8.

[9] "Rhetoric and Reality in the American Revolution," *William and Mary Quarterly*, 3rd Ser., 23 (1966), 3–32.

[10] Rev. Jacob Duche, in *Pennsylvania Journal*, March 25, 1756.

way out of this maze, some historians, most of them working in the last two decades, have attempted a more systematic analysis of the structure of American colonial society. As the following selections will show, they have relied far more upon quantitative measurement and statistical analysis than upon contemporary comments found in public and private documents. They have attempted to develop empirical indices of social change rather than to offer contemporary opinion on it. A new methodology, borrowed primarily from other disciplines, is being devised in order to escape the impasse created by the earlier reliance upon literary evidence.

One of the significant side effects of this kind of analysis has been to throw light on the large mass of lower- and middle-class individuals whose inconspicuous position in society has ordinarily hidden them from the historian's sight. Men who wrote letters, participated in legislative and legal proceedings, published sermons and political pamphlets, or whose names appeared in newspapers and the reports of colonial officials have previously monopolized our attention for two reasons: first, because they were the most visible members of the colonial society, constituting the elite; and second, because they seemed to be the prime movers in the growth of institutions and in the political and intellectual life of the society—areas historians previously have considered of greatest significance. But with the use of new sources—birth, marriage, and death records, census reports, land records, tax lists, probate documents, and the records of local communities—we are learning much more about the quality of life and significance of change within society as a whole —the part of the iceberg beneath the surface.

Students should not be misled into thinking that the new methodology can resolve all the old enigmas or solve all the problems of historical interpretation. Far from it. In some cases historians have advanced statistical calculations only to be attacked by fellow scholars who find their manipulations crude or naive. Often the new approaches seem as subjective as the older ones. Despite the appearance of mathematical precision and scientific objectivity, errors of measurement and method creep as readily into quantitative studies as into nonquantitative studies. More deceptive, interpretations often are advanced on the basis of insufficient data. Not every question regarding the structure of society can be answered by the accumulation and quantification of data. And even those problems that do lend themselves to statistical analysis are often unworkable because of the fragmentary state of seventeenth- and eighteenth-century records.

Despite these qualifications, historical debate clearly is being elevated to a new plane by the use of fresh evidence. Historians are still developing the sophisticated research techniques that ultimately may enable them to chart the transformation of European society in its American setting. American historians have lagged behind European scholars in interdisciplinary studies, only recently embarking on the kind of illuminating analyses that have commanded the European field for a quarter-century. But as the following selections indicate, work now underway promises to deepen our understanding of the direction, degree, and quality of social change in colonial America and the relationship of these changes to other aspects of early American history.

2

historical background

As suggested in the preceding pages, generations of historians have probed the roots of our society in their search for the meaning of the American experience. Though the focus of their inquiries and the modes of their analyses have changed frequently, questions concerning class structure and class consciousness have long concerned them. Before studying the development of new approaches to these important problems, a short and suggestive interpretation of the "colonial experience" may aid the student.

By the beginning of the eighteenth century, the twelve English colonies in America, stretching from North Carolina to Maine, had a combined population of about 250,000, including some 28,000 black slaves and a lesser number of Indians living within or near the white settlements. Most of the colonies had endured a variety of problems in the first years—undercapitalization, periods of starvation, conflict with the Indians, social and religious tension, political instability, and periodic friction between and within colonies. Still, the colonists had thrived, at least in an economic sense: the land proved bountiful, trade with the mother country and with her colonies in the West Indies expanded rapidly, and the institutional framework of organized society took shape, crystallizing and slowly gaining strength. By the end of the seventeenth century, men could take satisfaction in the receding forests, the small but thriving colonial ports, the establishment of churches and agencies of local government, and the growing strength and sophistication of provincial legislatures.

The success of the American colonist in mastering his physical environment and in recreating in modified form the institutional apparatus of English life cannot disguise the fact that the New World settler was no stranger to social and political unrest, much of which can be understood in terms of an underlying tension between the individual and the community. Many Englishmen had supposed they were going to America to build new social organizations, suffused with the spirit of community. But others, confronting a new land where resources were abundant, the land sparsely settled, and English traditions remote, saw release from the restraining bonds of civil and religious authority as the promise of the New World. It was the centrifugal forces that were destined to prevail as the colonies developed: colonial churches proliferated, political power devolved to its local sources, covenanted communities lost their exclusivity, and economic monopolies failed. Inevitably these trends engendered litigiousness and factionalism as men and groups contended for a place in the new order of things.

The last quarter of the seventeenth century seems to have been a period of unusual stress in colonial America. The threat of Indian attack reached a peak in 1675 when tribes from New England to the Carolinas fell upon the English settlements. In addition, difficulties in the mother country had reverberations in the colonies. Beset internally by political revolution and entangled in disruptive and costly wars with France, England pressed programs of colonial reorganization that threatened some elements of local and provincial government, rendered land titles insecure, imposed unpopular governors in several colonies, and tightened economic restrictions for the North American settlers. To all of this can be added the atomizing effect of aggressive individualism, seen in its least attractive forms in the ruthless slaughter of the Indian, in the expansion of a harsh system of chattel slavery, and in the incessant jousting for place and position that often made of colonial politics a disordered and disorderly game.

Thus, life for the early American was both promising and precarious. The colonist possessed an unusual degree of freedom in contrast to his seventeenth-century contemporaries in Europe. Land was readily available, enough so to guarantee a voice in government to a majority of adult white males. The pursuit of material gain was relatively unhindered, especially after the conservative values held by early New England leaders began to erode. In most aspects of life, the Englishman in America worked himself free of the restraining devices of corporate society and regarded his release from the forces of authority as only fitting. As the Quaker colonizer William Penn put it: "are wee come 3000 miles into a Desart of orig[inal] wild people as well as wild Beasts . . . to have only the same priviledges wee had at home?"[1]

On the other hand, life in early American society was often precarious, sometimes tumultuous, and frequently violent. Though much has been written of social deference and political acquiescence, there is much evidence to indicate that duly constituted authority was opposed frequently, vociferously, and sometimes violently. Outbreaks of disorder punctuated the last quarter of the seventeenth century, toppling established governments in Massachusetts, New York, Maryland, Virginia, and North Carolina. In other colonies, existing authorities governed uneasily. The use of force was endemic to colonial life, and in areas where the machinery of government had not yet been firmly established, violence sometimes became the customary means of problem solving.

In the first half of the eighteenth century, all the colonies experienced an acceleration in the rate of growth, the result of a somewhat increased birth rate and a substantially decreased death rate compared with Europe, and the rapid influx of African slaves and Scotch-Irish and German immigrants following the wars of Louis XIV in 1713. Where 250,000 had called themselves colonial settlers in 1700, 1,600,000 did by 1760. Boston, which ranked first among the colonial towns in 1700 with 6,700 inhabitants, had grown to 20,000 on the eve of the Revolution. New York, Philadelphia, Charleston, and other seaboard cities also tripled in size. During the same period the slave trade expanded so rapidly that the ratio of Negro slaves to the total population grew from

[1] Quoted in Gary B. Nash, *Quakers and Politics, Pennsylvania, 1681–1726* (Princeton, 1968), p. 162.

about 8 percent in 1690 to more than 21 percent in 1770, with blacks outnumbering whites by as much as two to one in some areas of the southern colonies. Perhaps never in our history has the population been so diverse as on the eve of the Revolution, when fewer than half of the inhabitants of British America, so far as we can estimate, were of English parentage.

Just as the first half of the eighteenth century marked a minor population explosion, it also represented an era of economic take-off. The economy retained its agricultural base, as it would throughout the colonial period, but the rise in productivity and the sharp increase in per capita imports of finished goods from England (from £344,000 in 1700 to £2,612,000 in 1760) testify to a period of unusually rapid growth. Agricultural production showed particularly impressive gains in the period from 1720 to 1760, reflecting not only the natural growth attributable to population increases but also the expansion of capital investment from abroad, further development of overseas markets, favorable natural conditions, and what one contemporary commentator called, the "restless energy" of the people.

While agricultural conditions remained bright throughout most of the pre-revolutionary era, the rapid growth and commercialization of the economy and the related growth of the seaboard towns may have left wealth less evenly distributed, society more layered, the poor more numerous and vulnerable, and power more consolidated in the hands of those in the upper stratum than at any previous time. One colonial writer stated before the Revolution that "you may depend upon it that this is one of the best poor man's Country in the World."[2] But we know that, beginning in the 1740's, the poor lists were swelling in the cities. "It is remarkable what an increase of the number of Beggars there is about this town this winter," wrote a Philadelphian in 1748. And the £900 allocated for the relief of the poor in Charleston, South Carolina in 1743 had multiplied to £6,000 seventeen years later.[3]

Certainly the embryonic provincial aristocracies of the seventeenth century had clearer definition by mid-eighteenth century. In all of the colonial capitals the wealthy modeled themselves after the

[2] Quoted in Carl N. Degler, *Out of Our Past: The Forces That Shaped Modern America* (New York, 1959), pp. 45–46.
[3] Bridenbaugh, *Cities in Revolt,* pp. 123, 126.

English upper class, carefully cultivating the arts and indulging in a life-style that differentiated them from the laboring and middle classes. To some degree this may have clarified the channels of political and social authority and lessened tension and social instability; but we cannot be sure about this. What does seem clear is that a consolidation of economic and political power was taking place and that the emergent elites, in their quest for power in each colony, were not timid about pitting themselves against royal governors and imperial bureaucrats.

What can be said about American society on the eve of the Revolution? Certainly it had become more than a mere extension of English society. The colonies had begun to assume their own contours, their own configurations, their own distinct social appearance, ideology, and institutions—all inherited at first from England, but gradually modified and subtly transformed after more than a century in the New World setting. Any attempt to portray the colonies as unified and homogeneous would be misguided. For instance, we find striking variations between tidewater and frontier, New England and the Carolinas, commercialized urban places and rural towns. Of course the colonies were not without their common elements. Everywhere colonial Americans exercised a large degree of political autonomy, and attempts to extend imperial control in the late seventeenth century were not notably successful. In the eighteenth century, the ambitious lower house legislatures steadily accumulated power, prestige, and experience, chipping away at the powers of royal or proprietary governors in the process. The opportunity for the common man to engage in politics was fairly widespread, since in a land-rich country most men could acquire the small acreage required for the franchise. In fact, political opportunity was more extensive than the desire to use it, because most men realized that the real issues in colonial society pivoted on the ability to hedge and restrain the power of the royal governors and other appointed officials of the Crown. Men were interested in power, but power of a negative sort: rather than the power to control government, the average settler was interested in the power to prohibit government from controlling him. He was fond of his freedom, impatient of authority, especially when exercised from afar, and jealous of his rights to pursue his own fortunes as undisturbed by the forces of authority as possible. As one British travel-

ler in the colonies put it about a decade before the Revolution, the
colonists "are haughty and jealous of their liberties, impatient of
restraint, and can scarcely bear the thought of being controlled by
any superior power."[4] Though they had not yet learned to think in
national terms, colonial Americans had developed ideas, values,
institutions, life-styles, and outlooks that distinguished them from
their fellow Englishmen at home.

[4] Quoted in Degler, *Out of Our Past,* p. 66.

3

---

traditional sources and traditional interpretations

Until recently, historians of colonial America have relied almost exclusively upon literary evidence in describing the contours of eighteenth-century society. Travel accounts, the reports of provincial governors and English colonial officials, promotional literature (usually written for consumption in England), sermons, diaries, letters, and other personal documents made up the raw stuff of social history. While these sources allowed historians to *describe* colonial society, they could rarely be used to *analyze* its social composition, measure changes in the division of wealth, trace the formation of economic groups, or chart patterns of mobility. Even those historians who portrayed the history of early America as a clash between social classes were forced by the limitations of their evidence merely to divide colonial society into social categories and to infer that these groups were fixed in size, strength, and status. Carl Becker's *The History of Political Parties in the Province of New York*, published in 1909, is a classic formulation of this "class conflict" interpretation of eighteenth-century American history. In the opening chapter, devoted to the period from 1700 to 1769,

21

Becker attempts to link the development of an aristocratic form of politics to the stratified nature of society. But restricted to literary evidence, Becker could not go beyond this assertion of class division to describe movement within and between classes or to specify the effect of seven decades of population growth and economic development on the class structure.

There have been a few exceptions to this reliance upon non-quantitative sources in the historiography of colonial America. The most conspicuous are two historians of colonial Virginia, Philip A. Bruce and Thomas J. Wertenbaker. In his *Economic History of Virginia in the Seventeenth Century,* published more than seventy years ago, Bruce drew upon land and probate records to sketch the contours of the tobacco-planting Chesapeake society. The chapter entitled "Relative Value of Estates" was a forerunner of modern social and economic analysis. A generation later, in 1922, Wertenbaker published *The Planters of Colonial Virginia.* Using rent rolls, tax lists, deeds, and wills. Wertenbaker gave meaning to what had been regarded previously as inert data outside the range of the historian's concern.

The following selections indicate the kinds of sources traditionally employed by historians in describing the profile of colonial society.

A. SOURCES

1. | CADWALLADER COLDEN
   "State of the Province of New York" (1765)

Cadwallader Colden, lieutenant governor of New York from 1761 to 1776, lived for 56 years in America. Aristocratic, but sensitive to the difficulties of eighteenth-century colonial life, he was known as one of the most versatile men of his day. As merchant, writer, scientist, philosopher, and politician, he towered above most figures in pre-revolutionary America. Colden's own attitudes can be discerned in this description of class structure in New York, included in a report written in 1765 for the Board of Trade, one of the most important cogs in the English imperial system. In describing colonial society, historians have mined the accounts of royal governors and colonial officials like Colden, whose reports to superiors in England were sometimes detailed, often colorful, and almost always subjective in their treatment of the structure and dynamics of English society in the New World. Reprinted from *Collection of the New-York Historical Society,* X (1878), 68–69.

The People of New York are properly Distinguished into different Ranks.

1. The Proprietors of the large Tracts of Land, who include within their claims from 100,000 acres to above one Million of acres under one Grant. Some of these remain in one single Family. Others are, by Devises & Purchases claim'd in common by considerable numbers of Persons.

2. The Gentlemen of the Law make the second class in which properly are included both the Bench & the Bar. Both of them act on the same Principles, & are of the most distinguished Rank in the Policy of the Province.

3. The Merchants make the third class. Many of them have rose suddenly from the lowest Rank of the People to considerable Fortunes, & chiefly by illicit Trade in the last War. They abhor every limitation of Trade and Duty on it, & therefore gladly go into every Measure whereby they hope to have Trade free.

4. In the last Rank may be placed the Farmers and Mechanics. Tho' the Farmers hold their Lands in fee simple, they are as to condition of Life in no way superior to the common Farmers in England; and the Mechanics such only as are necessary in Domestic Life. This last Rank comprehends the bulk of the People, & in them consists the strength of the Province. They are the most usefull and the most Morall, but allwise made the Dupes of the former; and often are ignorantly made their Tools for the worst purposes.

2. | *American Husbandry (1775)*

The following selection is taken from *American Husbandry,* published in London in 1775 as a guide to agricultural life in English America. Many such books and pamphlets were published as promotional tracts to be used in recruiting prospective settlers and investors. In many of these, America was depicted

as a vast horn of plenty, an earthly paradise where economic opportunity was unlimited and poverty unknown. The dangers of
relying upon this kind of evidence for social analysis are obvious.
The excerpt reprinted here describes conditions in Virginia and
Maryland.

In the plantations every man, however low his condition and rank
in life, can obtain on demand, and paying the settled fees, whatever
land he pleases, provided he engages to settle on it in ten years a
certain number of white persons; and when he has got his grant, it is
a freehold to him and his posterity for ever. In this circumstance
nothing can be more different, or in more direct opposition than
the two cases. The wastes in Britain are all private property, generally belonging to men of fortune, who, so far from being ready to
make presents of them to whoever demands them, will scarce be
prevailed on to let them on long leases: but suppose they gave leases
at a trifling rent, they would not build and inclose them, and that is
too great an expence here for a new settler, who could build a handsome house in Virginia for less than a beggarly cottage would cost
in England. Thus therefore there are many essential reasons for
men's preferring the wilds of America to the wastes of Britain, in
relation to the state of the land; and the ease and plenty of living
makes another object highly advantageous in Virginia, but by no
means so in Britain.

The pleasures of being a land owner are so great, and in America
the real advantages so numerous, that it is not to be wondered at
that men are so eager to enjoy [them], that they cross the Atlantic
ocean in order to possess them; nor is it judicious to draw compari-
sons between our British wastes and these, between which there is
no analogy in those essential circumstances that are the foundation
of the great population of America; and at the same time that this
is the case with our waste lands, it is the same with our cultivated
ones which are equally different.

It is true that many of the good farmers in Britain will make
more per cent. for their money than is done in America; but this
singly is not the enquiry: in all the articles of living while the
money is made, the state of the farmer and planter is very different:
the one lives penuriously and with difficulty, the other on comparison riots in plenty; the poorest villager in some of our colonies lives

better than a farmer of 200£. a year in Britain, that is frugal enough to save money. Besides this, what a difference there is between living in one case on their own freehold, and in the other on the grounds of a landlord! But the great point is the advantageous disposition of the savings or other money which a Virginia planter can apply annually to an increase of culture; this is a point deserving the highest attention. . . .

The tobacco planters live more like country gentlemen of fortune than any other settlers in America; all of them are spread about the country, their labour being mostly by slaves, who are left to overseers; and the masters live in a state of emulation with one another in buildings (many of their houses would make no slight figure in the English counties), furniture, wines, dress, diversions, &c. and this to such a degree, that it is rather amazing they should be able to go on with their plantations at all, than they should not make additions to them: such a country life as they lead, in the midst of a profusion of rural sports and diversions, with little to do themselves, and in a climate that seems to create rather than check pleasure, must almost naturally have a strong effect in bringing them to be just planters as foxhunters in England make farmers. To live within compass, and to lay out their savings in an annual addition to their culture, requires in the conduct a fixed and settled economy, and a firm determination not to depart from it, at least till a handsome fortune was made.

3. | MICHEL-GUILLAUME JEAN DE CRÈVECOEUR
Letters from an American Farmer (*1782*)

Michel-Guillaume Jean de Crèvecoeur, a French aristocrat, settled briefly in French Canada in the 1750's before migrating to New York where he established himself as a landowner and farmer in 1759. Crèvecoeur traveled extensively through the colonies in the next two decades, adopting America as his country, and contributing in his *Letters from an American Farmer* a highly romantic description of colonial life. Though not published until 1782, the book apparently describes Crèvecoeur's impressions of American life before the Revolution. Traveling in America and observing Englishmen in their New World habitat was a favorite pastime of European aristocrats and natural scientists. Many published their observations, which have become a favored source of evidence for social historians. Travel accounts, like other forms of literary evidence, present the historian with the difficult, if not impossible, task of determining how much the descriptions tell us about the observer and how much about the observed. The following excerpt is reprinted from an edition published in 1911.

WHAT IS AN AMERICAN

I wish I could be acquainted with the feelings and thoughts which must agitate the heart and present themselves to the mind of an enlightened Englishman, when he first lands on this continent. He must greatly rejoice that he lived at a time to see this fair country discovered and settled; he must necessarily feel a share of national pride, when he views the chain of settlements which embellishes these extended shores. When he says to himself, this is the work of my countrymen, who, when convulsed by factions, afflicted by a variety of miseries and wants, restless and impatient, took refuge here. They brought along with them their national genius, to which they principally owe what liberty they enjoy, and what substance they possess. Here he sees the industry of his native country displayed in a new manner, and traces in their works the embryos of all the arts, sciences, and ingenuity which flourish in Europe. Here he beholds fair cities, substantial villages, extensive fields, an immense country filled with decent houses, good roads, orchards, meadows, and bridges, where an hundred years ago all was wild, woody, and uncultivated! What a train of pleasing ideas this fair spectacle must suggest; it is a prospect which must inspire a good citizen with the most heartfelt pleasure. The difficulty consists in the manner of viewing so extensive a scene. He is arrived on a new continent; a modern society offers itself to his contemplation, different from what he had hitherto seen. It is not composed, as in Europe, of great lords who possess everything, and of a herd of people who have nothing. Here are no aristocratical families, no courts, no kings, no bishops, no ecclesiastical dominion, no invisible power giving to a few a very visible one; no great manufacturers employing thousands, no great refinements of luxury. The rich and the poor are not so far removed from each other as they are in Europe. Some few towns excepted, we are all tillers of the earth, from Nova

Scotia to West Florida. We are a people of cultivators, scattered over an immense territory, communicating with each other by means of good roads and navigable rivers, united by the silken bands of mild government, all respecting the laws, without dreading their power, because they are equitable. We are all animated with the spirit of an industry which is unfettered and unrestrained, because each person works for himself. If he travels through our rural districts he views not the hostile castle, and the haughty mansion, contrasted with the clay-built hut and miserable cabin, where cattle and men help to keep each other warm, and dwell in meanness, smoke, and indigence. A pleasing uniformity of decent competence appears throughout our habitations. The meanest of our log-houses is a dry and comfortable habitation. Lawyer or merchant are the fairest titles our towns afford; that of a farmer is the only appellation of the rural inhabitants of our country. It must take some time ere he can reconcile himself to our dictionary, which is but short in words of dignity, and names of honour. There, on a Sunday, he sees a congregation of respectable farmers and their wives, all clad in neat homespun, well mounted, or riding in their own humble waggons. There is not among them an esquire, saving the unlettered magistrate. There he sees a parson as simple as his flock, a farmer who does not riot on the labour of others. We have no princes, for whom we toil, starve, and bleed: we are the most perfect society now existing in the world. Here man is free as he ought to be; nor is this pleasing equality so transitory as many others are. Many ages will not see the shores of our great lakes replenished with inland nations, nor the unknown bounds of North America entirely peopled. Who can tell how far it extends? Who can tell the millions of men whom it will feed and contain? for no European foot has as yet travelled half the extent of this mighty continent!

B. INTERPRETATIONS

4. | JAMES TRUSLOW ADAMS
   | *Provincial Society, 1690–1763*

One of the most explicit attempts to describe the anatomy of colonial society was contained in James T. Adams's *Provincial Society, 1690–1763* (1927). Already a noted historian and recipient of a Pulitzer Prize for an earlier volume on New England in the colonial period, Adams drew upon a wide range of literary sources in delineating, primarily in non-quantitative terms, the social arrangement of pre-revolutionary society and in tracing the changing role of social groups. In two chapters entitled "Aristocrats" and "The Common Man," Adams attempted to describe the social dynamics of America before the Revolution.

It was not by chance that this attempt at social analysis was at the heart of his book, since *Provincial Society* was one of twelve volumes in the *History of American Life* series, published under the editorial direction of Dixon Ryan Fox and Arthur M. Schlesinger, who intended to give new thrust and interpretive power to American history by utilizing what they termed the "social approach," descriptive of a new genre of analysis which deemphasized conventional political and institutional history and focused upon social change and social process. In 1937, when the series was completed, Schlesinger affirmed that the authors recruited for the project had amply demonstrated their sensitivity to the new social history by exploiting a wide range of sources, including "diaries, personal correspondence, travel accounts, advertisements, pictures, artifacts and other museum objects, books of etiquette, popular songs, cookbooks, works of fiction, scientific publications and a wide variety of ephemera."* As Schlesinger's remarks make clear the authors of the *History of American Life* were attempting to wring answers to new questions from traditional kinds of literary evidence. The following excerpt illustrates the point, though the student should consider the possibility that while he relied primarily on traditional kinds of evidence, Adams was able to capture the essence of colonial society.

From the very beginning of settlement there had been marked social distinctions between the colonists. Those who came as immigrants in every decade differed among themselves in wealth, family position, education and the various means of acquiring and maintaining influence. Although the icing may be said to have been left off the American social cake owing to the fact that none of the titled members of the aristocracy came as permanent residents, that merely created a vacuum in the accustomed social structure which was immediately filled to their own satisfaction by those whose claims or aspirations, buttressed by native ability or acquired capital, enabled them to rise to the top.

* William E. Lingelbach, ed., *Approaches to American Social History* (New York, 1937), 85.

Compared with a later age or even with the England of the later Stuarts, the differences in social classifications were, indeed, slight. Instead of ascending by a multitude of gradations from the plowman or artisan through the yeomanry, several grades of gentry, large county families and a half dozen ranks of nobility to a duke, one climbed from indented servant to the middle gentry, and there one abruptly stopped. There never was an aristocracy, speaking strictly, in the colonies and perhaps never more than a few score at most of genuine aristocrats permanently domiciled there. Nevertheless, the term in its denatured form is a convenient one to use for colonial social figures of a certain type, for what is frequently, and obviously incorrectly, referred to as the colonial aristocracy was something more than a plutocracy. Breeding, learning, length of residence, political control and other factors all combined to establish a social position based upon something more than mere wealth. The fact, however, that the entire population of the colonies, English or foreign and practically without a single exception, were from the middle or lower classes was a social fact of great importance.

The abbreviation of the social scale did not prevent such distinctions as there were being taken with extreme seriousness. "Mr." and "Gent." were insisted upon in life and carved upon the tombstone in death. Place at table, position in the college class room in New England, seating in church, and many other minor matters were regulated with a nicety of regard for social status that was equaled only by the minuteness of the differences upon which it was based. This was probably due to the extreme rarity of the social atmosphere. Frontier existence always tends to obliterate certain aspects of social cleavage. In its simplest form, that of a wilderness which must be subdued by the hand of man and from which a subsistence must somehow be wrung by physical toil, claims of social consideration grounded on conditions existing in the country left behind suffer short shrift. Even the power of money goes under a partial eclipse where money no longer can buy service and where everyone works for himself. The trappings of every sort which in the complex society of the older settlement covered one so comfortably, and perhaps disguised one so conveniently, tend to fall away or be pulled off, and leave one socially naked to the critical eyes of one's fellow pioneers; and one clings to such shreds as may remain.

In the first two generations of settlement along the coast, this frontier tendency toward social denudation had been operative to a considerable extent, but had also been offset to some degree by the strong inherited sense of social stratification which the settlers had brought with them from Europe. Moreover, many of the leaders of the first settlements had been worthy pioneers as well as socially superior to the bulk of the colonists in their respective settlements. In addition, during the earlier part of the seventeenth century the enforced simplicity of life in America prevented to a large extent that flaunting of the advantages of wealth and privilege which is more irritating to the common man than the mere knowledge of their existence.

In a new country the possibilities of making a fortune are by no means commensurate with those of making a living. It might in a sense be true, as Franklin said a half century later, that any man who could bait a hook or pull a trigger could get food in America, but this brought him no nearer to becoming a mercantile magnate or an opulent planter. For that he needed political influence with the authorities, the luck of inherited capital or the always rare ability to acquire it rapidly for himself. For the first, he had in some way to gain access to official circles, which was not easy without some money or social position to begin with. For the last, the way then as always was much easier for those who had some capital to start with than for those who had none. This was obviously true of the increasingly mercantile North, and in the change soon to come over the agricultural South the way to wealth lay through the control of slave labor, and slaves cost money. By the first decade of the eighteenth century, therefore, the possession of money in the older seaboard settlements was becoming more effective, and the differences between the man who started with advantages and the man who did not, more definite and more fixed. On the other hand, the democratic and leveling tendencies of the frontier were also becoming more effective than had been the case earlier because the new frontier was two steps removed from the life of old England instead of one, and because the leaders of colonial life no longer lived among the people there but remained behind in the more comfortable seaboard districts. . . .

At the opening of the eighteenth century two of the professions were in an interesting transition stage with regard to differentiation and social status. Throughout all the colonies it was customary for litigants to be represented in court by attorneys in fact but there was a strong feeling against attorneys at law, not seldom leading to statutes inimical to their pursuing their calling. This was true even in Maryland where they rose to prominence earlier than in any other colony. In 1700, and perhaps down to the Revolution, there was scarcely a single well educated colonial lawyer in all New England or, with a few brilliant exceptions, in New York. In the period covered by this chapter [1690–1763], the Marylander, Andrew Hamilton, who became attorney-general in Pennsylvania and whose later reputation was to become not only intercolonial but international, was first rising into prominence. The Welshman, David Lloyd, was also doing much in the Quaker colony to develop its crude legislation into a system of jurisprudence. At the beginning of the century, however, there was neither large fortune nor high fame to be won at the bar. Consequently that absence of specialization which is characteristic of all colonial life at this period is noticeable here as elsewhere. In Connecticut, for example, attorneys at law seem to have been first authorized in 1708, and such men as Roger Wolcott, Thomas Welles and Edward Bulkeley were admitted to the bar, but Bulkeley's grist and fulling mills were his primary concern, and the law occupied but little of the time of the others. In Virginia, William Fitzhugh had received a professional training in England and practised actively after coming to America, but his wealth and social standing were derived rather from his occupations as merchant, shipper and planter than from his legal work.

The period we are considering was one of transition in the medical profession as in so many other phases of colonial life. In New England it had early been the custom of the clergy to minister to the bodily as well as the spiritual ills of the parish and to apply mustard or hell fire according to the need. To the southward, the owners of large plantations included the care of their slaves, servants and poorer neighbors in their multifarious duties, and everywhere the women of the households practised the simpler forms of physic. Nevertheless, physicians who occupied themselves either mainly or wholly with their profession were becoming numerous. It is notable, however, that most of the leading men were not American born but newcomers from Europe. Thus one of the ablest men who were connected with the profession was Dr. John Mitchell, a member of the Royal Society, who came to Virginia in 1700. Dr. William Douglass, educated at Leyden and Paris, arrived in Boston in 1718. Dr. Cadwallader Colden, educated at Edinburgh, emigrated to Philadelphia a few years earlier, later moving to New York where he had a distinguished career as one of the most intellectual men in the colonies. The French were found practising in many places, and Doctors Porchier of Charleston, South Carolina, Jerauld of Medfield, LeBaron of Plymouth, Massachusetts, Pigneron of Newport, Rhode Island, and Gaudonnet of Newark, New Jersey, were only a few of those practising and teaching their apprentices along the whole seaboard. There were some native-born, however, such as Jared Eliot of Connecticut and Zabdiel Boylston of Massachusetts, who rose to prominence. The fame of both of these lay still somewhat in the future in this period. . . .

Although we still find frequently the combination of the pursuits of clergyman, planter, farmer, lawyer and various political offices such as sheriff with medicine, nevertheless the physician is clearly beginning to emerge as an independent entity and, at least in the case of men who were particularly successful, to occupy a social position of some eminence due solely to success in his profession.

The clergyman had always done so, though his established position varied much in the different colonies, and had been highest in New England. There, indeed, Cotton Mather was beginning to note mournfully how times had changed since the people used to regard their ministers as "Angels of God" and how reverently they had formerly wished to have them provided for. At the end of the century he was right in believing that conditions were altering and that many things had combined to lower the prestige enjoyed by the clergy. In the South, although there were, of course, many earnest men in the church, nevertheless, it was too often considered in England that an inferior type was good enough to send out to the colonies, and in many a parish the cloth received no more respect than it deserved. In the Puritan colonies of the North, the first fervor of religious enthusiasm had long since evaporated, and the growth of other interests tended to dislodge the ministers from the remarkable position of leadership which they had occupied. It must be confessed, moreover, that in the latter portion of the century they had lamentably failed in the trust accorded them, and by their attitude at the time of the Baptist and Quaker persecutions and the witchcraft delusion, they had lost enormously in influence. In the earlier decades of settlement, the earnest and more or less intellectually inclined New Englander who aspired to be a leader in the community naturally turned to the pulpit as the seat of power. With the broadening and secularizing of the public mind, however, and the alluring opportunities for the acquisition of wealth, men of marked ability tended more and more to remain in secular life and to devote themselves to business pursuits or to the nascent professions. As yet politics, other than royal officeholding, offered no separate career. . . .

In all the colonies, land and ever more land was the goal of those who wished to advance in the most rapid way possible both their financial and social position. For this, influence in the right quarter was absolutely essential. It is a mistake to think that large landholdings were common only in the colonies from New York southward and that all the corruption was in royal officials. . . .

For the acquisition of a rapid fortune in land merely by standing well with the powers that be, New York offered a rich field. Among Governor [Benjamin] Fletcher's grants, for example, was one to his favorite and right hand man, Captain John Evans, of an area of indeterminate extent of between three hundred and fifty and six hundred thousand acres, at a quitrent of only twenty shillings a year for the whole, for which Evans alleged he was later offered £10,000 in England. [Governor] Bellomont indeed asserted that nearly three quarters of the available land in the province had been granted to about thirty persons, many of poor character, before Fletcher finished. Lord Cornbury's grants while governor from 1702 to 1708 were equally extravagant but were made to companies of speculators rather than to individuals. They included such grants as that of the "Little Nine Partners" of ninety thousand nine hundred acres, Wawayanda of three hundred and fifty-six thousand, and Great Hardenburgh of two million acres, and were so loosely worded that sometimes the original intention as it appeared was so stretched as to result in claims of a hundred times the original acreage. [Governor Cadwallader] Colden cites one ostensibly for three hundred acres under which sixty thousand were claimed later. In the Southern colonies, more particularly Maryland and Virginia, political influence resulted in enormous grants to favored individuals, such as sixty thousand acres to Charles Carroll, and there were large grants in Carolina, in addition to the "Baronies," of twelve thousand acres each. The same influence which secured the grants also resulted in many cases in evading completely the payment of quitrents.

As has already been said, access to official society was a prerequuisite to the securing of this influence, and as that society was comparatively limited, intermarriage among its members became increasingly frequent and everywhere added its weight to the building up of local aristocracies of wealth. The financial standing of their members thus increasing also enabled them to strengthen their position as merchants. In all the colonies, the councils were almost wholly made up of the members of these small aristocracies, or plutocracies, and as the suffrage was very limited, their influence extended to the assemblies as well. By means of their large land holdings, their possession of a considerable portion of the cash capital of America, their position as merchant creditors of the smaller people, their control of the councils, and their privileged situation with regard to the dispensers of patronage and favors, as well as the more intangible influences always appertaining to a distinguished social position, the aristocrats by 1700 were fastening a firm grip both upon the political management and commercial exploitation of the New World. . . .

Although the group [of aristocrats] exerted great influence, it was, numerically, a small one compared with the total population. Economically, societies are always like a pyramid, and the mass of men at the opening of the eighteenth century was composed of those who had made only a moderate success or none at all in the art and practice of living. Outside the select group of the mercantile and landed "aristocracy" were the smaller merchants, shopkeepers, farmers, planters, artisans, mechanics, pioneers, fishermen, free day laborers, indented servants and slaves.

Although the "gentlemen" drew sharp distinctions, not seldom legal, between these smaller fry and themselves they could hardly be accused of snobbishness by the farmers, tradesmen and others who in turn insisted just as rigidly upon distinctions among themselves. In fact, perhaps snobbishness has never been more rampant anywhere in America than it was in the small Puritan villages of New England, where it received an added and ugly twist of Pharisaism.

This came out most clearly in the meticulous measurement of the personal and social qualifications of every member of a congregation before he or she could be assigned a sitting in church. Age, estate, "place and qualification," were weighed with the utmost care to determine the conflicting claims to precedence of the various small farmers who made up the bulk of every rural village. Infinite were the rulings giving each seat its specific social rank, such as that the "fore seat in the front gallery shall be equall in dignity with the second seat in the body," the front seats in the gallery with the fourth seats in the body, and so forth, as was painstakingly worked out in Deerfield even while facing annihilation by the Indians. Not infrequently the settlement of such vexed questions, when disputed, was referred to the town meeting for decision. On the other hand, within the households of the tradesmen or small farmers there was little of that distinction between master and man or mistress and maid which developed later. Indeed, when crossing Connecticut, Madam [Sarah] Knight was somewhat scandalized to find the farmers were equally indulgent to the negro slaves, "permitting them to sit at table and eat with them, (as they say to save time), and into the dish goes the black hoof as freely as the white hand."

Immediately below the "aristocrats" . . . were the richer town merchants or planters who had not yet fully arrived in a social sense but whose wealth and general position placed them between those above them and the smaller people of the descending economic scale. There was nothing essentially characteristic of them as a class, setting them off from others, and this chapter is concerned with those still lower for whom the New World offered special opportunities, and with those lower yet for whom it offered none.

Although luxury, of course, was limited to the wealthy, there was ample comfort for those who were able to do moderately well for themselves. The small shopkeeper or tradesman of the towns and the farmer or planter of the rural districts were well housed, clothed and fed. As was pointed out in the last chapter, their houses differed as yet in little but size from those of the ranks above them. The materials of which they were built were, in most colonies, the same, although from 1700 there tended to be a distinction in the South, as we have noted. Within, of course, there was a noticeable difference. Pictures were naturally absent from the walls of the more modest homes. The several fireplaces of the rich were represented by the one great one in the poor man's kitchen. Although occasionally pieces of furniture might be found that had crossed the ocean, most, when not all, of the furnishing was colonial-made, if not, indeed, made by the owner himself and his family.

In fact such a household, particularly in the country, was self-sustaining to a remarkable degree. A few things, like the iron pots in the kitchen, the pieces of pewter—if the household boasted of them—the materials for the best clothes, a few of the necessities for the table, such as salt, came from outside but otherwise almost every article consumed or worn was the produce of the farm or the immediate neighborhood. The beef and bacon came from the owner's cows and hogs, slaughtered in the fall and salted down. The former also supplied his leather. The wool, which the women of the household carded and wove and spun, was from the sheep of his own fields. The cider was pressed from his own apples. The winter's fuel was from the woods of his own woodlots or the village commons. The candles were made from tallow, produce of the farm, or from bayberries gathered by the children. The clothes worn by the entire household were frequently made by the women and even sometimes by the men. During the long days of winter, the men and boys fashioned the wooden farm implements, made innumerable utensils for the kitchen or built and carved and painted the beds, chests and chairs which slowly filled the rooms and added to comfort. . . .

Almost all, except the very poor, in the older portions of the colonies, seem to have had at least one slave, indented servant or the "help" of the daughter of some neighbor. There was little if any stigma attaching to such a position as the last under the conditions of the time, and the unmarried girls of fairly good families frequently went out to service. In this grade of society, although woman's work in the house was heavier than for the wives of the aristocrats, she had rather more freedom of occupation, and there are not a few instances at the beginning of the century, rapidly increasing as it advanced, of women in various lines of small business, more particularly as shopkeepers, petty merchants and innkeepers.

The clothing of this class was in marked contrast to that of their wealthy neighbors. With the exception of a better suit for church or other high occasions, it was mostly made of coarse heavy clothes, such as "ozenbrig" which we find constantly in use throughout the whole eighteenth century. The skins of animals, particularly deer, were much used as furs and as tanned leather. Leather breeches, indeed, sometimes adorned even the legs of ministers in New England for their rougher work. . . . The stockings were heavy woolens and were worn to the knee as a rule, but in summer both these and shoes were discarded even by men and women throughout the rural sections. In Pennsylvania . . . they could be worn only in the evening, and by day the only costume of the men was a shirt and "thin long pantaloons which reach down to the feet." . . .

Farther out on the frontier of all the colonies conditions of every sort were, of course, much more primitive, even the costume changed and the use of the Indian hunting shirt was general. Indeed, in the later years of the Indian wars many of the younger pioneers adopted more of the native dress, making the leggings longer so as to reach over the thigh and replacing drawers with the Indian breechclout. On account of their costume the frontiersmen were called "buckskins" and it is a fact of no little significance regarding the relations between tidewater and frontier that the residents of the former used the term as one of obloquy.

The first shelters erected by the frontiersmen were merely temporary and need not be described, but the permanent homes were log cabins, usually about sixteen feet by twenty, and when done by community labor took only two or three days to build. The type scarcely varied either in different localities or decades, and William Byrd has described it for us in southern Virginia at the time of surveying the boundary line between that colony and North Carolina in 1728. "Most of the Houses of this Part of the Country," he wrote, "are Log-Houses covered with Pine or Cypress Shingles, 3 feet long and one broad. They are hung upon Laths with Peggs, and their doors too turn upon wooden Hinges, and have wooden Locks to secure them, so that the building is finished without Nails or other Iron-Work." In most places the shingles would have been considered luxurious, the chinks between the logs being filled only with mud and moss and plastered over with clay. The doors and windows were sawed out after the logs were laid, and there was no glass for the latter. When there was any covering at all for the windows, other than solid shutters, it was paper smeared with hog's lard or bear's grease. Light in the evenings came only from the blaze on the hearth or from pine knots which served as candles. . . .

To return to the settlements, we have still to consider those there who ranked below the shopkeepers, small farmers and others who had achieved a certain amount of capital and independence. Although we now have available a dozen or more careful studies of the indented servant and slave in the colonial period, no thorough examination has yet been made of the position and numbers of the free whites of the wage-earning class, and it is therefore difficult to estimate their importance. In the aggregate, however, the group must have been fairly large. For one thing, few indented servants or slaves were employed as sailors, perhaps because the chance of escape was too great, and the sailors who manned the many hundreds of little vessels engaged even by 1713 in colonial commerce must have numbered many thousands. A contemporary estimate places those of the ports of Salem and Boston in 1717 at over thirty-five hundred. Closely allied to these were the fishermen who served on the New England fishing fleet. These, perhaps, were not strictly speaking wage-earners, but nevertheless they had no capital in the enterprise. A boat's crew usually consisted of three men and the master, the crew receiving the value of one-half the catch, amounting sometimes to £8 or £9 a man for the voyage, of which three were generally made in a season to the banks. The smaller boats for the nearby fishing, of course, made frequent trips, staying out until full in summer or only for the day in winter. Whether justly or not, the moral character of the fishermen of the time was considered very low, and most of the money they made was probably spent quickly.

On shore almost every observer agrees as to the scarcity of free white labor. Nevertheless in the older settled portions of the colonies there must have been a considerable number of those who had to work for wages and yet who did not wish to sell themselves as indented servants for a term of years. In the town of Newbury, Massachusetts, for example, the interesting list of heads of families . . . shows that, out of two hundred and sixty-nine, twenty-seven possessed no land, and of these one had only one cow, one had two cows and a third had a horse. The remaining twenty-four had no property of any kind. Ten per cent of the heads of families in that village must therefore have been wage-earners and to these may be added such younger members of their households as were not serving as apprentices. Mere reference to artisans of various sorts means nothing in this connection for they may have been either indented servants or free, but other references indicate that however scarce such wage-earners may have been they, nevertheless, were everywhere present.

It may well have been that such a class was not recruited to any great extent from immigration at the opening of the century, but it must have received more or less constant accretions both from above and below in the colonial population. Contemporary observers agree that there was comparatively little extreme poverty in any of the colonies at this time, but the occasional laws for the relief of debtors, the frequent ones regarding poor relief, and the constantly expressed fear lest the poor become heavy charges on the communities, all indicate that there was more or less poverty in spite of optimistic descriptions. The obstacles thrown in the way of the poor taking up residence in a town, so that they might not become entitled to poor relief, must have tended to sink them lower where they had already begun to fall. Certainly all poverty was not limited to the frontier, and as an example of what might be found even on the Boston Post Road we have a description by Madam Knight of a household near the Pawcatuck River. The building was made "with Clapboards, laid in Lengthways, and so much asunder, that the Light came throu' everywhere; the doors tyed with a cord in the place of hinges; the floar the bear earth; no windows but such as the thin covering afforded, nor any furniture but a Bedd . . . an earthen Cupp, a small pewter Bason, A bord with sticks to stand on, instead of a table and a block or two in the corner instead of chairs." Yet these were not shiftless people for she adds that "bothe the Hutt and its Inhabitants were very clean and tydee: to the crossing of the Old Proverb, that bare walls make giddy Howswifes.". . .

If misfortune or lack of ability thus added recruits to the wage-earning class from above, it must also have been receiving constant accretions from below. . . . The great servant-importing provinces were Pennsylvania, Maryland and Virginia, but the need and desire for such servants in the North were great, and in Massachusetts, in 1710, the legislature passed an act offering a bounty of forty shillings a head to any ship captain who would bring into the colony any male servants from eight to twenty-five years of age. In Maryland, the proportion of indented servants and convict laborers to the entire population seems to have remained fairly constant at about nine per cent, but as the figures for servants include practically no small children whereas these are included in the population figures, the proportion of servants to all adults in the colony would be much greater, perhaps twenty-five per cent. As the average period of servitude was five years, one fifth of the servant class, or five per cent of the total adult population, was passing annually from that status to the one of free whites. Of these, some, for one reason or another, reëntered upon a new period of servitude, and others became land owners but a very large proportion must have become wage-earners. The fifty acres of land which in many of the colonies were given as a "head-right," that is, fifty acres for every servant brought into the colony, inhered in the person importing the servant and not in the servant himself. It is therefore a mistake to think that on completion of his or her term of service the servant at once and automatically entered upon the status of freeholder. The indenture usually called only for clothes, a little ready money, and an axe or hoe. It was, however, not difficult for the new freeman to acquire the fifty acres upon application if he so desired. The instructions to the governors of North Carolina, for example, from 1667 to 1681, required them to grant to freed servants fifty acres, and this was occasionally done as late as 1737. The same instructions were issued to the governor of Virginia and probably complied with. In Maryland the old system of granting the importer of servants the fifty acres per head was abolished in 1683 and thereafter all land was sold, but there seems to have been no case in which the freed servant did not receive the fifty acres if he demanded them. . . .

Beginning with this period, . . . although the servant was gaining in legal rights, he was, speaking broadly, losing in social position. Throughout all the colonies, the increase in wealth and the growing distinctions between those who possessed it and those who did not tended to lower the servant's position as compared with the previous century when all alike were more under the leveling influence of the frontier. In Maryland, the increase in the number of convicts shipped by the British government brought the indented class in general more and more into disrepute, a condition affecting all the colonies to a lesser degree. In those in the South, however, the factor which operated most to lower the position of the white servant, as well as of the white landless wage-earner, was the enormous increase in the number of Negro slaves in that section which began in this period. Up to about 1700 the great majority of the laboring class had undoubtedly been indented servants with a smaller number of free wage-earners on the one hand and Indian or Negro slaves on the other. From that time on the slave for life rapidly tended to displace the indented servant and free white wage-earner in the colonies from Maryland southward and to differentiate that section economically and socially from the North.

With regard to enslaving the Indians, New England had early taken the lead and throughout the colonial period held more Indians in slavery than any of the other colonies except South Carolina, where in 1708 there were fourteen hundred Indian slaves against forty-one hundred Negroes. As late as 1706 Massachusetts provided for the sale of Indian children under twelve years of age taken in war. With the chartering of the Royal African Company in 1672, however, the traffic in blacks had entered upon a more active stage. The greatest demand came from the sugar islands, where the Negroes soon outnumbered the whites several times, and it was probably the very close connection between South Carolina and the West Indies, as well as the nature of its crop, which caused that colony early to become a leader in the use of Negro slave labor. By 1715, with a white population of sixty-two hundred, there were over ten thousand black slaves there, a much more rapid increase than in any other colony. In the same year it is estimated that there were twenty-three thousand Negroes in Virginia with a white population of a little more than seventy-two thousand, and in Maryland, three years earlier, eight thousand Negroes against thirty-eight thousand whites. In succeeding years the proportion of blacks rose rapidly and the type of agricultural labor under Southern conditions thus became definitely determined. . . .

Of the details of the trade, the capture of the blacks in Africa, their purchase by the dealers, and the often described horrors of the passage overseas, there is no need to speak again. Once arrived in the colonies and sold to his new master, the slave found kind or harsh treatment depending more upon the character of the master than upon the laws of the colonies. From the beginning to the present day, and occasionally for the better as well as frequently for worse, it must be recognized that the Negro has never been treated upon a basis of strict legality but according to the dictates of white sentiment. In some respects his position was similar to that of the indented servant. As the colonial system of labor based upon indentures was a development of the apprentice system, so was the system of slavery, in a way, a development of the indenture system, in which servitude was for life instead of for a fixed number of years. Although from one aspect slavery at first differed from white servitude, mainly in the mere extension of its period, the results of this extension were so great as gradually to alter the whole conception of the system and to change fundamentally the legal status and social position of the slave.

This change was marked in the years [from 1690 to 1763] . . . during which, in spite of many cross currents of opinion, slavery began definitely to crystallize into the system of later periods. Although there had been more or less legislation from 1660 onward tending to define and somewhat to alter the status of the Negroes, it was only after they became numerous in proportion to the whites that we can trace the beginnings of the Negro problem, and that was in the first decade of the eighteenth century. Even as late as 1698, although there were many slaves in all the colonies, they were not coming in more rapidly than white servants, and Governor Nicholson of Virginia advised the board of trade that six hundred servants had recently been imported and that four or five hundred Negroes only were expected during the summer. The colonists, however, desired slaves, in the North mainly for house servants, and in the South for field labor also. Moreover, the English government, at the prompting of the merchants, was doing everything possible to encourage the trade, which received an enormous impetus in 1713 by the signing of the Asiento with Spain, giving the English a monopoly of the Spanish colonial slave trade. The New England traders too had been quick to seize upon their opportunity and by the beginning of the eighteenth century the "Guinea trade" was already enriching the merchants of Boston, Newport and other places.

The rapid increase in numbers of the Negroes in the colonies, however, brought some of the disadvantages of the system clearly before the settlers, and there was in consequence more or less difference of opinion as to its desirability. Of most importance was the question of safety. It must be recalled that the Negroes of this period were far from being the good-natured, tractable, often devoted and loyal beings into which, in many cases, they developed after a generation or more of living in America. By 1700 there were many American-born Negroes but those constantly being brought over from Africa were still savages, unable to speak English and naturally rebellious at their new condition. As the numbers increased, the possibility of a general uprising against the whites or of the massacre of white families on isolated plantations was a real one. Even by 1712 in three of the southern counties of Virginia the black outnumbered the white population, and throughout the early eighteenth century there were a number of attempted insurrections in several of the colonies, which kept the whites in terror. Moreover, along the entire border, until the Peace of 1713, there was the menace and often the presence of warfare with the Indians. The various acts passed by one colony and another, in the South as well as the North, during this period, and which were aimed at restricting the importation of additional Negroes undoubtedly had their origin in the fear of their increased numbers. All these laws, however, were disallowed in England as interfering with a lucrative trade, the fostering of which was beginning to be one of the prime commercial concerns of the merchants of the mother country.

On the other hand, in spite of his dangers, the Negro unquestionably filled both an economic and social need of the colonists. The supply of domestic servants, either free or indented, was inadequate. In the South, white labor was not adapted to the cultivation of rice, which was rapidly becoming the leading source of wealth in Carolina. The development of large tobacco plantations depended upon the presence of a correspondingly large labor supply. So long as a planter was limited to tilling the soil himself with the help of only a few others, there was no possibility of rising above the grade of yeoman farmer. Although the economic development of America would have been impossible without the indented servant, nevertheless there were distinct drawbacks to that type. The first year was usually lost to the Southern employer while the newcomer was becoming acclimated. There was also the necessity of an annual turnover of a part of the labor owing to the fulfilling of the term contracted for and the impossibility of replacing the laborers thus lost except by a new importation from England. These conditions made the slave for life appear an attractive asset in spite of his drawbacks. The conflict of opinion on the part of employers is evidenced by the laws to hinder importation, which represented fear, and the continued purchase and demand, which represented economic necessity. . . .

Having thus reviewed some of the main groups of colonial society in a rapidly descending scale, we may inquire what were the possibilities open to the colonist starting in any of these ranks to advance himself above it. The most hopeless position, of course, was that occupied by the slave. Following earlier laws passed in Maryland and Virginia, it was enacted by Massachusetts in 1698, Connecticut and New Jersey in 1704, Pennsylvania and New York in 1706, and South Carolina in 1712, that a child of a slave became himself a slave, thus apparently closing the avenue of escape for the future as well as the present. In the same period new laws were also passed which made manumission more difficult. Moreover, the slave could not legally own any property. Although in practice he was allowed to gather together some personal belongings and occasionally given a patch of ground which he might plant for himself, nevertheless, in spite of rare cases in which he made money enough to buy his freedom from a willing master or was manumitted for other reasons, the odds against this new recruit to civilization were too heavy, and there is no case during this period of a free Negro having achieved anything beyond the position of a wage-earner or the owner of a small farm with, very rarely, a slave of his own.

For the indented servant, the case was very different. He could look forward at the end of a few years to becoming free to work for himself, and practically no social disability seems to have been attached to his former period of servitude, which was merely a contractual relation entered into voluntarily by himself (with the exception of the convicts), usually as a means of defraying the cost of his emigration to America. When his contract time expired, he was therefore in the same position as any other freeman with little or no capital. For such there were ample opportunities depending upon ability and inclination. If he had the luck to have a good master who became interested in him, his progress might be made easy in many ways. In the South, he might often become an overseer and, if industrious and saving, could accumulate enough in a few years to start a small plantation of his own, though an observer in South Carolina said that few did so on account of their shiftlessness. For those with less administrative ability and only their trade or labor to offer, the wages were high and the demand for their services practically unlimited.

Many of the contemporary descriptions must not be taken too literally as they were written for the purpose of inducing immigration and were no more reliable than such literature in our own day. Against such it is well to set the less optimistic utterances of occasional homesick souls. "O these Liars," writes one of these, who says that they described the climate and country only to lure others over. "If I but had wings to fly, I would soon hie myself from hence to Europe, but I dread the tempestuous ocean and the pirates." "Whosoever is well off in Europe better remain there. Here is misery and distress, same as everywhere, and for certain persons and conditions incomparably more than in Europe." The cost of all manufactured articles is high, he says, and the administration of justice speedy and good, "otherwise we have the same old world as in Europe."

On the other hand, wages were three times as high as in England, wrote another, and although this was an exaggeration, the high wages did make the accumulation of a modest property possible for the skillful and industrious. Letters from immigrants to their relatives picture the conditions. "It is a great deal better living here than in England for working people," wrote one. "Poor working people doth live well here as landed men doth live with you thats worth £20 a year. I live a simple life and hath builded a shop, and doth follow weaving of cloth, but I have bought 450 acres of land in the woods." Another, evidently under the influence of the new freedom, wrote that "the farmers or husbandmen live better than lords. If a workman only work for four or five days in a week, he can live grandly. The farmers here pay no tithes or contributions. Whatever they have is free for them alone. They eat the best and sell the worst." Still another wrote that "here is no want of victuals or clothing. Here it is a good Country for you people to come into" and offered to take care of one of his young cousins should he be sent over.

The high wages both for labor and all sorts of craftsmen and artisans, the fishing on shares, the possibilities for the adventurous in the fur trade, positions for the clerically minded in a shop or the office of a merchant, the welcome accorded the country peddler, the small scale on which foreign commerce might be begun—all these and many other ways of beginning modestly with large possibilities made America a land of opportunity for those with energy and industry. It was above all else, however, the chance to secure land that attracted the majority of the immigrants, as it became the ambition of most Americans themselves. This was, perhaps, particularly true of the Germans, and in one list of twenty-nine hundred and twenty-eight adult males passing through England on their way here in 1709, eighteen hundred and thirty-eight were farmers. In another list there were one thousand and eighty-three out of fifteen hundred and ninety-three. In this regard, however, in spite of ample land yet available here and there, the land accumulations of the very rich and the desire on the part of the well-to-do to keep as much in their own hands as possible, were beginning to have their effect on the opportunities for the small man. In local struggles against new methods of the rich engrossers or in the diversions of the streams of migration and settlement, we can trace the beginnings of such effects, although in the next period this struggle was to become sharper, more bitter and more vocal.

In New England the custom had been to grant lands to new groups of settlers who would establish a new town and church, divide among themselves without cost part of the land allotted and retain the remainder in common ownership. From time to time this might be divided again or from it allotments made to newcomers. We have already seen, however, how this system, so favorable to the small man without capital, was being altered by the new policy of granting or selling large tracts to individuals or companies who held them for speculation. In the case of the tract owned by John Reed we have also seen how he tried, and to some extent succeeded, in introducing the English system of long-term leases instead of sales, thus doing away with the freehold so dear to the heart of the New England pioneer. It would be a mistake, however, to give the impression that the very rich formed a separate predatory group attempting to loot the continent, as contrasted with generous or public-spirited classes below them. In 1700, for example, when the little farming town of Hatfield in Massachusetts decided to open more land for new homesteaders, the older proprietors violently opposed giving up any of the undivided commons according to former usage, insisting that the new settlers or the young men of the village who were growing up and starting households of their own, should be required to lease the land and become permanent tenants of the older group of settlers. On this occasion the new men won after a two years' struggle but the episode was symptomatic of more general and bitter agrarian contests which we shall note in the next period.

In New York, the engrossing of enormous tracts permanently retarded the settlement of the province. The dislike of new settlers to becoming mere tenant farmers, the terms on which the speculators offered the lands for settlement, and the growing confusion with regard to titles owing to the loose wording of overlapping grants, all helped to divert to Pennsylvania immigration which otherwise would have poured up the Valley of the Hudson. In Maryland the system which developed of speculating in lands by means of taking out warrants for tracts but not carrying the process so far as to get the grants issued, thus saving the payment of quit-rents, tied up enormous amounts of uncultivated lands. Although Charles Carroll, then agent in control of land affairs, was instructed in 1712 to stop this speculation, the trade continued and reached very large proportions. Not only was the actual amount of land thus covered by these warrants enormous but the committee of the assembly which was appointed to examine into this grievance twenty years later found that, owing to the indefiniteness of the location of some of the warrants, three or four men held options on all the vacant lands on the Potomac between the Monocacy and Susquehanna and back of the Eastern Shore settlements from the Pennsylvania line to Dorchester County.

In Virginia, [Governor] Spotswood said that servants whose terms were finished and who became small farmers settled out on the frontier. About the same time, the council writing to the Board of Trade said that the chief cause why many of the families of older settlers, whose lands were worn out, "as well as great numbers of young people and servants just free," were crossing over to North Carolina was the lack of land to be had on fair terms in Virginia, though they also suggested it was to avoid creditors. As we shall see later, the increase in slave labor was probably another cause, but the inability to get fresh lands well located and on easy terms was undoubtedly an important factor in the emigration. As the older portions of the colonies became more crowded and even the wilderness far beyond the range of settlement became preëmpted by those fortunate or astute enough to secure title, the small man without capital or influence began to feel himself more and more hemmed in and enmeshed in the power of those who had both. Little by little the resentment over the land situation, combined with other factors which one by one came into play as the century advanced, tended to bring classes and sections into sharp alignment, and to create a smouldering fire of resentment on the part of the frontiersmen and frequently the small farmer or landless man of the older settlement against the rich, which was to create a fertile field for propaganda in the days to come.

4

new sources and
new interpretations

Only in the last two decades have scholars resorted to quantitative analyses and new conceptual models in their attempt to define and bring new insights to the functioning of early American society. In most cases the new modes of inquiry have been borrowed from other disciplines where social scientists, especially sociologists, have been developing analytical techniques in order to study contemporary societies. For social historians the resort to new approaches has offered the opportunity to go beyond contemporary opinion, which is subjective by nature, and to make actual measurements of the movement and grouping of people in the colonial past.

As the selection by Bernard Barber indicates, students of contemporary society, initially inspired by Karl Marx's signal work on class and class conflict and Max Weber's explorations of bureaucratic structures, have developed new analytic models that permit them to discover what literary sources rarely disclose: the precise economic and social composition of society; the divisions of wealth, power, and prestige within it; the degree and rate of movement within and between classes or groups, and the pattern of recruitment of economic, political, and professional elites.

Thus social historians are utilizing approaches borrowed from other disciplines in order to ask new questions. And for answers they are working with evidence only occasionally considered by their predecessors. Of course the historian studying the seventeenth or eighteenth century faces a relative scarcity of data, since many of the indices of wealth, class, or status available to the sociologist who probes the mechanisms of contemporary society are unavailable to the student of the past. Census reports, income tax statistics, mortgage records, and the mass of economic data collected today by private enterprise and city, county, state, and federal governments are generally unavailable for the study of early American society. On the other hand, colonial historians are beginning to examine documents that have survived the passage of time—land records, tax lists, probate records, and other materials—with interesting results. What once was regarded as inert, intractable, and hopelessly fragmented data, has gradually assumed an important place in the research of colonial historians.

Several cautionary notes must be added. First, it is far easier to abuse than to use statistics, as most historians who try their hand at quantitative analysis learn sooner or later. Becoming acquainted with sampling techniques and the laws of statistical relevance and error probability is the first step in approaching any data. Second, quantitative analysis and conceptual models drawn from other disciplines dictate no particular interpretation of colonial society. As the reader will see, the area of disagreement among the "new" social historians is broad; in fact the reader may conclude that James T. Adams, though innocent of quantitative analysis and cross-disciplinary approaches, understood the anatomy of colonial society as fully as any of the new practitioners of social history. But at the very least, the past has been reopened to investigation.

The following chapter is divided into two sections, the first giving examples of the new data used by social historians, and the second composed of seven theoretical, empirical, and methodological studies of social structure and class consciousness. The reader may wish to turn first to the articles on pages 75–188 and then return to the examples of new sources upon which these studies are based. Because of space limitations, most citations of source materials and references to the works of other scholars, which support and amplify the arguments, have been omitted from the reprinted articles.

A. SOURCES

Tax records

While tax records are perhaps the most accessible and important source for the study of social structure in colonial America, they are also the most difficult to use. In fact one is tempted to suggest that historians employing tax records in recent years have more often misused than used them.

The first caveat in approaching tax records is to realize that great variations in the manner of levying taxes can be found from colony to colony or from year to year. Most taxes assessed in the American colonies were based on real property, that is, on land and personal possessions; but even within this classification many variations occur. In New Hampshire, for example, taxes were assessed on the estimated income which land and buildings produced. In other colonies, taxes were levied on the assessor's evaluation of land and other real possessions. Because of this lack of uniformity, comparative studies of colonial social structure based on tax data must be made with great caution.

A second characteristic of colonial tax records is that they seldom reflect the real value of property or the full extent of individual estates. Unimproved or marginal land was not usually taxed, and since the wealthy often invested in land for speculative purposes, their actual wealth is understated in contemporary tax records. Slaves, livestock, buildings, tools, and household effects were generally taxed, though variations from province to province are common. Money wealth—income from trade, fees and emoluments, bank credit, notes, bonds, mortgages—was often excluded from assessors' lists, again presenting problems for those who are studying class stratification or the distribution of wealth. It can ordinarily be assumed that tax lists reveal only a portion of the individual's wealth and that a proportionately larger part of the assets of the rich is concealed than of the middling or poor.

Another difficulty in using tax lists rests in identifying the size and composition of the taxpaying segment of the community. Women were excluded, unless they maintained their own households, as in the case of widows. Slaves and indentured servants were not included, although they were often listed and their value sometimes assessed to their masters. Grown sons living at home, apprentices of adult age, and inmates (married artisans or laborers living in houses owned by others) were rarely taxed. Independent adult males without taxable property were customarily listed and assessed a "head tax" or "poll tax." In analyzing the social spectrum, each of these groups needs to be considered.

The following examples indicate some of the problems inherent in tax lists. In the first selection, a fragment of the Philadelphia County tax list of 1693, the total assessed wealth of the taxpayer is listed in the first column and the tax paid in the second. The list is for several streets at the commercial center of Philadelphia. Several of the taxpayers, like Samuel Carpenter and Griffith Jones, were merchants and were apparently assessed not only for land and buildings but also for merchandise in stores and warehouses. One method of using tax lists of this kind to trace changing patterns of stratification or wealth distribution is to divide the list into tenths or fifths according to assessed wealth and then to calculate the fraction of total assessed wealth controlled by each decile or quantile of the taxpaying population, from wealthiest to poorest. This kind of analysis, applied to tax lists over a period of years, will reveal the changing economic leverage of each layer within the community. However, only a detailed knowledge of the particular community and its residents will eliminate flaws in this approach. For example, in the Philadelphia tax list of 1693, the property of Joseph Pidgeon & Company was assessed at £1300. To count Pidgeon among the wealthy of Philadelphia would be an error, however, since he was merely the agent of the New Pennsylvania Company, a joint-stock company of London merchants exporting finished goods for retail in Philadelphia. The assessment of £1300 was for the Company's warehouse, store, merchandise, and property. Thus to include Pidgeon as a taxpayer with assessable property of £1300 would badly skew the stratification pattern of the county. The list is reprinted from the *Pennsylvania Magazine of History and Biography*, 8 (1884), 85–105.

The second example is a fragment of the tax assessor's return for one township of Chester County in 1759. Far more information is available than on the Philadelphia tax list: the amount of land owned and under cultivation, the number of indentured servants and slaves, and data on livestock and mills. In addition, inmates and freemen are listed separately, allowing for a more precise analysis of the social structure. The list is taken from the Shippen Papers, Historical Society of Pennsylvania, Philadelphia, Pa.

5. | *Tax List, Philadelphia County, Pa.* (*1693*)

By Virtue of a law made at Philadelphia by a Gen:ʳˡˡ Assembly held the 15th May 1693

For Granting One penny ℔ pound to King William & Queen Mary &c Wee the Assessors under Written have Taxed and Assessed the Inhabitants the respective Sums following

Samuel Rowland	£100	£ —	8s.	4d.
Peter Sherbone	—	—	6	—
Thomas January	—	—	6	—
Thomas Bud	400	1	13	4
Joseph Kirl	250	1	—	10
Abraham Carpenter	350	1	9	2
Andrew Derickson	800	3	6	8
John Fisher	72	—	6	—
Edward Shippy	200	—	16	8
Patrick Robinson	400	1	13	4
John Cox	50	—	4	2
Henry Flower	150	—	12	6
Arthur Cook	200	—	16	8
Thomas Harding	—	—	6	—
William Coleman	—	—	6	—
Carried over		£13	11	8
Brought from other side		£13	11	8
Thomas Lacey	—	—	6	—
Augustine the Trumpeter	—	—	6	—
Francis Little	30	—	2	6
Fran: Jobson Lott & Land	100	—	8	4
Richard Basnett	150	—	12	6
Richard Whitpains Building	500	2	1	8
Jasper Yates	500	2	1	8
Peregrine Stockdale	—	—	6	—
Francis Jones & Compaʸ	800	3	6	8

John Songhurst	30	—	2	6
Charles Goss	800	3	6	8
John Whitpain	100	—	8	4
James Claypoole	50	—	4	2
Edward Claypoole	100	—	8	4
John Claypoole	100	—	8	4
Griffith Jones Front & Second Str^{t}s	1000	4	3	4
Thomas Parsons	80	—	6	8
Widdow Dean	30	0	2	6
Abraham Hooper	150	0	12	6
John Felles	70	—	5	10
Bentall & Harts Brewhouse	500	2	1	8
Thomas Griffith	50	—	4	2
James Piller	30	—	2	6
W^m. Salsbury	30	—	2	6
John Shippy	—	—	6	—
Sum carried over		£36	09	—
Brought from the other side		£36	09s.	—d.
Joseph Pidgeon & Compa^y	1300	5	8	4
Anthony Burgis	100	—	8	4
Widdow Delaval	250	1	—	10
Thomas Morris	60	—	5	—
Samuel Cart	150	—	12	6
Samuel Carpenter	1300	5	8	4
Samuel Jennings	150	—	12	6
Wid: Eckley	200	—	16	8
Ben: Waller	—	—	6	—
John Fleckny	60	—	5	—
John Philpott	—	—	6	—
John Crapp	80	—	6	8
Hermon Johnson	30	—	2	6
Tho: Hooton & Moth^r	400	1	13	4
John Deplove	200	—	16	8
Thomas Wharton	100	—	8	4
Arthur Holdens	—	—	6	—
Joshua Carpenter	1000	4	3	4
Sam:^{ll} Holt	70	—	5	10

James Wood	—	—	6	—
Jeremiah Price	—	—	6	—
Peter Goit	300	1	5	—
Richard Kees	800	3	6	8
Summ carried over		65	4	10
Brought from other side		£65	4s.	10d.

6. | *Assessor's Return, Chester County, Pa.* (*1759*)

	Land	Sou'd	Servants	Negroes	Ages	Cattle	Horses	Sheep	Mills	£	S	D
Burnett James	200	12	—	—	—	7	4	8	—	1	17	9
Barnard Isaac	160	5	—	1	16	5	2	6	—	1	8	—
Connaly Edward	7	—	—	—	—	2	2	—	—	—	5	—
Carter Jacob Stiller	66	6	—	—	—	3	2	4	—	—	10	—
Carter Joseph	66	—	—	—	—	2	4	—	1	—	13	—
Crage James	50	6	—	—	—	3	2	9	—	—	12	—
Carter Joseph Smith	150	10	—	—	—	4	3	—	—	1	7	—
Cambel John	50	6	—	—	—	2	2	6	—	—	11	—
Chamberlin Joseph	200	—	—	—	—	—	—	—	—	1	7	—
Chamberlin Isaac	141	16	—	—	—	2	2	6	—	1	5	—
Carter Samuel	90	8	—	—	—	2	3	—	—	—	15	—
Caldwell Margrat	100	—	—	—	—	1	—	—	—	—	12	6
Dinge Christopher	120	15	—	—	—	4	3	7	—	1	4	—
Dutton Joseph Mill wright	68	4	—	—	—	1	1	4	—	—	9	9
Darragh John	100	10	—	—	—	2	1	4	—	—	18	—
Dutton Kingsman	6	5	—	—	—	1	1	—	—	—	3	6
Dutton Richard	200	12	1	—	—	5	3	8	—	1	19	—
Eleson Jared	100	6	—	—	—	1	1	—	—	—	14	9
Farra Oliver	—	—	—	—	—	2	1	—	—	—	2	6
Gillieson John	50	—	—	—	—	4	2	—	—	1	Free Man	
Griffith William	150	10	—	—	—	3	2	6	—	1	2	—
Harclay Thomas	100	11	—	—	—	—	—	—	—	—	14	—
Johnson James	—	—	—	—	—	1	1	—	—	—	5	—
Linn Hugh	100	7	—	—	—	4	2	6	—	—	17	6

Name													
Lindsay James	150	10	—	—	—	6	3	12	—	1	9	—
Martin Abraham	200	12	1	—	—	5	3	8	—	1	19	—
Myer Hanry	100	9	—	—	—	3	3	—	—	—	18	3
McCloskey Joseph	130	10	—	—	—	2	2	2	—	1	1	
McMinn John	50	8	—	—	51	—	—	—	—	—	12	—
Noblet William	100	—	—	—	47	4	2	—	—	—	11	9
Peters William	300	20	1	4	36	9	4	14	2	3	13	9
Pike Abraham	29	10	—	—	12	2	2	2	—	—	7	6
Perkins John a house and Garden	—	—	—	—	—	—	—	—	—	—	3	9
Richards Edward	—	—	1	—	30	2	—	6	—	—	7	6
Reed John	—	9	—	—	—	2	1	—	—	—	2	—
Richards Jacob	170	13	—	—	—	6	4	7	—	1	12	9
Richards John	80	—	—	—	—	—	—	—	—	1	Free Man	
Richards Jonathan	130	8	—	—	—	5	1	4	—	1	1	—
Ratten John	100	8	—	—	—	3	2	5	—	—	16	—
Shelley Nathan	—	—	—	—	—	1	—	—	—		Poor	
Smith Richard	100	3	—	—	—	2	1	2	—	—	12	—
Thomson William	100	8	—	—	—	2	2	2	—	—	18	—
Tayler Elizabeth	125	—	—	—	—	—	—	—	1	—	15	—
Withrow Alexander	—	—	—	—	—	2	1	—	—	—	5	—
Withrow William	—	—	—	—	—	2	1		—	—	5	—
Phillip Taylers Children	180	—	—	—	—	—	—	—	—	1	3	—

	Land	Cattle	Horses	£	S	D
INMATES						
John Bean	—	—	—	—	3	6
Samuel Farra	—	1	1	—	5	—
John Farra	—	2	—	—	4	—
Jacob Pike	—	1	1	—	5	—
FREEMEN						
Thomas Johnson				1	—	—
Andrew McMin				1	—	—
Hugh Redden				1	—	—
Thomas Marshall				1	—	—
Rees Peter				1	—	—
John Lindsey				1	—	—

Land records

"God Land will be as great a God with us English as God Gold was with the Spaniard," wrote Roger Williams in 1664.[1] Forty years later, a Quaker magnate in Pennsylvania, James Logan, observed of the colonists that "earth, as 'tis their employment, so 'tis the principal object of their thoughts."[2] As both these colonial leaders noted, the activities and aspirations of Englishmen in America focused on land. Thus records of land distribution, land holding, and land exchange are essential to the study of colonial society.

Records of land allocation and distribution are extensive and are to be found in the town, county, and provincial archives as well as in proprietary records of provinces like Maryland, New York, Pennsylvania, and the Carolinas where property was granted by or leased from proprietors but subject to an annual quitrent. More useful in measuring individual wealth are rent rolls, since they usually specify land warranted and surveyed for actual use, while records of land distribution usually indicate "rights" to land, or land options, which could be taken up, held for speculative purposes, or sold. Another category of land records is deeds and mortgages which enable the historian to trace the transfer of property.

Establishing landholding patterns in the eighteenth century is an enormously complex task, involving a careful sifting and collating of tax lists, land records of all types, and probate records. For example, a study of landholding in Philadelphia in the eighteenth century would require an analysis of extant tax lists, rent rolls, deed books, records of proprietary agencies—the Board of Property, the Proprietary Secretary, and the Surveyor General—and wills and inventories of estate. Work of this sort has been undertaken only in a few cases, usually with the aid of electronic computers. Yet for many areas of colonial America the surviving records are too fragmentary to permit thorough analysis of this kind.

The first document is a small portion of the list of "First Purchasers" of Pennsylvania—Englishmen who bought land from William Penn in 1681 and 1682, even before the colony had been settled. Many never immigrated to America but purchased land only for investment. Later it would be sold by their relatives,

[1] Quoted in Wesley Frank Craven, *Diversity and Unity—Two Themes in American History* (Princeton, 1964), p. 8.
[2] Logan to William Penn, April 5, 1705, Edward Armstrong, ed., *The Correspondence of William Penn and James Logan . . .* (Philadelphia, 1879–80), II, 10–11.

friends, or agents in the colony. The list is published in Samuel Hazard, ed., *Annals of Pennsylvania, from the Discovery of Delaware, 1609–1682* (Philadelphia, 1850), pp. 637–42.

The second example is a small section of William Penn's proprietary rent roll, prepared by Governor John Blackwell in 1689. The original document is in the Penn Papers, Historical Society of Pennsylvania, Phildelphia, Pa. Because the rent roll lists land "taken up" or warranted for use it is far more valuable than the list of land purchasers in studying the actual social differentiation of society. Some landowners are listed several times since they held land in various parts of the county.

The third document, a deed from Peter Dalboe to Reece Preiss in 1688, is a typical legal record of land exchange, useful not only for tracing patterns of land ownership, but also for identifying the occupation of members of the community and charting changes in land values. The document is taken from Deed Book E2–5, pp. 21–23, Department of Records, City Hall, Philadelphia, Pa.

7. | *List of First Purchasers of Pennsylvania* (1682)

An Account of the Lands in Pennsylvania Granted by William Penn, Esqr, Chief Proprietary and Governour of that Province, to Several Purchasers within the Kingdom of England, Ireland, and Scotland, &c:

[1.]		[3.]	
Philip Ford	5,000	Edward Jefferson	1,500
Thomas Rudyard	2,000	Thomas Scot	500
The Same	2,000	John Goodson	500
Harbert Springet	1,500	John Beckley	250
	10,500	Daniel Quare	250
[2.]		John Stringfellow	250
James Claypoole	5,000	Richard Townsend	250
John Moore,		Caleb Pusey	250
Joseph Moore,	1,000	John Hicks	250
Sabian Cole	1,000	Edward Blake	250
Thomas Baker	1,000	William Moore	500
Humphrey South	1,000	Henry Sleighton	250
Samuel Jobson	1,000	John Pusey	250
	10,000	Thomas Virgo	500
		Thomas Burbary	250

John Alington	250
Richard Jordan	250
Samuel Benet	250
Thomas Cobb	250
John Tibbey	250
Elizabeth Shorter	250
Amos Nicholls	250
Jn° Barger	250
Jonathan Stanmore	250
John Spencer	125
Mark Keywton	125
Edward Crow	250
William Bosswell	500
Edward Simkins	250
	9,500

[4.]

Thomas Farnborrow	5,000
Hugh Chamberlaine	5,000
	10,000

[5.]

Nicholas Moore	10,000

[6.]

William Bowman	5,000
Griffith Jones	5,000
	10,000

[7.]

William Kent		1,250
Benjamin East		1,250
Charles Bathurst		1,250
John Toovey		1,250
William Philip, Jos. his son		1,250
Nath¹: Harding	500	is 1,000
Wᵐ. Carter	500	
ffrancis Harrison	250	750
John Carver	500	

John Swift	500	1,000
&		
Wᵐ. Lawrence	500	
		9,000

[8.]

Robert Dimsdale	5,000	7,500
Hugh Lambert	2,500	
Thomas Rudyard	1,000	1,500
Harbert Springet	500	
William Busel		1,000
		10,000

[9.]

William Markham	5,000
Henry Waddy	750
John Day	1,250
ffrancis Clumstead	2,500
William Haige	500
	10,000

[10.]

George Fox	1,250
Alexander Parker	1,000
Robert Lodge	500
John Buryeat	500
Thomas Zachary	500
James Parks	500
Thomas Longhorn	250
Thomas Lawson	250
Christopher Taylor	5,000
A. B.	250
	10,000

[11.]

Wᵐ. Bacon	10,000

[12.]

Nathaniel Allen	2,000

John Hartt	1,000	Joan Dickson	500
Henry Comley	500	James Petre	500
William Smith	500	John Jennet	500
James Wallis	1,000	Roger Drew	500
Richard Coslet	1,000	Edward Erberry	500
Edmund Benet	1,000	William Lane	500
William Smith Mariner	1,000		
Margaret Martindel	1,000		10,000
John Love	1,000		
		[16.]	
	10,000	Edward Martindel	1,000
		Philip Th. Lehnman	1,000
[13.]		Arnold Brown	
Charles Marshall	1,000	William Cole	
Charles Jones		N.	5,000
Charles Jones Junior,	2,000	N.	
Robert Vickris		Peter Young	500
Richard Vickris	2,000	Tho: Bailey	250
John Moon	500	Joel Jelson	250
William Brown	1,000	John Bristow	500
Charch Harford	1,000	Tho: Priggs	500
Richard ·Sneed	1,500	George Keith	500
John Jones		A. B.	500
Michael Jones	1,000		
			10,000
	10,000		
		[17.]	
[14.]		George Powell	500
Richard Marsh	5,000	John Clare	500
The Same	5,000	John Hill	500
		Christopher Forford	500
	10,000	William Beaks	1,000
		Samuel Allen	2,000
[15.]		Walter King	1,000
Thomas Callowhill	5,000	John Passons &	
The Same	500	Abram Hooper	500
Nathaniel Evans	500	Thomas Plaice	250
Thomas Pagget	500	Rich^d. Mills	250
Thomas Paschal	500		

8. | *Rent Roll, Sussex County, Del.* *(1689)*

	acres		
Thomas Hall	450	Henry Bowman	3000
Andrew Depree	645	George Yong	300
John Okey	800	Wm Kenny	300
John Cropper	1000	John Sturges	1000
Luke Watson	600	Wm Arundell jun^r	300
Henry Smith	600	John Avery	210
John Vines	500	Francis Williams	400
John Kiphaven	500	Robt Hart jun^r	900
Alex^r Mouleston	1000	Robt Hart jun^r	30
Jn & Sam^{ll} Watson	600	Nathan^{ll} Walker	96
John Okey	400	Tho: Nixon	400
Luke Watson Senr	600	Mathew Osborne	300
Tho: Welborne	775	Richard Shoulter	300
John Bellarmy	1000	Arth^r Johnson Van Kerk	375
Wm Bellarmy	1000	Wm Spencer sen^r	500
John Hill	430	Steph: Whitman	600
John Hill	50	Wm Jerman	400
Alexand^r Draper	1000	Arthur Woolgast	400
Luke Watson	2049	Richard Battye	200
Mathias Everson	375	Halmanus Woolbank	400
Abraham Clement	400	John Haggister	400
Robt Bracye	300	Ja Rodes & Richd White	500
		John Avery	300

Lotts sett out in the Towne of Lewis in the County of Sussex
att one bushell of wheate each Lott except Court & meeting houses

The first Streete
Lots upon ye River or front street

Henry Stretcher	2 Lots	Wm Darvall	2
John Kiphaven	2	W^m frampton	1
Wm Ourian	1	Wm Clark	2

Ralph Rawson	1	John Browne	2
Josh Barkstead	1	Cornel	2
Jerem: Scott	1		

Lots in ye back
Street

Arthur Starr	2 Lotts	Albertus Jacob	1
Wm Carter	2	Tho: Oldman	1
Wm Ourian	1	The Court house	1
Jerem: Scott	1	The meetinghouse	1
Paynter	3		

9. | *Deed of Property, Philadelphia, Pa. (1688)*

This Indenture made this sixth day of the fourth month June Being the Fourth year of the Raign of James the Second . . . in the year according to the English accompt One thousand six hundred Eighty Eight. Between Peter Dalboe of the Province of West new Jersey in the parts of America yeoman of the one part and Reece Preiss of the County of Philadelphia in the province of Pennsilvania . . . yeoman of ye oth^r pt. Witnesseth that for and in consideration of the sume of thirty four pounds fifteen shillings silver Lawfull mony of the sd province on hand payd by the sd Reece Preiss to the sd Peter Dalboe . . . the sd Peter Dalboe Hath given granted aliened bargained sold enfeoffed and confirmed . . . to the sd Reece Preiss his heires and assigns a certain piece or parcell of Land scituate lying and being on the west side of the Delaware River and on the East side of the Skullkill within the sd Country Beginning at a corner marked Tree by the sd Skullkill being the corner Tree of Daniell Pastorius and Runing by the Land of the sd Daniell southeast two hundred and forty eight perches to a corner marked tree from thence South West nineteen perches and 11/31 parts of a perch . . . containing thirty and six Acres and a half . . .

In Witness whereof the parties first above written to these presents have to these present Indentures their hands and seals interchangeably sett and putt the day and date first above written. . . .

Probate records

Probate records, like tax records, yield to analysis reluctantly. In the first place a large minority, and in some areas even a majority, of heads of families did not leave wills. Inventories of estate, required by law in most colonies, are more common, though a recent survey of probate records in selected areas of New England indicates that inventories were made for fewer than 50 percent of deceased heads of household. Compounding the difficulty is the unpredictable pattern of these wills and inventories: who left wills and who did not? Though only a careful comparison of death records and probate records will establish the degree and nature of the distortion, it seems probable that the impoverished were far less likely to provide for the disposition of their property than the rich, just as the illiterate were less likely to leave wills than the educated. Similarly, inventories of estate were less frequently made for the poor, for indentured servants, or for subsistence farmers in remote frontier areas than for men in the upper half of society or for persons living in commercialized areas.

A second distortion inherent in probate records is that they rarely account for all forms of wealth or indicate the actual estate of the individual at his economic prime. Massachusetts probate records list real and personal property, for example; but in New Jersey and Pennsylvania only personal property was evaluated. Furthermore, many men disposed of part of their estate before death, passing on land and personal property to children or others.

Despite these limitations, probate records provide important data for studies of social stratification and social mobility. The will of David Reece, taken from Philadelphia Will Book C, #17, and the inventory of estate of Jonathan Dickinson, published in *Pennsylvania Magazine of History and Biography*, 59 (1935), pp. 422–28, are good examples of probate records. Though tax lists provide, as probate records cannot, an overall view of the relative wealth of each member of the community at one moment, probate records are far more precise in evaluating individual wealth at one moment in time.

10. | *Will of David Reece, Chester County, Pa.*

Know all men by these presents that I David Reece of the Township of Newton in the county of Chester yeoman, being weak in body but of perfect memory do make and ordain this my Last Will and Testam^t in manner & form following. Annulling and revoking all other Wills heretofore made by me and this only to be taken for my Last Will and Testam^t. I will that all my just Debts and duties wch I shall owe at my Decease and all my funerall debts be first fully paid and discharged by my Executors hereafter named. Item I give and bequeath unto my wife Elinor the Annual or yearly Sum of Six pounds Current mony of Pensilvania . . . Item I give and bequeath unto my sd wife the use and occupacon of one feather Bed and its furniture for her Naturall life and after her decease I give & bequeath the sd Bed & furniture to my Son Thomas . . . Item I give and bequeath to my sd Two Sons Thomas & Lewis all the rest & Residue of my goods & chattel to be equally divided between the sd Two . . . Item I give & bequeath to my Son Lewis all such sums of mony wch are due to me either Bill Bond or any other Specialty whatsoever. Item I give devise & grant unto my Son Thomas and his Heirs forever all that moiety or half-part of that messuage & Tenem^t of Lands whereon I now dwell the sd moiety or half part to be alotted & Laid out for him on that end of the sd Messuage next adjoining to the Creek or Rivulett called Crum Creek. Item I give and devise to my Son Thomas & his Heirs and Assigns for Ever one moiety or half part of that piece of Land by me purchased from Francis Howell late of Landisho in Carmarthenshire in South Wales containing Two hundred acres . . . Item I give devise and grant unto my Son Lewis & to his Heirs for Ever all the other moiety or half part of the sd Messuage and Tenem^t of Lands wch sd moiety is to contain all the Houses Edifices & Buildings whatsoever to the sd messuage belonging or appertaining and also all the other moiety or half part of that Two hundred acres of Land by me purchased of Francis Howell aforesd. Item as Touching all Corn & Grain that now

I have growing on yᵉ sd Messuage my Will is That my son Lewis shall have the Two third parts of all such grain and my son Thomas but one-third part of the Corn & grain . . . In Witness whereof I have hereunto sett my hand & seal this fourteenth day of the Eleventh month Anno Dni One thousand seven hundred & five. David Rees.

11. | *Inventory of Estate, Jonathan Dickinson, Philadelphia, Pa. (1723)*

Inventory of the Goods & Chattels of Jonathan Dickinson late of the Citty of Philadᵃ. Merchᵗ. deed taken this twentieth day of ffith Month Anno Domini 1722.—

In the best Parlour

Mohogony Chest Drawers and Table	£7.10.—
6 foot Table ditto	5.
4 foot Dᵒ	2. 5.
6 Elbow Cane Chairs at 20/	6.
8 Common ditto at 16/	6. 8
Brass hearth Tongs Shovel and Doggs	3.
Large Looking Glass	8.10.
4 Scones	5.
Brass knobb'd Iron Tongs Shovel and bellows	12.
Stand	14.
Tea Table and fframe	2. 5.
Sett large Tea Cups & Saucers	2.
Sett Small Dᵒ	1.18.
Dᵒ Bason	9.
Sugar Cop 9/milk pot 12/& 3 large saucers 6/	1. 7.
4 Dishes 12 plates edged and 2 Basons	5.
China Bowl Stand	1.
2 doz. Courser China plates at 36/p.Doz.	3.12.
3 China Chocolate Cups	6.

8 fine earthen plates & 12 Saucers sorted	10.
3 Blew Stone Galon Juggs and 3 doz.Glass ware	15.
2 Brushes and Glass ware	4.
Cash	42. 2.7½

Front Parlour

5 foot Mohogony Table	4.
4 foot ditto	2. 5.—
Looking Glass	6.
2 pᵣ Scones	2.10.
Clock & Case	22.10.
Cane Couch and Squab	3.
12 Cane Chairs at 22/6 pc.	13.10.
Pair Doggs Tongs & Shovel	10.
Mohogony Cloaths Press	5.
2 Cane Chairs	1.12.
2 Quart & 2 Pint Decanters 2 Crewetts 4 cups & Brush	12.

Green Room

Old Broken Escrutore wch Joseph claims	2.
Brass knobbed Doggs Tongs shovel & bellows	15.
3 Decanters 2 Crewetts & Glass	8.
Old Leather Chair	3.
2 Skins	5.

Front Chamber

Mohogany Table and chest of Drawers	7.10.
Looking [*glass*] with part of Top Broken	4. 2.
Swing Glass & drawers	1.
Japann'd Stand	10.
2 Scones	1. 4.
2 Elbow Cane Chairs with blew Harateen Cushions	2.10.
2 Common Ditto at 16/each	6. 8.
Brass knobbed Doggs Tongs shovell Bellows & 2 brushes	17.
10 Glasses on Mantle piece	4.
Large sliding Brass & Iron standing Candlestick	1.10.
Joynt Stool	2.
Largest feather bed bolster 2 Pillows cased wt 85. at 21/p.£	7. 8. 9

Sacking bottom screw bedstead & Iron Rods	1.15.
Inside & outside Curtains Vailings head & Tester	
Clothes all of red & white Callicoe	6.
Suit Blew Harateen Do wth bases	5.10.
2 pair Dowlas sheets	4.
Quilt & old Blankett	2. 6.
Feather Bed Bolster 2 pillows cas'd w^t 45 ^{lb} at 21^d p.£	3.18.
Sacking bottom screw bedstead & Iron Rods	1.10
Suit Callicoe Curtains head and Tester Cloth	3.
Suit Blew Harateen Ditto	4.10.
Quilt 35/& pair blanketts 24/	2.19.

Best Chamber

Mohogany Chest Drawers and Table	7.10.
Looking Glass	7.
2 Scones	1. 5.
Easy Chair 12 cushions Court Squab 3 pillows all flower'd Sattin	20.
Cane Couch	2.10.
12 Elbow Cane chairs at 22/	13. 4
Swing Glass & drawers	1.15.
Brass hearth Doggs Tongs shovell Bellows & 2 brushes	3.
2 Cane Stools	1.
23 pc^s. China ware on Mantle peice	1.
Tea Tray and 16 p^s. China ware	1. 1
Feather Bed Bolster 2 pillows cas'd w^t 69^{lb} at 2/3	7.15. 3
Suit fine Callicoe Curtains & inside Damask Ditto with Vailings bases & head & Tester Cloth Quilted	12.
Fine Callicoe Quilt	3.10.
India Quilt much worn	2.15.
Quilted Silk head Cloth lin'd with Strip'd Holl'd & Silk Tester Cloth qt. 15 yds. with remnant	5.
Large Quilt. one Cinamon Colour'd Persian & fine Callicoe the other side	6.10.—
Blankett	8.
Sack bottom Screw bedstead and Iron Rods	2. 5
Close Stool and pewter Pan	15.

Two Quart Tankards 3 Salvers p^r Candlesticks Snuffers
& Stand 12 Spoons all with the family Arms 2
plates 2 lamps 6 sweetmeat forks 6 salts 1 p^r Candlesticks Salver Tankard & flower'd Cup all
called new plate w^{tt}. 390 oz. 15 dwt. at 7/pr. oz.   136.15. 3

3 Pint Tankards Wine Quart Ditto Tea pot with fam-
ily Arms 3 porringers 1 small D^o H D 1 eard
Cup shallow Salver pepper Box marrow Spoon
Ladle Lamp wth family arms 8 large Spoons 6
Tea Ditto Tongs Strainer Childs Spoon and
Noodle Cap all worn plate q^t 165 oz. 17 dwt at
6/6   53.18.

Wine Quart Tankard 1 porringer 2 spoons left in Jo-
sephs Custody and now at Vineyard supposed to
weigh 38 oz. at 6/6   12. 7

Chamber over Upper Kitchen

Mohogany Chest Drawers & Table	5.10.
Looking Glass	6.
Cane Couch and blew silk Squab	2.15.
6 Elbow Chairs D^o with blew Cushions at 24/	7. 4.
4 other Cane Chairs at 16/	3. 4
Swing Glass & Drawers	1. 8.
Brass hearth Doggs Tongs Shovel bellows Iron Tongs and Shovel with Brass knobbs and brush	2.10.
Warming Pan	15.
Feather Bolster 2 pillows Casd w^t 60 ^{lbs} at 21/	5. 5.
Suit Camblet Curtains Vailings bases & Quilted head & Tester Cloths	5.
Callicoe Quilt & Blanket	2.
Blew silk Quilt lin'd with strip'd Holl'd	5.
Sack Bottom Bedstead and Iron Rods	1.15.
11 Large Double flint drinking Glasses	9.

Red Room

Mohogany Chest Drawers and Table	4.10.
Swing Glass and Drawers	1. 5.

7 Cane Chairs at 16/	5.12.
Doggs Tongs Shovel brass knobbed bellows & brush	18.
Feather bed bolster 2 pillows cas'd w^t 68 ^{lb} at 21d. pr.	5.15.
Sack bottom Screw bedstead & Iron rods	1.12.
Double Suit Callicoe Curtains and Vailings	4.
Quilt and Blanket	2.

Stair Head

Mohogany Cloaths Press	5.

Long Room

Feather bed Bolster 2 pillows cas'd w^t 63^{lb} at 21d. pr.	5.10. 3
2 Sheets Blankett and Quilt	2.10.
Lightish Colour'd Suit Curtains Vailings head & Tester Cloth	3.
Feather bed bolster 2 pillows Cas'd w^t 60^{lb} at 21d. p.	5. 5
Green Rug	1. 7. 6
Sack bottom Screw bedstead and Iron rods	1.10.
Pallet feather bed and bolster w^t 46 ^{lb} at 21d.	4. . 6
Ditto bedstead	17.
2 Red Rugs 30/ and 2 Cotton hamocks £3	4.10.
Small Wallnut chest Drawers and Swing Glass	2.
7 Cane Chairs 1 damaged	5.
Small Quilt	1.
2 doz & 9 huggabag Napkins much worn at 10 d	1. 7. 6
31 very old Ditto	6.
2 doz. Diaper Ditto mark'd with blew silk at 2/	2. 8.
7 Course round Towells at 18 d	10. 6
12 Course small diaper Towells	10.
17 Oznabrigg Ditto	14. 2
9 Huggabag D^o at 20 d	15.
12 New Oznabrigg Napkins & 7 small old Table Cloths Ditto	18.
9 Diaper Towells	1. 2. 6
8 Damask Ditto	1.12.
12 D^o Chest Drawers Cloths	2. 8.
5 diaper D^o much worn	12. 6
Large Damask Table Cloths	3.

Small diaper Ditto	18.	
Suit Course Garlic Curtains Vailings & head Cloath	2. 5	
pair Ditto window Curtains & Vailings	7.	
Muslin Table border	4.	
Oznabrigg bolster and 2 pillow Cas'd	2. 6	
Child bed basket cover Quilted	3. 6	
8 p^r Garlit Sheets	10.	
23 Course Sheets	6.18.	
4 Oznabrigg bolster Cases	8.	
24 Pillow Cases sorted	1.10.	

Stair head

17 Blankets at 16/ p.	13.12.	

In Black Trunk I D N 3

11 p^r Holland Sheets at 50/	£ 27.10.	
28 p^r Pillow Cases sorted at 4/	5.12	
10 Huggebag Table Cloaths at 25/	12.10	
4 Doz. Ditto Napkins at 24/ p.Doz.	4.16	
1 Doz. Towells at 3/	1.16	
1 Doz. D° Damask at 4/	2. 8	
1 doz. D° Course	15.	55. 7.

In Red Chest

19 p^r Holl^d Sheets at 50/	£ 47.10.	
5 remnants holl^d q^t 72 y^{ds} at 5/	18.	
20 p^r Pillow Cases at 5/	5.	
Damask Table Cloath sideboard & 12 napkins	3.10.	
5 setts ditto at £3/10	17.10.	
4 p^r Muslin Window Curtains Valings	4.	£95.10.0

North Garret

Feather bed bolster 2 pillows cas'd w^t 60 ^{lb} at 21^d	5. 5.	
Lemon Colour'd suit Camblet Curtains Vailings Tester		
and head cloath	4.	
Sack bottom Screw bedstead and Iron rods	1.15.	
Small Wallnut chest drawers	2.	

6 Cane Chairs at 15/	4.10.
5 India Quilts mostly new at 3£	15.
Small white Callicoe Quilt for Pallet Bed	1. 6.
1 pr Blew window Curtains	2. 6
Doggs with Brass Knobbs	7.
3 Lemonade bowls and 8 Custard Cups	6.
Old Close stool and Earthen Pan	3.
1 pewter Chamber Pot	. . .

Long Garrett

2 Small Feather beds and Bolsters w^{tt} 51 ^{lb} at 18 ^{d}	3.16. 6
3 Small baggs Feathers w^{tt} 18 ^{lb} at 18 ^{d}	1. 7.
6 Cane Chairs at 16/	4.16.
2 small Stills	4.
3 p^r Doggs brass knobb'd 2 Tongs 2 Shovels Ditto	1.17. 6
16 Wicker baskets	1.12. —
Large Tongs & Shovells	7. 6
Speaking Trumpett	7. 6

Upper Kitchen.

7 Tin pudding pans at 18^d	10. 6
Tin dripping pan	2.
6 plates at 12^d & 2 dish covers at 2/6	11.
Old Apple roaster Cheese Toaster Saucepan & Cullender	4.
Candle box and [?]	2. 6
185 patty pans 3 naple bisketts Cont^g 12 each and 6 Tin plates at 18^d p. doz.	1. 7.7½
2 Copper Quarts at 4/ each 3 porringers 2/ each and Coffee pot 5/	19.
2 bed pans each 7/ and 2 pewter chamber pots 7/	1. 1. —
Brass dish Warmer 10/ Iron d^o. 7/6 plate d^o 5/6	1. 3.
Warming pan and 2 brass skimmers	16.
12 knives and 16 forks	4.
2 doz. Skewers	1. 8
Large Tin funnell and Rolling pin	2. 6
1 Stone Jugg 3 earth dishes	3. 6

Copper Fish Kettle and cover w^t 24 ^{lb} at 2/	2. 8.
Bell Mettle Skellet	1.
Copper stew pan and Cover	1. 2. 6
2 Marble mortars 30/ & 20/	2.10.
9 leather Chairs	5. 8.
Mohogany Ovall Table ab^t 4 foot	2.
ditto ab^t 3 foot	1. 7. 6
Looking Glass	1. 4
Large Doggs Tongs Shovell and bellows	1.
Large Copper Tea pot Hand brass Chaff. dish and small cast Ditto	18.
Copper Stew pan Cover. bell mettle pot & Skellet	2. 5.
Memo this is brought Over 5/ wrong	
Brass Kettle with Copperbail w^{tt}. 8^{lb} ½	16.
2 large pewter Cullenders	10.
11 doz. pewter plates & 2 doz. soop Ditto	13.
24 sorted pewter dishes w^{tt} 183 ^{lb} at 16^d p. £	12. 4
Pewter pasty plate	3.
7 Soop dishes 2 basons	2.10.
Earth Punch bowl 2 dishes 3 little basons 2 Sillibub potts 5 saucers 2 chamber potts	12.
6 Alchimy spoons	16.
2 box Iron heaters and Stand	10.
Large square pine Table	9.
2 brass Candle sticks	6.
2 p^r Bellows	7.

Lower Kitchen

8 pewter dishes Cheese plate 4 basons	3.
5 plates	4.
Cullender and old bason	3.
Jack w^{tts} & appurtinances	4.10.
Endirons doggs Tongs shovel 3 pott racks 2 Spitts & Fender	1.17. 6
Gridiron 2 frying pans and Ladle	10.
Large Iron pot 4 lesser ditto & 5 small	3.10.
Iron Pot and Kettle 7/ each	14.

2 Brass Kettles	3.
2 Bell mettle Skellets	1.
Old copper stew pan and cover	10.
9 Brass Candlesticks	1.
2 Brass Chaff dishes	12.
Cleaver	2.
Old Copper Sauce pan 5 pott hooks 3 Trevetts	10.
2 Dish and 2 plate Covers	4.
Brass Ladle Skimmer and Iron Flesh fork	3.

Cellar

Pipe Wine	20.
Pewter Gallon Pot	12. —

£ 1017.15.10

Census records

Although the first national census in the United States was not conducted until 1790, many local and provincial attempts at tabulating population were made before the Revolution. Some were assembled in response to requests for information by the English Board of Trade or other agencies of royal government; others were taken in order to compile provincial or local militia lists or to serve other internal purposes. Though sporadic and often fragmentary, census reports are an important addition to the mosaic of evidence that the student of eighteenth-century social stratification must work with. The best guide to census data before 1790 is Evarts B. Greene and Virginia D. Harrington, *American Population before the Federal Census of 1790* (New York, 1932). The example that follows, a portion of the Massachusetts census of 1765, is reprinted from J. H. Benton, Jr., *Early Census Making in Massachusetts, 1643–1765* (Boston, 1905).

12. Census Report, Suffolk County, Mass. (1765)

	Houses	Families	Whites under 16 Males	Whites under 16 Females	Whites above 16 Males	Whites above 16 Females	Negro & Molatos Male	Negro & Molatos Female	Indians Male	Indians Fe-male	French neutrals under 16 Male	French neutrals under 16 Fe-male	Ditto above 16 Male	Ditto above 16 Fe-male	Total
Boston	1676	2069	4109	4010	2941	3612	510	301	21	16					15,520
Roxbury	212	212	291	324	371	421	47	33			1	3	1	1	1493
Dorchester	204	245	292	284	343	404	23	14				1	1	1	1360
Milton	124	141	215	222	214	245	31	16			2	3	1	1	948
Braintree	327	357	571	590	555	651	31	35	1	1	1	3	3	3	2445
Weymouth	203	248	275	294	315	347	13	14					3		1258
Hingham	375	426	594	539	555	702	38	39			7	11	9	12	2506
Hull	31	33	31	27	39	57	9	7							170
Houghton	265	424	593	555	567	580	9	17	9	10					2340
Dedham	239	309	417	441	484	531	21	15	3	3		1	2	1	1929
Medfield	113	121	111	126	176	211	3	1	2	4	1	2	1	1	639
Wrentham	293	347	464	463	514	551	18	12	1		4	1	1	1	2030
Medway	123	138	165	178	215	210	10	7	1		1	1	2	3	793
Bellingham	72	82	119	111	116	108	8								462
Needham	129	168	209	226	246	250	8	6							945
Brookline	53	53	68	62	97	93	13	5							338
Chelsea	54	70	110	85	99	125	20	13							452
Walpole	100	106	188	177	207	209	2	2				1	3	3	792
	4593	5549	8822	8717	8054	9251	812	530	38	34	17	24	23	26	36,352

13. | BERNARD BARBER
     | *"Social Stratification"*

Bernard Barber, whose article is taken from the *International Encyclopedia of Social Sciences* (18 vols.; [New York, 1967], XV, 288–95), has made important contributions to the study of social structure. His *Social Stratification: A Comparative Analysis of Structure and Process* (New York, 1957) is an outstanding example of recent work in this field. Reprinted, with the omission of several sections, by permission of the author and the Macmillan Company.

Social stratification, in its most general sense, is a sociological concept that refers to the fact that both individuals and groups of individuals are conceived of as constituting higher and lower differentiated strata, or classes, in terms of some specific or generalized characteristic or set of characteristics. Borrowed by analogy from the earth sciences, the term "social stratification" has come into general sociological use only since about 1940, although the matters to which it refers have been discussed under the heading "social class" for a very long time. However, in contrast to its earth-science usage the sociological usage of the concept of stratification often includes, implicitly or explicitly, some evaluation of the higher and lower layers, which are judged to be better or worse according to a scale of values. Such matters as relative moral worth, relative equality and inequality, and degrees of justice and injustice are often involved in the concept of social stratification. The concept is therefore widely used in political, ideological, and moral debate and controversy, as well as in social science analysis. But despite the difficulty of separating the context of moral and ideological controversy, on the one hand, from that of social science analysis, on the other, considerable progress, both theoretical and empirical, has been made in the study of social stratification during the last one hundred years. A brief history of this progress provides some necessary background for assessing where social stratification theory stands today and for laying out a conceptual model of what that theory might be in the future.

ORIGINS OF SOCIAL STRATIFICATION THEORY

As a relatively undifferentiated notion, the idea of social stratification is found in the Judaeo-Christian Bible, the social thought of the Greeks, and the basic social and religious texts of the Indians and the Chinese. The idea has persisted, in relatively crude form, right up to the present day.

Marxian theory

In the history of the evolution of social stratification theory, Marx is the Copernican hero because his concept of social stratification, in contrast with all previous, common-sense notions in this area, emphasizes the basic importance, as a criterion of stratification, of the individual's or group's location in the economic structure. This emphasis contributed one of the essential foundations for all subsequent stratification theory and, indeed, for all other kinds of sociological analysis. In terms of their structural location in the social system, which is centered on the means of production, men in society are divided by Marx into two strata, or "classes," as he called them (following the generally preferred practice of his time). These two classes are the owners of the means of production and the workers whom they employ.

In the light of present sociological analysis and knowledge, this is too crude a concept of social stratification to cope with empirical social reality. First, it does not provide an adequate account of actual structural differentiation in what has been variously labeled the economic, the productive, and the occupational aspect of society. Modern students of the sociology of work and of social stratification have demonstrated not only that this aspect of society is structurally much more differentiated than Marx said but that actual behavior cannot be understood without taking this greater differentiation into account. For example, the analysis of social stratification needs to take into account such differences as those between owning and managing business roles, between business and professional occupational roles, and between skilled and unskilled labor roles. A second way in which the Marxian concept of social stratification is relatively crude is that it tends to minimize, and therefore has no systematic theoretical place for, a variety of other social-structural factors that are of the greatest importance in society, such as lineage and kinship affiliations in all societies or ethnic affiliations in societies that are ethnically differentiated. Modern theorists and researchers treat ethnic-group stratification, for example, as an important type of stratification in its own right—as indeed it is and has been throughout much of history in many parts of the world. Third, Marxian theory tends to minimize, and therefore has no satisfactory theoretical place for, a variety of cultural factors that are as important in the determination of behavior as is the single factor of social stratification. These cultural factors include values, religious ideas, scientific ideas, and legal norms. It is not correct, as Marxian theory holds in the explanation of social stability and change, that social stratification is always the independent variable and cultural factors always dependent variables. Both stability and change are as much determined by cultural factors as by the factor of social stratification. For example, science is probably as much a maker of the modern world as is social stratification.

Marxist analysis has also, of course, been vehemently ideological, in addition to claiming to be scientific. It has always sought to make moral judgments of the world and to change it. Some of the resulting ideological distortion has hindered the progress of social stratification theory. For example, social science has taken a long time to shake off the conceptual confusion resulting from the Marxian moral disapproval of the entrepreneurial and managing roles in society. Similarly, the excessively simplified dichotomization of the social stratification structure in the Marxian picture of modern society has exaggerated the amount of class conflict that has occurred and that is inevitable in such a society. To be sure, some conflict is endemic in the structure of every society; and the productive, or occupational, aspect of modern society is certainly one structural source of conflict. But there are other sources, such as religious and ethnic differences, and it may be that these differences have actually engendered more conflict in the modern world than has the occupational difference. In any case, this is a matter for empirical analysis, not for ideological preconception, while Marxian theory has tended to take its stand on the latter.

Max Weber

After Marx, the next great figure in the history of social stratification theory is Max Weber. He made progress in several ways, probably in part because of his desire to correct Marx, who was one of the dominant intellectual figures when Weber's thought was taking shape. Weber's trinitarian model of social stratification— based on the concepts of class, status, and party—introduced a systematic, explicit, and necessary differentiation into stratification theory. Although Marx knew about such "status groups" as the aristocracy and the peasantry, he chose to neglect status as an explicit and independent dimension of stratification. Weber improved stratification theory by making both status and party (or power, as he also called this factor) as independent in principle as class, which for Marx was the sole independent factor. With this trinitarian view, Weber was able to show that any one of these three factors could independently affect the other two and that any one of them could often be translated into, or exchanged for, either of the other two. Even Weber, however, as we now see, did not go far enough in differentiating his conceptual model of social stratification. There are more than three important and independent dimensions of social stratification. We have already referred to two of these other dimensions: kinship and ethnic stratification. Educational stratification is still another dimension that independently affects behavior in society.

Weber's view inevitably had ideological implications; many took this view as a counterideology to the Marxian view of society. At least implicitly, Weber was justifying the functions of the high-ranking status groups, especially those that performed political, military, and civil-service functions. According to Marxian ideology, these groups are viewed as useless, at least for positive tasks; it is their negative function—that is, their "exploitation" of the lower classes—that is of importance. The classic Marxist proposition that in a socialist society the state will wither away is a result of the view that the high-ranking military, political, and civil service roles (and, in some societies, their associated status groups) are essentially useless.

As a product of his times, Weber was not very much concerned with how to make a more precise ordering of social behavior along the three dimensions of social stratification that he analyzed. For example, he defined "class" as "chances on the market," but he said little about the measurable indicators of this concept or about problems of measurement in general. We now feel it necessary to ask Weber a series of questions: how does one measure "chances on the market"? just by current income? by earned or inherited capital as well? by some application of social power, as through influence of the government or of trade unions? Similarly, Weber defined "status" in terms of "honor" and "style of life," but he did not tell us how either is to be reliably and precisely measured. Indeed, it is obvious that he was thinking only of the *higher* ranges of the "honor," or "status," dimension of stratification, not of the middle and lower ones. Present analysis is interested in the whole continuum of "honor," or "prestige," as it is now usually called. And prestige measurement scales range from the least to the most highly ranked points on this continuum. Finally, Weber said little about how to measure "power," and we have had to wait until the recent studies of local-community influence structure to see some improvement in this area.

THE MULTIDIMENSIONAL APPROACH

In the contemporary period, conceptual developments in stratification theory have come most notably from [Talcott] Parsons and from [Kingsley] Davis and [Wilbert] Moore. Influenced in part by the general interest in the study of values in modern social science, these theorists have stressed the prestige dimension of social stratification and have treated what Weber called status as a generalized social phenomenon applying to all positions in the occupational structure of society. Prestige is the resultant of two factors: a system of values, and the functional significance of roles as embodied in the occupational structure. Functional significance is determined by the relative capacity of a role for "producing" some service or good in society—services and goods being construed in the most comprehensive way possible, not in the limited economic way intended by Marx when he spoke of production. For example, governmental, religious, artistic, and ideological roles are as functionally significant, as subject to evaluation, and as "productive" in some measure as are the roles of owning capital, managing a business, or tending a machine in a factory.

Parsons, in addition to his interest in the dimension of prestige, has also been interested in the power aspect of social stratification. In this area he has stressed two general propositions, neither of which has been universally accepted in social science theory. One is that power is a positive social phenomenon—the capacity for achieving goals in social systems—and not just a negative phenomenon—the capacity to prevent others from acting as they wish. The second proposition is that power is not a zero-sum phenomenon, in which if A has more, then B necessarily has less. Rather, power is a phenomenon that allows increments and their social consequences to be shared by both A and B, although not always in complete equality, of course.

Parsons, Davis, and Moore have sought to be scientific about social stratification theory or at least to reduce its ideological bias when presenting it as scientific theory. But they have had many critics who have charged them with a number of ideological commitments nonetheless—for example, with favoring inequality in social systems, underemphasizing the conflict and power aspects of social stratification, and favoring social stability rather than social change. . . .

A CONCEPTUAL MODEL

A conceptual model for contemporary social stratification theory should be highly differentiated—that is, it should be multidimensional. It should also have good measurement techniques for each of its differentiated dimensions and be as free as possible of ideological bias. There seem to be at least two sources of resistance to the adoption of such a model. One source is ideological. There are still sociologists who resist a highly differentiated social stratification model because, for ideological reasons, they want the term "class" to refer to some single, simple, and all-explanatory notion. Such a simplistic approach would be more difficult to sustain in the face of a social stratification model that captured the full complexity of social stratificational reality. Another source of resistance is connected with methodology and with resources for research. The more differentiated the conceptual model for stratification analysis, the greater the resources needed for research studies and the more difficult such studies are likely to be. Up to now, studies using oversimple stratification models and poor measurement techniques have been made by a number of poorly trained sociologists. Such researchers are now conceptually and technologically obsolete, and, like all workers who see their skills being reduced in value or discarded, they resist new ideas and methods.

It is fundamental that social stratification is multidimensional. Contrary to a view held by some, this is the case not only for contemporary industrial societies but for other types of societies and in other historical periods as well. For example, studies of stratification in Hindu caste society and in seventeenth-century England demonstrate the necessity of a multidimensional model. But it is not only on empirical grounds that the several dimensions of a multidimensional stratification model are justified. On theoretical grounds, each of the dimensions has to be, and can be, justified in terms of the special and independent functions that the specified dimension plays in society. It is desirable, of course, that the analysis of these special and independent functions be derived from, and integrated in, some systematic general theory about behavior and social systems, rather than constructed *ad hoc*. But this is not always possible. Where it is possible, general theory and social stratification theory are the more fruitful for one another.

To say that the several dimensions of stratification are independent of one another, both theoretically and empirically, does not mean that they are not also interdependent—that is, that they affect one another to some extent and yet retain a measure of autonomy. For example, the dimensions of occupational prestige, power, income, and education are to some extent independent. That is to say, in some measure occupational prestige is respected regardless of the amount of power or income. Contrariwise, power or income may achieve goals despite low occupational prestige. But the different dimensions also affect or limit one another because of their interdependence. A certain level of educational attainment may not be able to express itself without a certain level of income. And a certain level of occupational prestige may find itself ineffective because it does not have a certain amount of power. One of the important tasks for a multidimensional theory is to conduct research that leads to more and more precise statements, probably in quantified form, of the various measures of independence and interdependence that the several dimensions of stratification have in regard to one another.

Both theoretical analysis and empirical research have already made quite clear what some of these multiple dimensions, or independently functional variables, of social stratification are. Though the list below includes the most important of these dimensions, it is not necessarily complete. Nor is the order in which they are listed meant to imply any order of relative importance. In principle, each dimension is as important as every other. In any concrete social situation, of course, one may be more important in the determination of behavior than another, but this greater importance holds only for those specific circumstances.

SOME DIMENSIONS OF SOCIAL STRATIFICATION

Power

One way of defining "power" is as the capacity for achieving goals in social systems. Power in this sense is obviously functional for all social systems, large and small, and for all types of societies. In all social systems, some roles have more power, others less, and the result of this differential distribution is a stratified structure of power. Sometimes an individual's or group's differential capacity for power extends over a broad range of social situations, sometimes over quite a narrow one. The degree of specialization, or division of labor, in a society will affect the typical distribution of these ranges that exists in that society. When power is exercised against the moral feelings of the relevant other actors in a social system, it is perceived by these others as illegitimate; when exercised in accord with such feelings, it is perceived as legitimate, or, as it is usually called, authoritative. Power, legitimate and illegitimate, has a number of different social sources in all societies. Therefore it does not stand in any simple one-to-one relation with any of the other dimensions of social stratification.

Occupational prestige

The different more or less full-time "productive" roles in a society are of differential functional significance for the society and therefore obtain a higher or a lower evaluation, or amount of prestige. In different societies and in different historical periods, the relative amount of prestige obtained by a specific "productive" role may vary somewhat, though not nearly so much as some ideological views of society have held. This variability is a result of the fact that the same necessary function in a social system—for example, the military function and roles—may be somewhat differently valued according to the different sets of values that prevail in different social systems and at different times. However, since the differences among these sets of values are often much exaggerated for ideological purposes and since even such relatively small differences as do exist have to accommodate themselves in some measure to the necessary functional significance of particular roles, it follows that the same specific "productive" role in different societies usually has much the same prestige everywhere. We have already seen that the results of occupational-prestige studies in 24 societies (all contemporary but representing quite different types) show considerable consensus in the relative evaluation of the same role in societies of different types. We have also seen that research shows the stability over time, at least for the United States, of occupational-prestige ratings for specific occupational roles. Prestige, too, of course, to some extent varies independently of the other dimensions of stratification.

Income or wealth

Different roles in society offer different possibilities for earning income and accumulating capital wealth; so too, different roles have different chances of inheriting wealth. Sometimes, highly prestigious and also powerful roles—for example, religious leaders such as "medicine men" in primitive societies or the Catholic pope in modern society—can earn or accumulate little money in their own right or for their own use. Conversely, sometimes roles of low prestige—for example, bandits or thieves—can accumulate large amounts of capital wealth. In the modern type of society, an example of differential chances for earned income can be seen in a comparison of business with professional "productive" roles. On the whole, and partly because of the differential symbolic significance of money as an indicator of achievement in the two areas, professional roles earn less than business roles of equal relative prestige.

The stratification of income and wealth, whether earned or inherited, has considerable social and economic consequences in partial independence of the other dimensions of social stratification. For example, chances for education may be much influenced by relative income and wealth, so that individuals who occupy roles of the same relative prestige but of differential income may find themselves at an advantage or disadvantage vis-à-vis one another in affording educational opportunities to their children. Differential amounts of disposable income are also important in determining differential access to those "style of life" items that are taken as symbolic, sometimes accurately, sometimes inaccurately, of a given amount of occupational prestige or power or education. This is what [Thorstein] Veblen was concerned with in his discussion of patterns of "conspicuous consumption." Both economists and sociologists have studied the independent significance of disposable income as a dimension of social stratification, but much more study, preferably by the two disciplines jointly, would be valuable.

Education and knowledge

The amount of knowledge that individuals have acquired, either formally, through education, or informally, affects the way in which they behave. As a result of differential amounts and types of education, and of other learning experiences, the amount of knowledge is differentially distributed and may be conceived of as forming a stratified structure among the individuals in a society. This dimension of stratification produces effects independently of the other dimensions. For example, in studies of the use of psychotherapeutic facilities and of behavior toward relatives who have been released from mental hospitals, it has been shown that amount and type of education and knowledge is the significant determinant of behavior among people of the same level of occupational prestige or income.

Religious and ritual purity

In terms of the functionally significant religious ideas that prevail in every society, individuals and groups can be regarded as possessing either more or less religious or ritual purity. In a religiously homogeneous society, of course, there is greater consensus about where individuals and groups should be placed with regard to this dimension of stratification; in religiously heterogeneous societies, there is usually more dissensus. Hindu caste society has probably been the society in which religious and ritual purity have been most important in comparison with the other dimensions and structures of stratification. But even in Hindu society the religious dimension has not been all-important (although some religious and literary ideology has held that it has been), nor is it in any one-to-one relationship with other dimensions. Clearly, this has been even truer of other types of society.

Family and ethnic-group position

In all societies, kinship groups and their extensions in the form of ethnic groups perform important functions: procreation, socialization of children, and provision of moral and psychological support between parents and children and between husbands and wives. Families, because of their varying success in performing these functions and because the other services that they perform for the national and local communities also vary, are differentially evaluated. This evaluation results in a stratification of higher-ranked and lower-ranked families, which in turn has an important and independent influence on the way in which members of particular families treat one another and are treated by others. Moreover, family and ethnic-group position (where there is ethnic heterogeneity in a society) does not stand in a one-to-one relationship with other dimensions of social stratification.

Local-community status

All but the very simplest societies are subdivided into communities that have special problems for which the contributions of local individuals and families are needed. These individuals and families are given a higher or a lower evaluation in the local community in proportion to their contributions to that community's welfare and quite independently of their evaluation on the other dimensions of social stratification. Differential evaluation of position in the local community is an important determinant of the behavior of self and others in the local community and sometimes of behavior outside it as well, when local-community position becomes known in other local communities or in the society as a whole.

CORRELATIONS AMONG RANKINGS

According to the multidimensional approach to social stratification, each individual or group in society is conceived of as ranked along each of the several dimensions of social stratification discussed above, as well as along others. The study of social stratification should therefore involve investigation of the ways in which these different relative rankings are correlated with one another, whether positively or negatively. The rankings may all be highly correlated with one another (all high, all medium, or all low in rank) or much less highly correlated (some high, some medium, and some low in rank). A series of analyses and researches have been undertaken to investigate social stratification in these terms. The task of explaining why the various rankings of groups and individuals are often *not* highly correlated has been called the problem of "status inconsistency." Two general hypotheses, or propositions, underlie the investigation of this phenomenon. The first is that status inconsistency results in types of behavior different from those caused by status consistency, with each specific pattern of inconsistency having its own specific consequences. Thus, it has been said that in the United States the combination of high occupational prestige and low ethnic position results in political liberalism. Unfortunately, this and other empirical generalizations in the study of status inconsistency have not yet been solidly established. For example, it has also been asserted that Catholics, many of whom experience the status inconsistency of having higher occupational prestige than ethnic position, tend to be politically illiberal. Further empirical work is necessary to arrive at more reliable empirical generalizations about the consequences of specific patterns of status inconsistency.

A second general proposition underlying work on status inconsistency is that there is a tendency toward status equilibration, that is, toward highly positive correlation among the individual's several rankings. This proposition should, however, still be taken as a working hypothesis and not as an established empirical generalization. In our own and other societies, various kinds of status inconsistency have lasted long enough—not only throughout an individual's lifetime but over several generations—to raise a strong doubt: are the social processes that maintain status inconsistency not at least as powerful in principle as, and sometimes more powerful in practice than, the processes that lead to status equilibration? The position of the Jews in most societies, the position of the many high-caste Brahman priests in India with low occupational prestige—these are the kinds of empirical phenomena that raise such a doubt.

In the light of this discussion of the problem of status inconsistency, a number of general points should be made as a basis for further work in this field. First, there is no question that for some individuals in all societies, even relatively simple societies, and for many individuals in some societies, there is considerably less than perfect correlation among their rankings on the several different dimensions of social stratification. Second, apparently there are social processes that are conducive to maintaining this lack of perfect correlation over a long period of time, as well as processes for increasing the degree of status consistency. If hypergamous marriage in caste societies or the marriage of the daughters of the *nouveaux riches* to men of distinguished lineage in modern societies are examples of the latter, then ethnic and so-called racial prejudice is an equally compelling example of the former. Still very much an open and important question for social stratification research is what the various empirical tendencies toward status consistency or inconsistency are in different societies and at different historical times. Third and last, it should be assumed in this research that there is nothing inherently or completely functional about status consistency. It may have its dysfunctions as well as its functions. For example, status consistency may lead to social stagnation as well as to social harmony. Contrariwise, status inconsistency may have its functions as well as its better-known dysfunctions. Those who experience status inconsistency may be the more socially creative and liberal, although they may also have the unhappiness and sense of social injustice that sometimes, though not always, comes from status inconsistency.

THE STRUCTURE OF STRATIFICATION SYSTEMS

When all the individuals in a society or all their associated solidary kinship groups are ranked along any one of the several dimensions of social stratification, there results a distribution of differential rankings that can be conceived of as having a certain structured shape. Because of the differential distribution of capacities among the members of any society and because of society's need for some measure of hierarchy in the patterning of its authority systems, the rankings tend to show some, and often a considerable, degree of hierarchy, which manifests itself in a tapering toward the top of the various stratification structures. If some tapering is universal, the shape of the rest of the structure is more variable. There seem to be two basic shapes, the pyramid and the diamond. The latter is the typical pattern for modernized societies, where there are strong pressures toward social equality as well as a need for increasing numbers of middle-ranking functionaries. In other types of societies, where the opposite forces prevail, the standard shape of the stratification structures has been more pyramidal, the majority of roles (and therefore the individuals who occupy them) ranking very low. In the modern world, a number of fundamental social and cultural changes are resulting in what seems to be a general trend in all societies toward an increasingly diamond-shaped distribution of roles along many of the dimensions of their social stratification systems. In some cases, aspirations toward this type of stratification structure outrun actual achievement. This leads to much social unrest as well as to great efforts to make social fact conform to social aspiration.

STRATIFICATION AND SOCIAL MOBILITY

Social mobility consists in the movements of individuals up and down along any one or several of the dimensions of social stratification. Because there are several different dimensions of social stratification in any society, the relative importance of different processes of mobility and also the relative amounts and degrees of mobility will vary in different types of social stratification systems. Any discussion of the processes and amounts of social mobility should always make very clear whether they are occurring within an over-all stratification system that is relatively stable in type or in one that is changing (whether slowly or rapidly) from one basic type to another. Otherwise, the phenomena of individual mobility may be confused with those of basic social structure. For example, in both seventeenth-century England and eighteenth-century France only certain individuals were rising from lower strata into the bourgeoisie and the aristocracy. Contrary to what has sometimes been said, the aristocratic stratum itself was not disappearing, nor was the bourgeois stratum becoming highly evaluated or more politically powerful than the aristocratic stratum. It was a case of individual mobility in both places, not of basic change in the system of social stratification. With regard to social mobility—as is also true of other dynamic social processes—it is necessary to see that individual processes and basic structural processes are different matters, though not, of course, unrelated.

14. | NORMAN H. DAWES
      "Titles as Symbols of Prestige in Seventeenth-
      Century New England"

In his study of honorific titles in New England, Norman H. Dawes has combined quantitative and qualitative analysis to show that while social customs inherited from England continued to have meaning in the New World, the compulsion to rank men in the social order gradually eroded. Reprinted with omission of notes by permission of the author. From *William and Mary Quarterly*, Third Series, 6 (1949), 69–83.

Prominent among the evidences of social prestige that were important to the New England colonists were titles indicative of rank. A strenuous attempt was made to maintain traditional titular honors that had long flourished in the mother country, but the conditions of frontier life made it difficult to perpetuate niceties of usage much though they were cherished by those who loved the stately ways of the past. Consequently there was an interplay between heritage and environment in New England which developed a unique attitude toward honorifics, albeit one that was not always consistent.

The titles and prefixes of respect that comprised the nomenclature of honor in New England were complex and utilized with a punctiliousness which was more apparent than real. Official memoranda clearly indicate an attempt by clerks and recorders to use titles as a means of designating the quality of an individual. An entry, under date of December 19, 1671, in the court records of Middlesex County referred in one sentence to "the Reverend Mr. Charles Chauncey," the "Worth(y) Daniel Gookin Esqr." and to two presumably less dignified individuals, "Jno. Greene and Joseph Hawley." Another entry in the same records for 1686, noting the renewal of seventeen innkeepers' licenses, apparently distinguished among the applicants by the prefixes to their names. One Mistress, four Mr.s, one Widow, two Lieutenants, and nine unqualified names composed the list. Most of the official records and documents of early New England, by displaying a discrimination in the use of titles similar to those noted, create the illusion that they were carefully regulated in accordance with a definitely prescribed rule of social etiquette. But a more exhaustive study of the records reveals no standardized relationship between the title and the specific social standing of the person to whom it was applied.

It is obvious from the list of tavern keepers in the Middlesex court records that occupational status did not determine the nature of the title accorded. All artisans were not bulked under one title, all merchants known by another, nor did any title accruing from occupational status carry with it a connotation of specific social significance. Similarly the socially dignifying titles that were used in association with holders of similar political offices did not conform to a standard pattern related to the given civic post. Common titular designations did not accrue to all freemen in the Bible Commonwealths or elsewhere in New England, for additional social dignities ranged them variously from Esquires at the top to Goodmen or untitled persons at the bottom. In fact New England society was in no way so organized as to present any definite formula by which the proper title for any particular man or woman might be derived from the mere juggling of any one neatly circumscribed constant. Rather, titles were accorded for a complexity of reasons rooted in historic tradition and colored by the peculiarities of the contemporary society.

The high-sounding titles which designated the English nobility were but infrequently employed in New England, for the colonists who were entitled to such designations were very few in number. Arbella, the wife of Isaac Johnson, and Susan, the wife of John

Humphrey, were both referred to as Lady. The title of Lord applied to but one New England resident of the seventeenth century; namely, to Richard Coote, Earl of Bellomont, Governor of New York, Massachusetts and New Hampshire. The prefix Sir adorned the Christian name of both Thomas Temple, created baronet in 1663, and John Davy who fell heir to a baronetcy in 1707; "Bart." was appended to both names in written or printed reference. Sir was likewise accorded the knights, Richard Saltonstall, Edmund Andros and William Phips, and "Knt." followed their names as "Bart." followed the baronets'.

The Esquire that dignified not a few New Englanders had its origin as a title in the military pratices of medieval Europe. It derived originally from the Latin *scuto* or *scutum* meaning "having to do with arms." The generalized significance of *scuto* became somewhat lessened in scope when, with the passage of time, it came to apply chiefly to the young men of gentle family who gained proficiency in the art of combat by serving a military apprenticeship before assuming the dignity of knighthood. *Armiger, scutifer, scutarius,* and *ecuyer* were the various names by which these young bloods were known. The title of Esquire, derived from the French *ecuyer,* by the seventeenth century had passed from the military into the political sphere and was generally applied to anyone of gentle birth active in governmental affairs. Squire seems to have obtained chiefly in oral address and to have been confined to local officials, particularly to the Justices of the Peace, while the written "Esq." was used for those in higher political office.

The exact significance of Esquire in seventeenth-century New England is difficult to determine. Although it continued to be associated with political honor, its use was somewhat erratic. Some Assistants and Councillors, for example, were granted the dignity of an Esq., but not all were so honored. Thomas Welles was a Connecticut magistrate for seventeen years, Deputy-Governor for one year, and twice elected Governor before he was referred to in the records as Esquire. To the year 1665 the only Assistants of Connecticut whose names were recorded with an Esq. were George Fenwick of Saybrook and John Winthrop, Jr., of New London. Nor did all Assistants in Massachusetts receive the coveted title, for in 1646, twelve were listed and but six designated as Esq. In 1654 out of thirteen, there were only six Esquires. In Rhode Island, prior to the year 1663, Edward Hutchinson was the only Assistant who received the distinction. Subsequent to that date William Brenton and Benedict Arnold joined the ranks of Rhode Island's Esquires. The designation of all magistrates as Esquires that came in vogue later in the century must have indicated a relaxing of the former usage, for a careful analysis of the various records will not allow the conclusion that any definite relationship ever existed between the magistracy and Esquire as a title in New England. It was not unusual, moreover, to find an "Esq." appended as something of a social distinction to the names of a few who had never held the office of magistrate.

While no conclusions can be drawn concerning any definite link between Esquire and high political office, the general social significance of the title is evident. The sparing use of Esquire in the early years must indicate that it was an honorific that could not be lightly bestowed. Whatever may have been the peculiar attributes that originally prompted the early New Englanders to pay a man the social compliment of an Esq., there is little question that later usage was somewhat broader. The Esquire that was not accorded even as a courtesy title to Thomas Welles during his term as Governor of Connecticut and that until 1654 was permitted to adorn the names of but six of the Massachusetts Assistants, became in the Bay Colony between the years 1693 and 1696, the property of no less than nine men who claimed as their greatest honor a Deputyship. Either through having lost an early concept of "esquireness" or through mere carelessness in the application of the title, the colonial society of New England gave some impetus to a connotative change in the word that was eventually to leave it without any definite social import in the future society of America.

The present loose social connotation of Gentleman may also in part be attributed to early New England experience. Gentleman derived from the French *Gentile-homme* and seems to have been brought into England after the Norman Conquest. In its broadest meaning the designation applied to all those of titled rank including the royal family. By the fifteenth century the title had come to apply chiefly to the lowest group of the minor aristocracy. The quality which marked this group was the ability to live without manual toil. During the next two centuries the title came to apply to a wide variety of persons who in the earlier years would not have been deemed of gentlemanly rank. Writing in the opening years of the seventeenth century, William Harrison described the diversity of meanings which the title then carried:

> Whosover studieth the laws of the realm, whoso abideth in the university (giving his mind to his book), or professeth physic and the liberal sciences, or beside his service in the room of a captain in the wars, or good counsel given at home, whereby his commonwealth is benefited, can live without manual labour and thereto is able and will bear the port, charge, and countenance of a gentleman, he shall . . . be . . . reputed for a gentleman ever after . . .

The use of the written "Gent." in New England added a still broader basis to the usage which had grown up in England by the early seventeenth century. None of the pre-fifteenth and but little of the fifteenth and early sixteenth-century concept of a Gentleman lingered. For the obvious reason that New England was wanting in a full-fledged aristocracy the title did not apply exclusively to a well-born, hereditary, ruling social group. A few of the New England colonists who bore the title could, in perfect accord with traditional standards, claim their right to it by virtue of aristocratic lineage; among them were Leonard Chester, George Wyllys, Samuel Wyllys, Henry Bode, Thomas Cammock, Francis Champernowne, George Cleeve, Henry Josselyn, Francis Neale, Thomas Bradbury, Joseph Cooke, Samuel Danforth, William Hooke, John Humphrey, John Pynchon, William Pynchon, Robert Saltonstall, Adam Winthrop, Deane Winthrop, John Winthrop, Sr., and Samuel Dudley. It is significant that gentlemen of good blood in New England usually possessed additional qualifications for the social dignity which their title represented. By their ownership of large landed estates, by occupancy of high civic office, by superior education or a combination of several such characteristics, they were able to bear the all-important "port, charge, and countenance" of their distinguished rank.

Apart from its application to those of aristocratic pedigree the use of Gent. in New England was somewhat ill-defined, except in so far as it connoted social superiority in a general way. Ministers not infrequently were accorded the title, doubtless on the score that their education and professional activity contributed to a life divorced from manual toil. Many also were those who, oftimes coming from little, celebrated their social ascent by assuming, apparently with public consent, the title which in feudal Europe had been the prerogative of aristocrats. New-World-created barons of the earth and princes of the sea whose lofty place had been won by diligent and fortunate enterprise could find in New England no purchasable Knt. or Bart. to act as a badge of the social eminence to which they had attained, but Gent. was theirs for the taking, provided of course that their qualifications for the distinction did not cry the assumption. With successful landowners, merchants, and businessmen in ever increasing numbers acquiring or assuming the title, it could not long keep its aristocratic flavor.

The varied implications of the title in seventeenth-century New England came fundamentally from a growing change in its basic meaning from a designation implying legal status to one connoting ethical qualities. In the early decades Gent. was employed chiefly to indicate one's social rank with only an occasional use of the term as implying ethical attributes. After the middle of the century Gentleman as a title indicative of personal virtue came into wider use. An epitaph of Master Henry Flint, pastor of the Braintree church, written about 1668 praised the departed as "a gentleman remarkable for his piety, learning, wisdom and fidelity in his office." Cotton Mather, writing at the end of the century, expressed the pious hope *"that there yet be found among the sons of* New England, *those young gentlemen"* who would emulate the goodness of the ministers and magistrates and thereby bring true *"that saying of old* Chaucer . . . To do the genteel deeds, that makes the gentleman."* The title of Gentleman also came into some use as a form of polite address, particularly for a group. In addressing a company of fishermen and sailors in 1644, John Dunkin, Master, started his speech with words which would have sounded strange in the ears of a fifteenth-century Englishman: "Gentlemen, I have given you three or four days." When Richard Coote, the Earl of Bellomont, gave a dinner in honor of the Massachusetts Deputies in the Spring of 1699 he turned to his wife and remarked: "Dame, we should treat these gentlemen well; they give us our bread."

The oral form of address used for a gentleman was most commonly Master. But Master had also an independent use as a socially dignifying honorific, particularly when employed in written designation. In such instances, the word was abbreviated to Mr., and its implications of social quality were somewhat less than those accompanying Gent. Since its broadest application in New England seemed to be to those of professional standing, Master probably connoted a social worth such as that which accrued to those just above or within the very upper limits of the middle class. Ministers were almost universally addressed as Master, sometimes in place of, sometimes in addition to the more specific title of Reverend. Schoolteachers and all those who held the M. A. degree were customarily honored socially with a Mr. or Master. Apart from those whose Master distinguished them as of professional standing, the Mr.s were usually men of considerable wealth. Landowners, successful merchants, and men prominent in economic spheres generally were deferred to as Mr. The title with the passage of time, came to be spelled and pronounced Mister and with the etymological change its import of social dignity was lessened. Since the abbreviation Mr. served for both Master and Mister, it is often impossible to determine from a study of original records which title was intended. Subsequent usage would tend to indicate that Mister became the more generalized title and progressively less important as a socially dignifying agency.

Less socially significant than Mr. was the title of Goodman, also used as a designation for some members of the middle class. In fact, Goodman had the least social import of any of the general honorifics, but even Goodman had lost some of the definite social implication that was its characteristic in English society. As a title it, in common with Yeoman, traced to the Saxon word *zeoman* which indicated a person who was settled, staid, married and engaged in earning a living from the soil. By the thirteenth century the title had changed into *gea-mann,* the *gea* deriving from the archaic German form *gau* meaning *region* or *country.* Since G very easily changes into Y in linguistic developments, the word *yeoman* came to obtain by the seventeenth century and as such appeared in legal documents. From *gea-mann* emerged also *goodman* a title used both in legal documents and in direct address as a term of civility. The New England influence upon the connotative trends of the two titles was somewhat abrupt, for while Goodman in the records of the seventeenth century was used both frequently and indiscriminately as applicable to rural and urban dweller alike, Yeoman was relatively rare as a specific title. A study of the use of Yeoman in the primary sources would seem to lead to the conclusion that the title tended toward becoming an occupational designation rather than an indication of social or legal status. Richard Cutts of Portsmouth, N.H., for example, who was generally accepted as a Gentleman, was designated as a Yeoman in a deed of 1698. Another example to the point is a Bay Colony record wherein William Cole was referred to both as Gentleman and as Yeoman in the same document. Apparently yeomen were any who derived a sizeable income from agriculture. There is no evidence to indicate that Yeoman ever applied to petty farmers or to any below the Goodman status. Goodman, save for its newly acquired characteristic of embracing the moderately prosperous townsmen along with the substantial farmers, continued to function as an indication of respectable yet not greatly elevated social station.

An episode related by Cotton Mather concerning a dispute which arose in Plymouth over the implications of the title of Goodman furnishes rather direct information as to its meaning among the New England people. Attempting to impute moral worth to the title, two ministers of Plymouth denied to non-churchmembers the right to be designated as Goodman. A storm of protest followed their action, and Governor John Winthrop of the Bay Colony who was in Plymouth at the time, clarified the issue by publicly defining the term. Winthrop contended that the title implied not moral worth but worth as a citizen capable of serving his community in civic matters. He stated that

when *Juries* were first used in *England;* it was usual for the *crier,* after the names of persons fit for that service were called over, to bid them all, *Attend, good men,* and *true;* whence it grew to be a civil custom in the *English nation,* for neighbors living by one another, to call one another *good man such an one* . . .

Since, as an indication of minimum civil competency, the title could and did apply very widely, it was not always meticulously accorded either in oral address or in official records. The tendency with the passage of time was to omit it, although it had by no means passed out of existence by the end of the century.

In addition to the general titles implying varying degrees of social dignity and ranging from Lord at the top to Goodman at the bottom, New England had also collateral honorifics which, in being more specific and limited in application, had less exact social significance. When high officials of state were addressed orally or in written form, Worshipful Sir, The Right Worshipful, Your Excellency and Honorable were the common indications of deference. Military titles were employed more meticulously than other forms of deferential address. The importance of military leadership in a frontier society gave to a military title a real significance lacking to many that were merely the preservation of English custom. Not infrequently titular designations of military significance clung tenaciously to men whose qualifications for more dignifying forms of address were unquestioned. John Leverett, even after he had held the Bay Colony's highest political office, continued to be referred to, and deferred to, as Captain Leverett, an honorable designation he had early won in the militia.

The church, too, had its honorable designations, but they were sporadic and the Brother and Sister which were used held no measurable implication of social worth. Yet, in the early years when church membership was so basic a requirement for any who would aspire to prestige in New Israel, a "Bro." or its feminine counterpart prefixed to a name must surely have imparted some dignity thereto. In much the same manner, the Sir that attached to the surname of candidates for the M. A. at Harvard College added social dignity, but was for the most part confined to the institution from whose practices it derived. Its only importance in general social intercourse lay in the fact that it acted as a symbol of the importance attaching to one who pursued higher learning in New England.

The title of Reverend as applied to ministers in New England was also limited in its scope and indefinite in implications of social worth. Reverend was not always used, yet a careful checking of primary sources reveals that the frequency of its use was far greater than has heretofore been noted. Professor Samuel E. Morison's statement that "The title Reverend was seldom if ever used for clergymen in England or New England before the close of the seventeenth century," is subject to modification. The more usual and more socially important title for ministers was, of course, Master, but it was not uncommon for that prefix to be preceded by a Reverend, most often without the capital letter. It is very possible that "reverend" was used to qualify Mr. merely to distinguish if from a Mr. attached to the name of any non-preaching Master of Arts or to others where good blood or affluence, rather than education, were implied by the title. Occasionally Reverend, with the capital *R*, replaced altogether Mr. or Master and, in such instances of course, took on the socially dignifying features of the more general title of Mr. which it implied.

Despite the difficulty of determining the exact social connotations of New England honorifics, there is ample evidence to show that titles in general were used sparingly enough to imply social exclusiveness. Random examination of primary sources reveals how few of the populace were honored with formal titles. Of the 95 men who took the oath of allegiance in Topsfield and Rowley in 1678, only 12 were given a prefix of respect, 6 being designated Mr. and 6 being accorded military titles ranging from Lieutenant to Corporal. Of the 139 men of Salem who were granted land in 1636 only 16, or about 12%, were honored with Mr. The listing of Ipswich's total electorate in 1673 contained 119 names and deferential prefixes were accorded to but 35 of them: 17 Mr.s, 14 with military titles, and 4 with titles derived from church office. The Mr.s among the 116 Marblehead residents who were entitled to a share of the common lands in 1675 were restricted to 13 men. A significant percentage regarding the total distribution ratio in the Bay Colony between the titled and untitled can be derived from calculations based upon the freeman lists. According to the count of the writer, of the 3440 Bay Colony residents admitted as freemen before the year 1686, only 225, or 6½%, were recorded as distinguished by title: 3 received an Esq., 209 Mr., 12 a designation of military rank and one a Doctor. The percentage is even more strikingly illustrative of the infrequency of titular designations in official records where freemen and non-freemen alike are listed. Unfortunately, such records exist only for scattered segments of the entire population, but even in limited scope they are indicative of the characteristic distribution of honorifics. A Suffolk County record of 1678 that included names of every inhabitant, freeman or non-freeman, who took the Oath of Allegiance, yields a count of titled and untitled that sets the ratio of the titled at the level of .037 or 3.7%: of the 729 listed, 10 were designated as Mr.s and seventeen as of some military rank. The not over-generous use of title was, of course, not confined to the Bay Colony, but obtained throughout all New England in the seventeenth century.

The relative scarcity of titled persons does not necessarily argue that deferential forms of address were applied scrupulously and consistently. In fact, an extraordinary degree of carelessness and irregularity in the use of titles was exhibited by the early writers and official scribes. The various prefixes and suffixes appended in different records to the name of Increase Nowell, an early magistrate of the Bay Colony, are examples to the point. In 1630, the Charlestown records listed him as an Esquire, as did the colony records also at an early date. In 1646, however, Nowell's name was included without any form of respectful address among those of twelve Assistants variously honored with Esq.s and Mr.s. The recorder of official events in 1654 appended a Gent. as his contribution toward the proper designation for the worthy magistrate. Yet another honorific was employed when in 1656 an entry in the records of the Great and General Court referred to "Mr. Nowell." William Coddington was similarly treated by the recorders of the Rhode Island Colony. Accorded an Esquire in one place, he was referred to in another with no distinguishing title. The Rhode Island records also deal in a most inconsistent manner with the name of the socially prominent John Coggeshall. His name appeared in the records under date of May 5, 1686, without any title of honor whatsoever. Elsewhere he was designated as Gent., Esq., or Mr. Even John Winthrop Sr., who might be expected to have observed exact rules of etiquette for the use of titles, had such existed, was not particularly scrupulous in the matter. His journal refers to "one Nicholas Easton" with apparently no intention of belittling the socially prominent citizen whose name the official records, more often than not, preceded with Mr.

The court records of Maine for the year 1640 that included the names of twelve grand jurymen and designated each as Gent. could hardly have been the work of a careful scribe, for with titles so sparingly accorded, it is unlikely that all twelve could have qualified as gentlemen. Clear-cut evidence of careless titling in official records was revealed by the case of a Joseph Rednape who was called before the Essex Court in 1644 to answer for his refusal to have his child baptized. In the three references made to the defendant's name, it appeared once as Mr., once as Goodman and once simply as Joseph Rednape. Moses Maverick, whose name appeared in official records twenty-eight times between 1648 and 1681, was sometimes honored and sometimes slighted by the Marblehead scribe or scribes. The first six times his name was entered without any respectful prefix, in the two succeeding entries he was accorded a Mr., the next four again omitted the Mr., while subsequent references alternated in such fashion as to indicate the carelessness generally characteristic of New England recorders of the seventeenth century. Ten times Thaddeus Reddan's name appeared in the same records between 1672 and 1681, eight times with a Mr. The two remaining untitled entries were interpolated separately without any apparent reason for an omission of title. The proportion of eight to two would seem to indicate that Mr. was Reddan's proper title and the omission of title mere oversight. Conversely the Mr. prefixed to Ambrose Gale's name might reasonably be concluded to have been a misapplied honor, for of thirty-three references to Gale, only four accord him the distinction.

A deep impression has been made on the minds of historians by the fact that Josias Plastowe of Boston, through an action of the Great and General Court of the Bay Colony, was officially deprived of his title of Mr. as part punishment for a criminal offense. In so far as the writer has been able to discover the Plastowe incident was unique. Although it may safely be construed as evidence that title was regarded as a symbol of prestige, a conclusion easily sustained by other evidence, it cannot, as one isolated example, argue against the testimony of the innumerable instances of careless usage in the original .early records. There is no denial of the fact that seventeenth-century New England was title conscious. But the lack of precise consideration given by the scribes to prefixes and suffixes as insignia of social value permits the deduction that society as a whole was tolerating many lapses from the demands of strict usage. Such toleration showed that inherited customs of exact niceties in titular designation were not being kept intact in New England and foretold an increasing degeneration of the social significance of honorifics.

15. | JACKSON T. MAIN
| *"The Economic Class Structure of the North"*

Jackson T. Main's *The Social Structure of Revolutionary America* (Princeton, N.J., 1965) was the first full-scale attempt to define and analyze social stratification in eighteenth-century

America. In chapter 1, reprinted below with some abridgements, Main describes the social structure of the northern colonies and suggests a correlation between the level of economic development and the degree of stratification. Reprinted with the omission of most notes by permission of Princeton University Press.

The existence of an economic class structure in revolutionary America may easily be ascertained through numerous tax lists and inventories of estates, but the interpretation of this data is not so simple. Far from revealing a society which was everywhere uniform, the records show a great diversity. Generalizations can indeed be made, but not until full justice has been done to the variety of class structures which characterized the new nation. Differences between the northern and southern colonies, originating in geography and reinforced by slavery, are obvious. Each of these sections contained smaller regions—New England, the Chesapeake, the Carolina low country—while such factors as the date of settlement, the pattern of property ownership imposed by the colonizers, and subsequent development or stagnation, created other sub-sections. Despite these local variant societies, certain general features were of particular significance because they occurred everywhere and resulted in the existence of social structures common to all sections. They permit the formulation of a synthesis.

One clearly identifiable type of society existed when an area was first occupied. Although the pattern of settlement was nowhere identical, ranging from the compact, pioneer villages of New England to the extensive land holdings of frontier New York, certain characteristics were always apparent. These tended to be modified or to disappear as the frontier stage ended. The social changes which then occurred depended upon a number of circumstances. If the region possessed inferior soils, or if it was remote from markets (as in the New England uplands), its economy produced little above subsistence. The primarily subsistence farm society also occurred when a scarcity of labor or of capital prevented the development of large-scale commercial agriculture, as was the case during much of the colonial period. However when the soil and transportation facilities were both good, and when capital and labor were relatively abundant, a commercial (or "plantation") farm society was created. A fourth type of social structure appeared with the rise of cities. Although every colony-state had its peculiar history, each possessed some variation of these four basic social structures: the frontier, subsistence farm, commercial farm, and urban.

The northern frontier was most commonly settled by the New England system, in which the people moved as a group and divided the land among themselves. Class distinctions were few. The rich stayed in the east, and although every frontier contained some poor men, the great majority of pioneers were property owners. The system of distributing land, at least in New England, often reinforced this relative equality, because during most of the colonial period every head of family had received a share. The proprietors of Wallingford, Connecticut gave to every "High rank man, or his hairs" 476 acres, to each "Middel Rank" family 357 acres, and to every man of "Loer Rank" 238 acres. Evidently the proprietors thought in terms of a social hierarchy, but economically the effect of such a division was to create or reinforce the existence of a society in which small farmers formed the great majority. When shares of land were offered for sale, the prices were low enough to encourage settlement and could be paid over a period of time. For example, original shares in the town of Kent, Connecticut, were offered for as little as £165 old tenor (which probably equalled about £50 sterling), and no payment had to be made for three years.

When the pioneers settled individually instead of by groups, the outcome was not much different. Land prices charged by northern speculators were low enough so that poor men could become farmers almost at once. Speculative tracts in Worcester County, Massachusetts, were valued at 7s per acre before the war.* Elsewhere in New England wild land was worth from 3s per acre (Henry Knox's price for Maine land) on up to 12s an acre (Jacob Wendell's large tract in Berkshire County). The better land, which was of course more valuable, could always be obtained on credit or even occasionally for nothing at all when a speculator was anxious to attract settlers. Pioneers in New York paid James Duane £80 for one hundred acres—a considerable sum, but he allowed ten years in which to pay. Newspapers advertised land for £30 to £75 the hundred (6s to 15s per acre) or at low rents with none at all for the first few years. A traveller reported that land near the headwaters of the Susque-

---

* All figures are in currency unless otherwise indicated. As a rule of thumb, sterling was equal to money minus one-fourth.

hanna, in New York, sold for £20 to £40 the hundred (4s to 8s per acre) and that Wyoming Valley land cost only £5 sterling per hundred, which could be paid over a period of fifteen years without interest, plus a small quit rent amounting to an additional £6 for the period. In Pennsylvania the government sold tax-delinquent unimproved land at an average price of 14s per hundred. Such land was probably inferior, not so much in quality as in location with respect to transportation. The farmer who hoped to prosper by the sale of his surplus crops or by the rising value of favorably situated land had to pay more. Land ten miles from the Mohawk was worth only 1½s per acre while that along the river sold for 5s or 10s. Still this was a cheap price for valley soil.

The pioneer therefore was able to obtain land easily. It is true that first-rate property required more cash than most settlers possessed, and that where speculators were permitted to engross large tracts the farmer had to pay the profit. Sporadic complaints indicate some dissatisfaction, but these were few enough to prove that the difficulty was not serious. Thus hardworking settlers with little or no money could acquire land and survive even though they might not have a cash income for many years.

The typical frontier society therefore was one in which class distinctions were minimized. The wealthy speculator, if one was involved, usually remained at home, so that ordinarily no one of wealth was a resident. The class of landless poor was small. The great majority were landowners, most of whom were also poor because they were starting with little property and had not yet cleared much land nor had they acquired the farm tools and animals which would one day make them prosperous. Few artisans settled on the frontier except for those who practiced a trade to supplement their primary occupation of farming. There might be a storekeeper, a minister, and perhaps a doctor; and there were a number of landless laborers. All the rest were farmers.

The scattered but numerous tax records of New England towns make possible a more detailed description of the frontier class structure there. Ordinarily only polls, land, and certain farm animals were taxed, but narrow though the tax base was, it is possible to determine the distribution of land and to identify, in part, the occupations of the settlers.

Warren, New Hampshire, was a typical frontier community.

Among thirty taxpayers in 1781 only one had over 500 acres. He and two other men, the "large property owners" of their town, formed the wealthiest 10 percent of the population. They owned about 30 percent of the taxable land and farm animals. This proportion, as will be seen presently, indicates a wide distribution of property. Seven heads of families (23 percent of the taxpayers) were landless, to which number may be added one person for whom a poll tax was paid, probably the son of the taxpayer. The rest of the men owned small farms. If, therefore, the word "small" is defined so as to include all farms of less than 500 acres—and this is a workable definition—73 percent of the community belonged to that class. Most New Hampshire towns, except those near the coast, conformed to this type.

The colony did, however, contain some towns which developed as a result of speculative activity. Wolfeborough contained in 1774 fifty-three taxpayers, of whom five held much of the property owned by residents—over half of the livestock and improved land. At the other end of the social scale, about half of the residents did not own land. In this frontier community, property was concentrated in the hands of a few; and instead of the small landowners forming a majority, there existed a large number of landless men. The reason for this inequality lay in the presence of very large speculative holdings, especially the "Abbot-Wentworth" farm, which contained nearly 3,000 acres and on which were employed a number of landless men. Wolfeborough was not unique, but it was not typical.

Towns of the Massachusetts frontier had a social structure like that of Warren. A good example is Ashfield, which was just emerging from the frontier stage in 1776. The tax lists of that year included no one who owned more than moderate property. The 10 percent who paid the largest tax held 36 percent of the taxable property, a low figure for the colony. About 30 percent of the taxpayers did not have land. One of these was a doctor, who reported only a horse. The community also contained another doctor and three mill-owners but apparently no artisans.

Highly informative are the town assessment lists taken in Massachusetts before the Revolution. These record the annual worth of the real estate, technically the yearly rent. Supposedly the total value of the property was six times the rent, but judging from land prices given in probate records the assessors considerably undervalued the property. Unimproved and other types of relatively un-productive land were not taxed. In addition to land, the value of stock in trade and money at interest, tons of shipping, houses, shops, mills, stillhouses, warehouses, and the like, and certain farm animals, are included. The total worth of this property is not given, but the distribution of land can be analyzed and the occupations of the men can be deduced.

The Berkshire County towns of Sandisfield, Williamstown, and Tyringham were all recently settled in 1771. In the last, indeed, nearly half of the houses were called "log huts," and several of the farmers (identifiable because they owned oxen) had not yet taken title to their farms. About thirty percent of the men in these communities did not own land. Some may have been renting a tract, but this seems unlikely since few owned farm animals. They made up a class of agricultural laborers which probably consisted principally of pioneers' sons. The great majority of the residents were small farmers whose land was assessed at less than £10 annual value and usually at less than £4. Williamstown contained four men who paid a tax on "factorage," which meant that they were selling goods as well as farming, but there were no professional men listed and no artisans except for one potash manufacturer and some mill owners who were primarily farmers. The property of the community was widely distributed, for there were no men of wealth. . . .

The typical frontier society as revealed by these tax lists was characterized by economic equality. Charles Grant, in his fine study of Kent, Connecticut, concluded that this frontier town was democratic. Land was cheap, property equally distributed, and classes scarcely existed. Towns of the Wolfeborough type, born of large speculative holdings, form exceptions to the rule. Such towns were, however, rare especially in New England, and equality was the normal characteristic of frontier society everywhere.

This equality did not exclude differences. The northern frontier community often contained all the elements of those complex societies which would ultimately develop. Here were the real or potential landed aristocrats—a Philip Schuyler of Saratoga, New York, William Butler of Warren, New Hampshire, with 620 acres, Colonel Henry Rust of Wolfeborough with 600. Here also were the creditors: John Mills of Kent was owed over £3,000 in 1760. Here were perhaps an innkeeper, a country storekeeper, a lawyer (Goshen by

1751), a doctor (Wolfeborough in 1774), or a minister. Here too were a scattering of artisans, especially millers, blacksmiths, and cordwainers (shoemakers). Many of these were farmers with a trade or artisans with a farm. Finally, every such society contained landless laborers and occasionally tenants. The generalized frontier society included a very few settlers who had a store or an inn, or practiced a profession, fewer than one in ten who followed a trade, one out of four or five who were laborers. The remaining 60 percent or more were farmers.

When the frontier stage of a northern community ended, farming continued to be its chief occupation, but society became more complex, more differentiated. Its growth and direction depended upon the nature of the land and the accessibility of markets: if the land was good and markets were close by, or if transportation to markets was cheap, commercial agriculture developed. Otherwise, the members of the community had to be largely, though of course never entirely, self-sufficient, which meant that most of them must be farmers. The availability of capital influenced a community's growth also, since a commercial farm required a large investment and higher operating costs, especially for labor. Even where both land and transportation were good, some time might elapse before capital could be accumulated. Meanwhile the farmer must supply most of his own needs.

The subsistence farm society was the most common type throughout New England and perhaps the entire North. The social structure, like that of the frontier, remained simple. Great wealth could not be or had not yet been accumulated; therefore no wealthy class was present. Neither did the landless laborers increase in numbers, for land was not very valuable and therefore could be easily obtained; besides, those who wanted wealth did not remain in such an area but sought richer lands. Accordingly a majority of the residents continued to occupy a middle-class position and to remain small farmers. It was a frontier in arrested development.

Examples of this type of society are numerous. The town of Goshen, Connecticut, had passed from the frontier stage by 1771, yet it had developed only a small class of well-to-do residents and no one of real wealth lived there. In 1787 there was still no upper class. The richest 10 percent of the taxpayers had paid, in 1751, 23 percent of the tax. This proportion now increased slowly, reaching 27 percent by 1787 (compared with 36 percent in Milford, an urban center on the coast). Although total wealth increased, the per capita wealth was actually declining slightly. The proportion of men without land was about the same in 1787 as in 1751. Twenty-one men—11 percent —paid a "faculty" tax on the profits of a non-farm occupation. Most of the assessments were small, indicating that the taxpayer was an artisan or perhaps had a share of a mill. Three men paid the much larger tax typical of a shopkeeper or lawyer, and the presence of innkeepers and doctors is also suggested. However the town remained primarily agricultural, having changed little from frontier days.

Simsbury, Connecticut, was located near Goshen in the northwestern uplands. Its society in 1782 was very similar. No one was rich or even well-to-do: the estate with the highest assessed value (which determined the tax, and was based upon polls, oxen, cattle, horses, swine, improved land, houses, and faculties) was £116, owned by a man who had 94 acres and 19 farm animals. Only 21 percent of the men lacked land. A faculty tax was paid by less than 10 percent. The community contained one doctor, a minister, and probably a justice of the peace, but it seems to have lacked a shopkeeper. The wealthiest 10 percent of the taxpayers owned 20 percent of the taxable property, including polls. In nearby Winchester the distribution of property was almost identical. Here the non-farm population included, out of 148 taxpayers, one storekeeper, who paid only a small tax; one doctor, also of average wealth; four men who had mills; two shoemakers; five tavernkeepers, one of whom was also a miller and farmer; and a blacksmith-farmer, the town's wealthiest citizen. . . .

Towns of the subsistence farm type were not limited to interior counties . . . but were found within twenty miles of Boston. In Suffolk County, which included the city, a group of inland villages near Rhode Island were actually more extreme examples of the type than were the towns of Worcester County. Although the region had been settled for decades, the distance from Boston and Providence, together with the rough terrain and lack of navigable streams, made transportation costly. One observer remarked that he "never saw a Country so full of rocks & Stones." The amount of good soil was so limited that the farmers, though they seem to have eaten well, could not acquire large property, nor were merchants, artisans, or professional men attracted.

The consequence was a society almost entirely rural. Probate records indicate that less than one-tenth of the men were artisans. There were few professional men, and fewer still in trade. A small class of landless laborers existed, but two-thirds of the men were farmers of whom a large majority had property worth less than £500. The inventories of nearly two hundred estates before and after the Revolution included no one who was well-to-do (more than £2,000) and only half a dozen who showed more than £1,000 worth of property. On the other hand fewer than one in five had less than £100. Further evidence for the equal distribution of property lies in the fact that the wealthiest 10 percent of the men held only one-fourth of the property. . . .

States south and west of New England had larger areas of fertile soil and better transportation facilities, so that commercial farming was more general. Indeed the distinction between commercial and subsistence agriculture was less significant than the contrasts resulting from different historical developments. In New York, the east bank of the Hudson always had been occupied by very large estates, whereas the west bank contained mostly small farms; and the most accurate dichotomy is perhaps between large- and small-farm societies. Yet most of the landowners, by necessity, had to be primarily subsistence farmers. Many towns in Ulster and Orange County, or east of the Hudson back from the river, were indistinguishable from the New England communities. The tax lists for Cambridge, Hosick, and Claverack East districts, near the Massachusetts border, for Salem and North Castle in eastern Westchester County, and for Cornwall, Goshen, and Hannover west of the river all reveal societies which resemble the frontier in their equal distribution of property, the virtual absence of a wealthy class, and the large proportion of medium-sized farms.

Similarly in Pennsylvania, Berks County conforms to the subsistence farm type of social structure. The tax lists do not encourage analysis of the distribution of property, but the occupational structure can be determined. About one-fourth of the men were laborers, most of whom owned no land. Artisans were increasing in number during the revolutionary era, but did not exceed 10 percent of the population, while a few innkeepers, shopkeepers, and professional men appeared. The great majority—nearly two-thirds—were farmers, almost all of whom held less than 500 acres, 100 acres being the most common amount. . . .

The characteristic feature of the northern subsistence farm towns, or of those resembling the type, was the presence of an exceptional proportion of small farmers, whose properties and geographical location prevented their producing any considerable cash crop. This fact required them to do most of their own work, so that their society contained a relatively small proportion of artisans and of laborers. Some of these communities contained a few men of considerable means, who used hired help, made purchases from artisans, and marketed a surplus; but many towns entirely lacked an upper class. Property was equally distributed, the typical resident owning about £100 worth of personal and over £300 worth of real property. It was a society which almost guaranteed a degree of comfort, but economic opportunities were slight. The path of wealth lay in the commercial farm area or in the city.

The commercial farm community, by definition, sold a much larger quantity of agricultural products than did the subsistence farmers. Good soil was of course a necessity, but most important was accessibility to market, either by being close enough to a major urban center so that goods could be carried easily (as was the case with towns near Boston, New York, and Philadelphia), or by being located on a navigable river or a good ocean harbor. In contrast to the subsistence farm villages, these towns had greater wealth, more rich men, a greater concentration of property in the possession of the wealthy, sometimes more artisans, professional men, and men engaged in commerce, a much higher proportion of large farmers, and fewer small ones. They also ordinarily contained more laborers. Examples are Groton, Connecticut; New Town and the Hudson River communities in New York; Waltham, Milton, and other Suffolk County towns in Massachusetts; most of New Chester County in Delaware; Burlington County, New Jersey; and Chester County, Pennsylvania.

Groton, Connecticut, was an old town near New London on the Sound, which in 1783 contained over 500 taxpayers (including one identified as "the old Virgin"). The tax basis was primarily improved land, assessed at a low rate. The median assessed valuation was £33, and most residents held not far from that amount. There were however a number of men with estates valued at more than £100. The wealthiest 10 percent held 29 percent of the wealth, compared with about 22 percent in Connecticut's subsistence farm towns. Groton's society was more diversified than that of the inland communities. It had a lawyer, a physician who was also a shopkeeper, seven other shopkeepers (none of any size), fifteen tavern-keepers, nine blacksmiths, seven shoemakers, thirteen carpenters and joiners, as well as clothiers, tanners, tailors, and a goldsmith. The artisans formed about 8 percent of the population. There were also sixteen mills belonging to the substantial farmers. A quarter of the men were rated at less than £20, which meant that they had almost no property since a poll was rated at £18. These formed the labor force for farmers and artisans. All told, the non-farm element totalled over one-third of the population. Most of the wealth, however, was owned by the large farmers. . . .

More representative, or perhaps extreme, examples of the commercial farm type of society were the Hudson River districts such as Kinderhook, Livingston manor, Claverack West, and the Manor of Rensselaer (or "Ranselear"). The tax lists of 1779 . . . do not indicate occupations nor is it possible to discover for certain the proportion of landless men; moreover the currency used varied and was obviously inflated in certain cases. The characteristics which everywhere distinguished the class structure of the commercial farm society from that of the subsistence farm and frontier are, however, obvious. Large farmers were much more numerous. About one in seven of the men held real estate worth £500 or more, twice as many as in subsistence farm areas, and many times the number of large owners on the frontier. Whereas the frontier almost never contained estates worth £1,000, they were common in the richer communities; and the proportion of taxable property held by the wealthiest 10 percent generally exceeded 40 percent, contrasted with 20 percent to 35 percent in the other New York districts. . . .

Chester County, Pennsylvania, was a rich farming region in the southeastern corner of the state, adjacent to Philadelphia. The colony-state as a whole contained a higher proportion of landless men than did New England, and Chester in particular included a large percentage of such men, which varied from 40 percent in some townships to over half in others, averaging 47 percent in 1765. The explanation probably lies in the presence of indentured servants employed by the well-to-do farmers, sometimes identified in the tax lists as "inmates" as contrasted with "freemen." These "inmates" totalled about 10 percent of the adult men. Some towns, however, did not distinguish between "inmates" and "freemen," so that the true proportion of the former is probably nearer 15 percent. Some of those who lacked land were artisans, but there remains a laboring class which formed at least one-third of the population.

The principal characteristics which distinguished commercial farm societies from the subsistence or small farm type are, first, the greater average wealth of the former; second, the presence of more large than small farmers (regardless of how these are defined), whereas in subsistence communities the reverse was true; third, a slightly larger proportion of laborers; fourth, a greater concentration of wealth in the hands of the large property holders; and finally, more artisans, shopkeepers, and professional men. The last three characteristics existed to an even greater extent in the cities.

Cities during the revolutionary era may be divided into the lesser and the greater urban centers. With certain modifications in the former, they shared the same qualities. Both exhibited one fundamental feature: a wealthy class larger and richer than elsewhere in the North, controlling a greater proportion of the property. The wealth of this class was gained primarily from foreign trade, but in addition some large landholders made their homes in the city. Since many merchants invested in land, the townspeople not only possessed far more personal property than did the country folk but owned a substantial amount of real estate as well, including some sizable fortunes.

A variety of data demonstrate the higher concentration of property in these urban centers. The towns of York, Maine, and Charlestown, Massachusetts, both suffered heavy fire losses in 1775 which were reported in detail. Nearly two hundred persons claimed damage in York. The twenty principal losers accounted for 43 percent of the total sum. None of these men was unusually rich, though three reported that they lost over £2,000. Charlestown's inhabitants claimed damage in excess of £100,000. The 10 percent who lost the largest amount owned 47½ percent of the total. Tax lists indicate the same concentration. In the trading center of Kittery, Maine, the 10 percent largest properties accounted for 45 percent of the total valuation, including polls. The 1770 tax list for Portsmouth indicates that 5 percent of the taxpayers owned 34 percent of the taxable property, which means that 10 percent held nearly half. According to the assessment list of 1771 for Waltham, Massachusetts, the 10 percent largest owners of real estate held 43½ percent of the total value. In Newburyport they held 40 percent, while in Salem the proportion was no less than 60 percent. In Milford, Connecticut, it was only 36 percent, but the figure is high for that state, where 25 percent was average. In Albany, New York, the concentration of real and personal property was 44 percent, about the same as that for the rich Hudson Valley districts. The top 10 percent of the town of New Castle, Delaware, received 49 percent of the income, the highest share in the state except Dover hundred. Even this great concentration of property is less than that in Boston, where, according to probate records, the richest 10 percent had 57 percent of the wealth; while in Philadelphia the same proportion paid over two-thirds of the tax.

Further evidence for the existence of an exceptionally wealthy class may be drawn from other sources. The commercial farm centers had a higher proportion of men owning property valued between £1,000 and £2,000, but the cities contained a far larger percentage of residents who had fortunes of £2,000 and almost all of those owning £5,000. The towns of Dover and New Castle, Delaware, contained half of the men in the state who were assessed for incomes of over £200. On the Massachusetts assessment list, there were as many men in Salem and Medford whose real estate was rated at £25 annually as in the commercial farm towns of Milton and Waltham; and in addition the two small urban centers contained practically all of the well-to-do merchants. Among a dozen Connecticut towns, the only important urban center, Milford, had incomparably the largest number of men with taxable estates of £200: more, indeed, than all the others combined. The nearest rival, Wethersfield, was itself a smaller mercantile community on the Connecticut. Finally in Suffolk County, fourteen out of fifteen estates valued in probate for £5,000 belonged to Bostonians, who also owned forty-five out of sixty-seven evaluated at £2,000, or 72 percent of the large properties. Most of these men were merchants, but many of them had land, and several, such as Jeremiah Preble, who had £6,000 worth of land in Maine, were very large landowners.

The social structure of the major cities also included an exceptionally high proportion of men at the bottom of the economic scale. The lesser towns did not always have as many poor. New Castle contained rather fewer than did the surrounding areas, as did Milford, Connecticut, and Newburyport, Massachusetts. On the other hand Salem, York, and Medford included an above average proportion of men with little real estate. The town of Chester, Pennsylvania, contained in 1765 the remarkably high proportion of 61 percent landless men, about one-third of whom were "inmates." In general the more populous towns had the most poor people. New Hampshire probate records show that 30 percent of Portsmouth's inventories were valued at less than £100 total property as contrasted with 17 percent in the surrounding country. Nearly 30 percent of the Boston estates were worth less than £50 and 40 percent were valued at less than £100, compared with 8 percent and 17 percent respectively in the nearby commercial farm towns. Urban society, therefore, tended to have relatively large upper and lower classes, so that the middle group of property owners was proportionately smaller than in rural areas.

The occupations followed by the city dwellers were, of course, much more diverse than was the case in rural societies. Salem's tax assessment roll for 1771 listed thirty-six merchants and shipowners owning £200 worth of stock in trade, comprising one-eighth of the population. Richard Derby, the richest man in town, had £6,020 in stock, a still-house, 5½ warehouses, a 5,300-foot wharf, and 415 tons of shipping, in addition to £160 annual value in real estate which was perhaps the equivalent of £6,000 worth. Another merchant had nearly as much land and stock and even more tonnage. In addition the town had thirty lesser shopkeepers and artisans with shops. The smaller center of Medford had a somewhat lesser proportion of merchants but even more shopowners. Nearly a third of Portsmouth's population were artisans. The probate records during the pre-revolutionary years indicate that perhaps an eighth of the men were merchants or shopkeepers ("traders" being the generic term there) and about a tenth were professional men. The town also had a large population of seamen (about one-fourth), and a lesser number of laborers who were landsmen. In contrast, the nearby commercial farm towns contained only a third as many artisans in proportion to their population, and far fewer traders. Similarly the artisans of Chester, Pennsylvania, comprised at least one-third of the population. The two major sources for a study of Boston's society give much the same results. The tax assessor's book for 1780 lists over 1,300 persons. Of these, artisans accounted for 36 percent. The same figure is derived from an examination of over 500 probated estates. The next largest class consisted of men in trade, including ship captains, traders, shopkeepers, and merchants. This group formed 26 percent according to the tax list and 29 percent in the probate records. Laborers are almost never identified as such, but they evidently comprised most of those whose occupations are not given and whose estates were small. Such poor men, together with the mariners, formed about one-quarter of the population in both tax and probate records. Since these records did not include indentured servants or slaves, the true figure is considerably higher. The assessment list of 1771 indicates that 39 percent of the population lacked property, but not all of these were laborers. Many artisans, of course, were skilled workers rather than independent entrepreneurs. Professional men formed 3 or 4 percent of the population. Most of the rest evidently were tavernkeepers, pilots, farmers, or miscellaneous white-collar workers. Urban society was highly diversified and offered opportunities to many skills. The chances for advancement were good because the rapid economic growth constantly created new demands and new wealth.

The four types of social structure during the revolutionary era had distinctive characteristics. The feature most peculiar to the frontier—high mobility—will be discussed presently. Newly settled areas often had a higher proportion of people without land than did older areas. This occurred most commonly in conjunction with land speculation, but was due also to the difficulty experienced by men trying to get started. The class of poor people in Kent, Connecticut (as defined by Charles Grant), was larger in 1740 than at any time during the next thirty years. Similarly in Goshen the proportion of landless men steadily diminished between 1741 and 1787 as the poorer people either moved on or secured land. As a rule, however, frontier communities had a high proportion of landowners from the start. Few pioneers had large estates, and property was equally distributed. The 10 percent of the men who owned the largest farms held about one-third of the total wealth.

Land in subsistence farm areas was cheap, so that even if many pioneers at first were landless, they soon acquired farms, until only one in five were still without one. Since the community produced little surplus, few men of wealth were present. Instead, an even larger proportion of the men were small farmers than on the frontier, and the concentration of property was about the same. Such a society was almost entirely agricultural because most of the men had to be as nearly self-sufficient as possible.

Commercial farm societies contained far more propertyless men than did other rural communities. The proportion was not high in New England because truly large-scale agriculture did not develop there (though there are exceptions such as the Narragansett "plantations" in Rhode Island). Elsewhere in the North farm laborers and indentured servants were common and even a few slaves were used. This landless class made up nearly half of the male population in regions such as Chester County, Pennsylvania, and southwestern New Jersey. The farmers owned more property than did those on the frontier or in subsistence communities and some became rich. The wealthiest 10 percent paid between 30 percent and 45 percent of the taxes and owned nearly half of the property.

Urban society had an even greater proportion of rich men and an even higher concentration of property, probably exceeding 60 percent in both Boston and Philadelphia. There were also many poor people in the towns, including most of the slaves. Whereas in the country the great majority were farmers, city folk had many occupations so that urban society was diversified.

The general class structure of the North during the revolutionary era may best be analyzed through probate records. Of these, the Massachusetts series is particularly useful because real as well as personal property was evaluated. Everywhere there were people without land or houses. Such men almost always had little property of any sort and composed, generally, between one-fourth and one-fifth of the population in Massachusetts. When indentured servants are included it is a fair estimate that the class of poor people in the North comprised nearly one-third of the whole white population.*

At the top of the class structure were men with fortunes of £2,000 or more. These totalled at most 3 percent of the population in

---

* Another 10 percent or so had very little real property and were little better off financially than were the landless.

New Hampshire, 7 percent in Massachusetts, and perhaps 14 percent in New Jersey, the average for the northern states being about 10 percent. Substantial property owners with £500 to £2,000 made up probably 30 percent or so, and small property owners about the some proportion. The wealthiest 10 percent owned about half of the inventoried property in Massachusetts, 40 percent in New Hampshire, and 45 percent in New Jersey, the last figure being average for the North. This appears at first sight to represent a high degree of concentration, but according to recent studies the wealthiest 10 percent of families in the United States had 64 percent of the wealth in 1929 and 56 percent in 1956. The outstanding feature of northern society was not its small wealthy class but the very large proportion of substantial middle-class property owners.

The middle-class character of northern society was also made clear by the occupations of its people. By far the largest number were engaged in agriculture as independent, though small farmers. Nearly 30 percent of New Jersey's men in pre-revolutionary probate records were denominated "husbandmen" or "yeomen," which almost always meant that they were farmers, and another 20 percent of the men were certainly farmers also. In New Hampshire half of the people were so identified and farmers probably made up 60 percent of the total number of men. Massachusetts assessment lists and probate records give a similar result, with the proportion rising to 70 percent outside the urban area. Certainly farmers comprised fully half of the population.

Artisans were also an important element. They comprised over 20 percent of the men in Suffolk County, 10 percent in Worcester County, and the same elsewhere in New England. In New Jersey also they formed about one-tenth of the people, and this figure is probably a fair average for the North as a whole. About one-third of the men in New Jersey were laborers.* The proportion was a little higher in Pennsylvania and New York, somewhat lower in New England. Men engaged in commerce scarcely made up more than 2 or 3 percent of the population, professionals formed a similar proportion, and the rest followed a variety of occupations

---

* I have added, to the data derived from probate records, an estimated 10 percent for indentured servants and 4 percent for slaves. Slaves comprised nearly one-eighth of the population in Pennsylvania and New York but not over 3 percent in New England, averaging 6 percent in the North generally.

principally of the "white collar" type. Perhaps 20 percent of the people received their principal income from a non-farm property. Many laborers did so too, but it seems likely that 70 percent of the population depended directly on the soil. Society was diversified, yet still predominantly agricultural.

The reason why historians have disagreed concerning the northern class structure is obvious: their conclusions depended upon which set of facts they emphasized. Whoever studied the New England frontier, as did Grant, or the subsistence farm communities—even, in some areas, the commercial farm towns—naturally saw a democratic society. On the other hand the student who fixed his attention on the towns, or on most commercial farm areas, perceived obvious economic inequalities and a distinct class structure. The same contradictions appear in the South.

16. AUBREY C. LAND
"Economic Base and Social Structure:
The Northern Chesapeake in the
Eighteenth Century"

In order to understand the nature of society in seventeenth- and eighteenth-century Virginia and Maryland, Aubrey C. Land has turned from traditional literary evidence to new kinds of data. By analyzing and comparing inventories of estate spanning a period of eighty years, he has discovered aspects of the social and economic life of Chesapeake planters that otherwise might have remained hidden. From the *Journal of Economic History,* 25 (1965), 639–54. Reprinted without notes by permission of the *Journal of Economic History.*

The *Maryland Gazette* for 18 October 1749 carried an obituary of more than common interest:

On the Eleventh Instant Died, at his Seat on Wye River in Queen Anne's County, Richard Bennett, Esq. in the Eighty-third Year of his Age, generally lamented by all that knew him. As his great fortune enabled him to do much good, so (happily for many) his Inclination was equal to his Ability, to relieve the indigent and distressed, which he did very liberally, without regarding of what Party, Religion or Country, they were. As he was the greatest Trader in this Province, so great Numbers fell in his Debt, and a more merciful Creditor could not be, having never deprived the Widows or Orphans of his Debtors of a Support; and when what the Debtors left, was not sufficient for that purpose, frequently supply'd the deficiency. His long Experience and great Knowledge in Business, as well as his known Candor and generosity, occasion'd many to apply to him for Advice and Assistance, and none were ever disappointed of what was in his Power, and several by his means, extricated out of great Difficulties. . . .

A later issue adds some particulars:

On Wednesday last was solemnized the Funeral of Richard Bennett, Esq. of Wye River, in a very handsome and decent Manner, by the Direction of his sole executor, the Hon. Col. Edward Lloyd. Mr. Bennett, by his Will, has forgiven above one hundred and fifty of his poor Debtors, and has made Provision for the Maintainance of many of his Overseers, and other poor Dependents, and settled a Sum of Money to be paid annually to the Poor of a Parish in Virginia: and done many other Acts of Charity and Munificence. He was supposed to be the Richest Man on the Continent. . . .

Bennett's obvious virtues as a Christian gentleman need no underscoring, but two comments of the eulogist should be noted: his great wealth and his calling as a "trader." Perhaps the enthusiastic editor went beyond the exact truth in estimating Bennett's fortune, though probably not much. The field certainly included a few other candidates for the richest man. A neighbor across the Bay, Charles Carroll, counted his total worth at something like a hundred thousand pounds sterling, including £30,000 loaned at 6 per cent interest. Robert Carter, south of the Potomac in Virginia, could reckon himself worth nearly as much. The second William Byrd had left an impressive heritage which his son of the same name had already begun to dissipate. Even by the standards of London these were wealthy men.

All three alternate possibilities for the title of richest man are better known than Bennett, because they have had biographers, or because they played important political roles, or both. They belong to what has been variously called the aristocracy, the ruling oligarchy, or the squirearchy. The pejorative connotations of all three terms incline me toward a label suggested by a profound student of early American social and cultural history, "the southern agrarian leaders." We can understand them in a sense as leaders of an agrarian area. But when we inquire about the economic milieu in which they flourished or seek the mechanisms by which they acquired their dominant positions, we are faced with some difficulties.

The traditional historiography has leaned heavily on literary evidence, and when it does not ignore these questions often gives impressions that are positively misleading. As sources, personal letters, travel accounts, and memoirs have the great merit of being relatively easy to put into context and ideal to paraphrase. A few dozen up to a few thousand items of this kind can be quilted into interesting and convincing patterns. The procedure has the limitations of the sources. Even the most acute observer focuses on objects of high visibility. The high tor eclipses the molehill in the landscape until the king falls to his death because of the "little gentleman in black velvet."

In the eighteenth-century Chesapeake, the "great planters" were the element of high visibility. They held slaves, owned vast estates, and built magnificent houses that have survived as showpieces. Visitors came under the spell of these gracious livers and left charming accounts of their balls, their tables, and their luxury. Planters themselves contributed to the effect. They wrote letters and a few left diaries that have survived along with their great houses. Viewed through these sources they cut large figures and play the star roles in the arrangements that the people of the Chesapeake made for themselves in that period. These personages are accurately enough drawn, but they are a detail, though an important one, in the total production. Unfortunately the supporting cast and stage hands that made the production possible receive next to no attention, sometimes not even the courtesy of a billing. Just as *Hamlet* cannot be successfully staged without Hamlet, there can hardly be a play with Hamlet alone.

Not much literary evidence for the minor figures has come down; but another kind does exist and, even though bristling with difficulties and overawing in bulk, it can be compelled to yield some data for a fuller view. This body of material has been brought together in two despositories, the Maryland Hall of Records and the Virginia

State Archives, and properly canvassed will fill in some gaps in our knowledge of Chesapeake affairs. It consists of inventories and accounts of the estates in personalty of all free men at the time of their death.* The argument in this paper applies only to Maryland, for which a statistical analysis has been completed. The Virginia counties that have been analyzed give me the clear impression that differences between the areas north and south of the Potomac are not very great in respect of the basic contention here. Both were a part of a single economic region which political boundaries could not split asunder and were treated as a unit in contemporary British commercial records.

To obtain from the voluminous Maryland records a sample that faithfully reflects conditions in the northern Chesapeake, some of the usual economies are not possible. Geographical sampling by selected counties is ruled out. The process of carving new counties out of large older counties went on continuously from 1690 to the Revolution. Consequently the county of one decade is not necessarily the same unit in a later decade. Accordingly, all counties of the province are included. Over the entire eighty-year period 1690–1770 for which the records are reasonably complete the alternate decades from 1690–1699 to 1750–1759 have been tabulated. If it can be assumed that these sizable samples reflect with reasonable accuracy the spectrum of planters' estates, then we have some basis for understanding an otherwise shadowy aspect of the Chesapeake economy.

The profile of estates in the decade January 1, 1690, to December 31, 1699, shows an unexpected imbalance. Three quarters of these estates (74.6 per cent, to be precise) are of the magnitude £100 sterling or less. In the next bracket, £100 to £200, the percentage drops to 12.1, and in succeeding hundred-pound brackets to 5.5 per cent, 2.7 per cent, 1.4 per cent, 1.3 per cent, 0.6 per cent, and 0.3 per cent. After a break in the distribution, a meager 1.5 per cent at the top are valued at £1,000 sterling or greater.

Beyond the obvious fact that the less affluent far outnumber the better off, this analysis tells us little. The estates, small or great, are all those of planters—a handful of physicians, mariners, and clergymen specifically excepted. "Planter," then, simply describes an oc-

---

* Women who had property in their own right were also included. Mainly widows and spinsters, they formed a tiny fraction of the total.

cupation without indicating economic status of the individual. To get at what this distribution means in terms of worldly goods, standard of living, and possibly social status, it is necessary to look at particulars in the inventories themselves. Here impressions become vivid.

The planters at the bottom of the scale, those with estates of £100 or less, have at best a "country living": a saddle horse or two, half a dozen or fewer cows, a few swine to furnish fresh or salt meat for the table according to the season, a modest assortment of household utensils—sometimes nothing more than a cooking pot or skillet, a few tools and agricultural implements. Many essentials of a household—for instance, plates and cups—are missing in fully half the inventories, an omission indicating that makeshifts such as wooden bowls and gourds took the place of these articles. The appraisers of estates overlooked no article, not even a cracked cup without a handle or a single glass bottle. In brief the standard of living might be described as rude sufficiency. The self-styled poet laureate of Maryland, Eben Cooke, calls planters at this level "cockerouses."

The inventories also speak to the productivity of these small planters. In those inventories made during the autumn and winter after the tobacco had been cut the appraisers carefully estimated the size of the deceased's crop. Crop entries range from twelve hundred pounds, a trifle over two hogsheads, up to three thousand pounds, or about six hogsheads. This represented the producer's cash crop, almost his entire annual income, excepting possibly the occasional sale of a heifer, a pig, or a few bushels of corn to a neighbor or local trader. Reckoning the price of tobacco at ten shillings a hundred, these small producers could count their disposable incomes at a figure between £6 and £15 a year.

Even taking into account the small planter's self-sufficiency in fresh vegetables from the kitchen garden, cereals from whatever field crops he grew besides tobacco, and meat from his own farm animals, an income of this size imposed iron limitations on him. Between investment and consumption he had no choice. Such necessities as thread, needles, powder and shot, coarse fabrics for clothing or featherbeds, and an occasional tool or a household utensil strained his credit at the country store until his crop was sold. For the small planter, provincial quitrents, church tithes, and taxes represented a real burden. He cast his ballot for a representative who could resist the blandishments of governors and hold public expenses to the barest minimum. In good part the pressures from men of this kind kept investment in the public sector to lowest dimensions, whether the object was a county courthouse, a lighthouse, or a governor's mansion. As a private person he could not invest from savings because he had none. With tobacco crops barely sufficient to cover his debt to the country merchant, a disastrous year could prostrate him. A lawsuit, the death of cattle in a winter freeze, or a fire in house or barn forced him to contract debts which had often not been paid at the time of his death and which ate up his entire personal estate, leaving his heirs without a penny. Not infrequently his administrator actually overpaid his estate in order to save trifling family heirlooms more precious than their valuation in the inventory. Investment in a slave or indentured servant to increase his productivity, though not completely out of the question, was very difficult.

The small planter clearly was not the beneficiary of the planting society of the Chesapeake. He bred his increase and added to the growing population that filled up vacant land from the shoreline to the mountains before the Revolution. In the language of the courts he qualified as a planter. Considering the circumstances of his life, it would stretch the usual meaning of the term to call him a yeoman, particularly if he fell in the lower half of his group.

In the brackets above £100, different characteristics of the estates immediately strike the eye. Sumptuary standards of planters above this line were obviously higher. Kitchens had ampler stocks of utensils; and for dining, earthenware and china replaced the gourds and wooden makeshifts that apparently were the rule on tables of families in the lowest economic bracket. Ticking stuffed with flock gave way to bedsteads and bedding. Even more striking is the prevalence of bond labor, both indentured servants and slaves, in this higher stratum. The transition comes abruptly. In estates below £100, servants or slaves rarely appear and then only in those within a few pounds of the line. In the estates at £100 to £200, the inventories of eight out of ten estates list bond labor—a higher percentage, actually, than in any of the succeeding £100 brackets up to £500.

In fact, these estates falling between £100 and £500 form a relatively homogeneous group. Altogether they comprise 21.7 per cent of all estates. Though existence for the planter is less frugal, his worldly goods show few signs of real luxury. Not a single estate was debt free, though fewer than a tenth had debts amounting to more than half the value of the inventory. The number of slaves in single estates does not run high: from one to five in 90 per cent of the estates that had them at all. Yet even this small number represented between half and two thirds of the appraised valuation. Reflecting the additional hands for husbandry, tobacco crops ran higher roughly in proportion to the number of slaves or indentured servants. Crops ranged from twelve hundred pounds (planters with no bond labor) up to nearly twenty thousand pounds, or from a little over two up to forty hogsheads. Again using ten shillings per hundred for transforming tobacco values to sterling, we can put the incomes from tobacco production alone between £6 and £100 a year. Other sources of income for families with bond labor should not be ruled out. Doubtless off-season occupations such as riving staves or shingles, sawing plank, and making cereal crops occupied some productive time. Unfortunately only occasional data on this type of product appear, enough to call for acknowledgment but insufficient for measurement.

Nevertheless, with annual incomes of these dimensions from their tobacco crops, planters in this group had alternatives not open to the lowest income group. As respectable citizens with community obligations to act as overseers of roads, appraisers of estates and similar duties, they might choose to lay by something to see their sons and daughters decently started in turn as planters or wives of planters. Or they might within the limitations of their estates live the good life, balancing consumption against income. Social pressure must have urged them in this direction, to a round of activities that included local politics and such country entertainments as dances, horseracing, and cockfights, occasionally punctuated with drinking brawls complete with eye-gougings and other practices not usually associated with the genteel life of the planter. Whatever the choice it is difficult to see how the planter in these circumstances could add appreciably to his estate in a short period of years, or even in a lifetime.

Still further up the scale, the estates appraised at sums above £500 form an even smaller percentage of the total. The five £100 brackets between £500 and £1,000 include altogether 2.2 per cent of all estates. At first glance this small group appears to be a plusher version of the preceding: somewhat more slaves, larger tobacco crops, more personal goods including some luxury items. These are planters of substance, much closer to the stereotype, as the character and contents of their inventories show. And in their activities they moved on a higher plane. One had represented his county for a term in the General Assembly and another had served on the county court as a justice of the peace. In the matter of indebtedness, however, some interesting differences appear. Just over half the inventories list debts owed to the estate among the major assets. In a few cases the portion of total assets in the form of debts owed the estate runs to half or more.

What I think we see here is an emerging business or entrepreneurial element, a small group of planters with sources of income other than planting alone. All were planters in the sense that they, or their bond labor, produced tobacco crops. But the appreciable number in the creditor category have other concerns. The nature of these concerns appears more clearly in the most affluent element, whose members can be studied individually as cases.

This element includes all persons with estates inventoried at more than £1,000 sterling. In the decade 1690–1699, they represent 1.6 per cent of the total. They were the "great planters" of the day.

The smallest estate in personalty, that of Nicholas Gassaway of Anne Arundel County, was inventoried at £1,017 14s. 11½d. sterling; the largest, that of Henry Coursey of Talbot County, at £1,667 17s. 1¼d. Perhaps estates of this size would have cut a mean figure beside those of the sugar planters of the West Indies. In the northern Chesapeake of the closing years of the seventeenth century, they loom high.

The composition of these largest estates varies a bit from what we might expect of the great planter's holdings. Slaves comprise less than a quarter of the assets and, in several, less than a fifth.* It should be remembered that this decade lies in the transition period when slaves were displacing indentured servants as field labor. Even so, the numbers seem unimpressive—often no greater than slave

---

* The single exception was the estate of Edward Pye of St. Mary's County, appraised at £1150 13s. 6d. He had 42 slaves and 2 indentured servants (twice as many as the next largest slave holder) valued at £783, or 67 per cent of his total estate.

holdings in estates a third as large. By contrast, the number and the amount of assets in the form of debts owed the state are striking. Altogether they comprised between a quarter and a half of the assets in individual estates. In one of the largest estates, debts owed the deceased came to 78 per cent of the total assets.

The inventories themselves give some clues as to how these large planters had become creditors. Occasionally an industrious appraiser included information on how the debtor had incurred his obligation: for a pipe of wine, for a parcel of steers, for corn, for rent of a certain property, for goods. In short, the great planter had also become a "trader." Frequently a portion of the inventory is simply labeled "in the store" and the contents of that room or building listed under this heading. Then the origin of the debts becomes clear. Sometimes they ran well over a hundred major items and were carefully listed under captions "sperate debts" and "desperate debts."

Putting this cross section or sample against the general outlines of the Chesapeake economy, I suggest the hypothesis that the men of first fortune belonged functionally to a class whose success stemmed from entrepreneurial activities as much as, or even more than, from their direct operations as producers of tobacco. The Chesapeake closely resembles pioneer economies of other times and places. It was a region with a relatively low ratio of population to resources and an equally low ratio of capital to resources. External commerce was characterized by heavy staple exports and high capital imports. Internally this flow created a current of high capital investment, full employment, profit inflation, and rising property values. The tobacco staple did not lend itself to bonanza agriculture, as did sugar in the West India islands where fortunes could be made in a decade. Consequently the Chesapeake planters did not go "back home," to dazzle the populace with their wealth. Their returns derived in the first instance from tobacco production, which afforded a competence, and secondly from enterprise, which gave greater rewards. As entrepreneurs, they gave the Chesapeake economy both organization and direction. They took the risks, made the decisions, and reaped the rewards or paid the penalties. And they worked unremittingly at these tasks, which could not be performed in their absence by the small planter or by overseers.

It is not easy to analyze the activities of this economic elite into neat categories. They were at once planters, political leaders, and businessmen. The first two roles tend to obscure the last. Their role in politics is a textbook commonplace. As planters they lived in the great tradition, some even ostentatiously. On this point testimony is abundant and unambiguous. Had they depended solely on the produce of their tobacco fields, they doubtless would have lived up to or beyond current income. And some did. But in fact many among them increased their fortunes substantially and a few spectacularly, while still maintaining their reputations as good livers. During the early years of the eighteenth century, when the tobacco trade was far from booming, some of the first families of the Chesapeake established themselves as permanent fixtures. Several had come to the first rank, or very near it, both in politics and wealth by 1700: the Taskers, the Catholic Carrolls, the Lloyds, and the Trumans. Others, less well known but eventually architects of equal or greater fortunes, were rising in the scale within another decade: the Bordleys, the Chews, the Garretts, the Dulanys, the Bennetts, and the Protestant Carrolls. The secret of their success was business enterprise, though almost to a man they lived as planters separated from the kind of urban community in which their more conspicuously entrepreneurial counterparts to the north had their residences and places of business. An examination of the chief forms of enterprise discloses the mechanisms by which they came to the top of the heap.

One of the most profitable enterprises and one most commonly associated with the great planters of the Chesapeake, land speculation, appears early in the eighteenth century in both Virginia and Maryland. The Virginia Rent Roll of 1704, admitted as imperfect but the best that could be done at the time, shows half a dozen holdings that suggest speculative intent. After these tentative beginnings, speculators moved quite aggressively during the administration of Spotswood and his successors, when huge grants in the vacant back country became commonplace events for privileged insiders, with the governors themselves sharing the spoils of His Majesty's bounty. In the more carefully regulated land system of Maryland, agents of the Lords Baltimore made a few large grants to favored persons like Charles Carroll the Settler in the first two decades of the century. During these same decades other wary speculators took up occasional large grants. The Maryland system compelled speculators to be cautious, because it exacted some money for the patents and made evasion of quitrents nearly impossible. But by the 1730's, eager speculators had glimpsed a vision of the possible returns and kept the land office busy issuing warrants for unpatented areas. For a relatively modest outlay a small number of Marylanders obtained assets with which they experimented for years before discovering the last trick in turning them to account.

Speculators capitalized their assets in two chief ways, both enormously profitable. First, as landlords of the wild lands, they leased to tenants who paid rents and at the same time improved their leaseholds by clearing, planting orchards, and erecting houses, barns, and fences. Almost exclusively long-term leases, either for years (commonly twenty-one) or for lives, these instruments specified the improvements to be made. Tenants who could not save from current income thus under compulsion contributed their bit to capital formation to the ultimate benefit of the landlord. Literary sources give the impression that tenancy was not very widespread, but the records tell another story. Something over a third of the planters in the lowest £100 bracket in Maryland leased their land. Secondly, the large landholder sold off plantation-size parcels as settlement enveloped his holdings and brought values to the desired level. Not content to leave this movement to chance, many speculators hastened the process by encouraging immigration and by directing the movement of settlers toward their own properties. Jonathan Hagar in Maryland and William Byrd in Virginia are two among many who attempted to enhance the value of their properties in this way. It is difficult to determine profits even for single speculators except for short periods. Experience must have varied widely, and undoubtedly some speculators failed. But some of the successful ones made incredible gains in a relatively short span of years.

Even more ubiquitous than the planter-speculator was the planter-merchant. The inventories and accounts contain much evidence on the organization of commerce in the tobacco counties of the Chesapeake. Hardly a parish lacked one or more country stores, often no more than a tiny hut or part of a building on the grounds of a planter who could supply, usually on credit, the basic needs of neighboring small producers—drygoods, hoes and other small implements, salt, sugar, spices, tea, and almost always liquor. Inventories show some small stores with a mere handful of those articles in constant demand. Others had elaborate stocks of women's hats, mirrors, mourning gloves, ribbons, patent medicines, and luxury goods. The names of several great families are associated with country stores, particularly in the earlier generations of the line. Frequently, store-keeping duties fell to a trusted servant or to a younger member of the family as a part of his training. Occasionally, an apprentice from one of the county families came to learn the mysteries of trade by measuring out fabrics or liquors and keeping the accounts.

As with land speculation, determining profits of merchants is next to impossible. Consumers complained bitterly of high markups, and a few storekeepers boasted of them. Even so, the country merchant's profits were not limited to sale of goods alone. He stood to gain on another transaction. He took his payment in tobacco, the crops of the two- to six-hogshead producers. The small planter participated directly in the consignment system of the early eighteenth century only to a limited extent. His petty wants and his small crop hardly justified the London merchant's time and trouble in maintaining him as a separate account. His nexus to the overseas market was the provincial merchant, who took tobacco at prices that allowed at least a small profit to himself on every hogshead.

Closely allied to merchandising, moneylending presents almost as great problems of analysis. The Chesapeake economy operated on an elaborate network of credit arrangements. Jefferson's famous remark that Virginia planters were a species of property attached to certain great British merchant houses may have been true of some planters, as it was of Jefferson himself. But the observation has created a mischievous view of credit relations between England and the tobacco colonies and does not describe the debt pattern within the area at all accurately.* A full account awaits the onslaught of an industrious graduate student armed with electronic tapes and computers. Meanwhile the accounts can tell us something. Country merchants had to be prepared to extend credit beyond that for goods purchased by their customers. They paid for some of their customers at least the church tithes, the tax levies, and the freedom dues of indentured servants who had served their terms. These petty book debts could be collected with interest in any county

---

* To be sure, some planters had been caught in the toils of debt both to English merchants and to provincial capitalists. They were exposed to such disadvantages and liabilities when indebted to English houses that their efforts to extricate themselves were often almost frantic. But there were also many, as the inventories show, who had sterling balances with one or more English houses.

court. Loans to artisans—the shoemakers, tanners, and blacksmiths who multiplied in number toward mid century—were of a different order. For working capital, the artisan in need of £5 to £20 and upward turned to men of means, the "traders." Far from abating, the demand for capital increased as the century wore on.

Investment opportunities were never lacking for planters with ready money or with credit in England. As lenders, they squarely faced the conflict of the law and the profits. By law they could take interest at 6 per cent for money loans and 8 per cent for tobacco loans. One wonders why the Carrolls chose to loan their £30,000 sterling at 6 per cent, even on impeccable securities. Could the answer be in part that returns at this rate equaled those from further investment in planting? At any rate they did choose to lend, following the example of Bennett and a dozen or so others.

Far more profitable as an investment opportunity, manufacturing exercised an enduring fascination on imaginative men of the Chesapeake. During Virginia Company days, before the first settlement of Maryland, glass and iron had figured among the projects launched under Company stimulus. Although these had come to ruin in the massacre of 1622, Virginians never gave up hope of producing iron. Their success was limited; but in the upper reaches of the Bay a combination of easily worked ore, limitless forests for charcoal, oyster shell, and water transportation from the furnace site invited exploitation. British syndicates moved first to establish the Principio Works and later the Nottingham and Lancashire works. These remained in British hands until the Revolutionary confiscations. Last of the big four, the Baltimore Iron Works (1733) became the largest producer and the biggest money-maker. Five Maryland investors subscribed the initial capital of £3,500 sterling. The Baltimore enterprise was a triumph for native capital, though technicians and technology were both imported from Britain. After the first three years of operation the partners received handsome dividends but always plowed a substantial part of the profits back into the enterprise. By the early 1760's the share of each partner was valued at £6,000 sterling. The five partners were among the first fortunes in Maryland.

Beyond iron making, other forms of enterprise (mostly small-scale manufacturing or processing) attracted investment capital. In nearly all areas of the Chesapeake some shipbuilding, cooperage, and milling establishments provided essential local services or commodities. None of these required either the capital outlay or the organization of an ironworks. Consequently, as enterprises they were attractive to investors with modest capital but large ambitions. In the area of Baltimore, flour milling developed major proportions after mid century, as the upper counties of Maryland found grain more profitable than tobacco as a field crop.

An astonishing percentage of the personal fortunes of the northern Chesapeake had their roots in law practice. While not entrepreneurial in a technical sense, the rewards went to the enterprising. During the seventeenth century lawyers were neither numerous nor always in good odor. Private persons attended to their own legal business in the courts. By 1700, the fashion had changed as the courts insisted on greater formality in pleading and as the cumbersome machinery of the common law compelled the uninstructed to turn to the professional. Pleading "by his attorney" swiftly replaced appearances *in propria persona*. Still the legal profession remained trammeled. Laws strictly regulated fees attorneys could take and kept these at levels low enough that the ablest members of the Maryland bar went on strike in the 1720's. What lawyers lacked in size of fees they made up in number of cases. An attorney might, and frequently did, bring thirty or forty cases to trial in a three- or four-day session of a county court. Had these been litigation over land, an impression widely held by students who use the *Virginia Reports* and the *Maryland Reports,* attorneys might have spent their entire time in title searches, examining witnesses, and preparing their cases. The court proceedings at large, however, show fifty cases of debt collection for every case over land; and sometimes the ratio runs as high as a hundred to one. One traveler to the Chesapeake, remarking on the "litigious spirit," wryly concluded that this spectacle of everybody suing everybody else was a kind of sport peculiar to the area. In fact, the numbers of suits grew out of the very arrangements—a tissue of book debts, bills of exchange, and promissory notes—that kept the mechanism operating.

In this milieu the lawyer had an enviable position. From his practice he derived a steady income freed from direct dependence on returns from the annual tobacco fleet. In a phrase, he had ready money the year 'round. Furthermore, he had an intimate knowledge of the resources and dependability of the planters in the county—and, indeed, throughout the province if he also practiced at the bar of the superior courts. Consequently he could take advantage of opportunities on the spot, whether they were bargains in land, sales of goods or produce, or tenants seeking leases. He could besides avoid the costs of litigation that inevitably arose as he involved himself in land speculation, lending, or merchandising, as many did. As a rule the lawyers did well, and the most enterprising moved into the highest brackets of wealth. Perhaps the most spectacular example, Thomas Bordley, a younger son of a Yorkshire schoolmaster, came from an impecunious immigrant apprentice in a Maryland law office to distinction in the law, in politics, and in Maryland society within the span of a short lifetime. After his premature death in 1726 his executors brought to probate the largest estate in the history of the province to that time.

Quite commonly, lawyers added a minor dimension to their income from office holding. A fair percentage of Maryland offices were sinecures that could be executed by deputies for a fraction of the fees. Most carried stipends, but a few eagerly-sought prizes paid handsomely. Baltimore's provincial secretary received £1,000 per annum.

This is not the place to argue the returns from planting, pure and simple. Many planters did well without other sources of income. But impressive fortunes went to those who, in addition, put their talents to work in some of the ways described above. A few engaged in all. The list is finite, for we are referring here to a small percentage of planters, those with estates above £1,000: in the decade 1690–1699 to 1.6 per cent, in 1710–1719 to 2.2 per cent, in 1730–1739 to 3.6 per cent, and in 1750–1759 to 3.9 per cent. When tabulated and examined for group characteristics, they resemble functionally a type that could easily come under that comprehensive eighteenth-century term, merchant. They look very unlike the planter of the moonlight-and-magnolias variety. It is a commentary on the prosperity of the northern Chesapeake that, as this favored category increased in percentage and in absolute numbers, so did the magnitude of its members' individual fortunes. The sample taken just before the turn of the century shows top fortunes between £1,000 and £2,000, with none above. The sample decade 1730–1739 includes an appreciable number over £2,000. The two largest were those of Samuel Chew ($£9,937$) and Amos Garrett ($£11,508$), both merchants. Even these did not match the fortunes left by Dr. Charles Carroll and Daniel Dulany the Elder in the decade 1750–1759, nor that of Benjamin Tasker in the next.

The poor were not excluded, individually or as a group, from the general prosperity of the Chesapeake. Four individuals—Thomas Macnemara, Thomas Bordley, Daniel Dulany, and Dr. Charles Carroll—moved up the scale from nothing to the top bracket of wealth, two of them from indentured servitude. These were extraordinary men, but their careers indicate the avenues open to their combination of talents for the law, land speculation, moneylending, merchandising, and manufacturing in which they engaged. Of course all were planters as well.

But for the mass, advance was by comparison glacial. The composition of the base on which such performances took place changed more slowly. In the fourth decade of the eighteenth century the percentage of planters in the lowest economic group, those with estates of $£100$ or less, had fallen to 54.7 per cent, in marked contrast to 74.6 per cent of the decade 1690–1699. Between the same two sample decades the percentage in the next higher category of estates ($£100$ to $£500$) had increased to 35.7 per cent from 21.7 per cent. If this means that the poor were getting richer, it also means for the great majority that they were doing so by short and slow steps. Together, these two lowest categories still made up 90.4 per cent of the planting families in 1730–1739, as compared with 96.3 per cent in the last decade of the seventeenth century. Nonetheless, the shift toward a higher standard of living within this huge mass of lesser planters is quite as important a commentary on the economic well-being of the Chesapeake as is the growth in numbers and magnitude of the great fortunes.

It is never easy to know just how much to claim for statistical evidence. Perhaps there is enough here to raise doubts about the descriptive accuracy of reports from Chesapeake planters themselves. These sound like a protracted wail of hard times, rising occasionally in crescendo to prophesies of impending ruin. Yet even during the early and least prosperous decades, the northern Chesapeake experienced some growth. During the second quarter of the century and on into the following decades the samples made for this study indicate a quickened rate. The results worked no magic change in the way of life or economic station for the small planter, the mass of Maryland. These were always the overwhelming percentage of the producers. As a social group they come in for little notice. Their lives lack the glitter and incident that has made the great planter the focus of all eyes. By the standards of the affluent society theirs was a drab, rather humdrum, existence bound to the annual rhythm of the field crop. The highest rewards were for those who could transcend the routine of producing tobacco and develop the gainful activities that kept the economy functioning.

17. JAMES A. HENRETTA
"Economic Development and Social Structure in Colonial Boston"

James A. Henretta has studied two Boston tax lists, for the years 1687 and 1771, as a means of charting the changing distribution of wealth in one of the commercial centers of colonial America. By focusing on a single community, he is able to bring considerable precision to his study and to suggest correlates of change which might not emerge in broader-based surveys. From the *William and Mary Quarterly*, Third Series, 22 (1965), 75–92. Reprinted with the omission of some notes by permission of James A. Henretta.

A distinctly urban social structure developed in Boston in the 150 years between the settlement of the town and the American Revolution. The expansion of trade and industry after 1650 unleashed powerful economic forces which first distorted, then destroyed, the social homogeneity and cohesiveness of the early village community. All aspects of town life were affected by Boston's involvement in the dynamic, competitive world of Atlantic commerce. The disruptive pressure of rapid economic growth, sustained for over a century, made the social appearance of the town more diverse, more complex, more modern—increasingly different from that of the rest of New England. The magnitude of the change in Boston's social composition and structure may be deduced from an analysis and comparison of the tax lists for 1687 and 1771. Containing a wealth of information on property ownership in the community, these lists make it possible to block out, in quantitative terms, variations in the size and influence of economic groups and to trace the change in the distribution of the resources of the community among them.

The transformation of Boston from a land-based society to a maritime center was neither sudden nor uniform. In the last decade of the seventeenth century, a large part of the land of its broad peninsula was still cultivated by small farmers. Only a small fraction was laid out in regular streets and even less was densely settled. The north end alone showed considerable change from the middle of the century when almost every house had a large lot and garden. Here, the later-comers—the mariners, craftsmen, and traders who had raised the population to six thousand by 1690—were crowded together along the waterfront. Here, too, in the series of docks and shipyards which jutted out from the shore line, were tangible manifestations of the commericial activity which had made the small town the largest owner of shipping and the principal port of the English colonies. Over 40 per cent of the carrying capacity of all colonial-owned shipping was in Boston hands.

Dependence on mercantile endeavor rather than agricultural enterprise had by 1690 greatly affected the extent of property ownership. Boston no longer had the universal ownership of real estate characteristic of rural Massachusetts to the end of the colonial period. The tax list for 1687 contained the names of 188 polls, 14 per cent of the adult male population, who were neither owners of taxable property of any kind nor "dependents" in a household assessed for the property tax. Holding no real estate, owning no merchandise or investments which would yield an income, these men constituted the "propertyless" segment of the community and were liable only for the head tax which fell equally upon all men above the age of sixteen. Many in this group were young men, laborers and seamen, attracted by the commercial prosperity of the town and hoping to save enough from their wages to buy or rent a shop, to invest in the tools of an artisan, or to find a start in trade. John Erving, a poor Scotch sailor whose grandson in 1771 was one of the richest men in Boston, was only one propertyless man who rose quickly to a position of wealth and influence.

But many of these 188 men did not acquire either taxable property or an established place in the social order of Boston. Only sixty-four, or 35 per cent, were, inhabitants of the town eight years later. By way of contrast, 45 per cent of the polls assessed from two to seven pounds on the tax list, 65 per cent of those with property valued from eight to twenty pounds, and 73 per cent of those with estates in excess of twenty pounds were present in 1695. There was a direct relation between permanence of residence and economic condition. Even in an expanding and diversifying economic environment, the best opportunities for advancement rested with those who could draw upon long-standing connections, upon the credit facilities of friends and neighbors, and upon political influence. It was precisely these personal contacts which were denied to the propertyless.

A second, distinct element in the social order consisted of the dependents of property owners. Though propertyless themselves, these dependents—grown sons living at home, apprentices, and indentured servants—were linked more closely to the town as members of a tax-paying household unit than were the 188 "unattached" men without taxable estates. Two hundred and twelve men, nearly one sixth of the adult male population of Boston, were classified as dependents in 1687. The pervasiveness of the dependency relationship attested not only to the cohesiveness of the family unit but also to the continuing vitality of the apprenticeship and indenture system at the close of the seventeenth century.

Yet even the dependency relationship, traditionally an effective means of alleviating unemployment and preventing the appearance of unattached propertyless laborers, was subjected to severe pressure by the expansion of the economy. An urgent demand for labor, itself the cause of short indentures, prompted servants to strike out on their own as soon as possible. They became the laborers or semi-skilled craftsmen of the town, while the sons of the family eventually assumed control of their father's business and a share of the economic resources of the community.

The propertied section of the population in 1687 was composed of 1,036 individuals who were taxed on their real estate or their income from trade. The less-skilled craftsmen, 521 men engaged in the rougher trades of a waterfront society, formed the bottom stratum of the taxable population in this pre-industrial age. These carpenters, shipwrights, blacksmiths, shopkeepers owned only 12 per cent of the taxable wealth of the town.* Few of these artisans and laborers had investments in shipping or in merchandise. A small store or house, or a small farm in the south end of Boston, accounted for their assessment of two to seven pounds on the tax list. (Table III)

Between these craftsmen and shopkeepers and the traders and merchants who constituted the economic elite of the town was a middle group of 275 property owners with taxable assets valued from eight to twenty pounds. Affluent artisans employing two or three workers, ambitious shopkeepers with investments in commerce, and entrepreneurial-minded sea masters with various maritime interests, bulked large in this center portion of the economic order. Of the 275, 180 owned real estate assessed at seven pounds or less and were boosted into the third quarter of the distribution of wealth by their holdings of merchandise and shares in shipping. (Table III) The remaining ninety-five possessed real estate rated at eight pounds or more and, in addition, held various investments in trade. Making up about 25 per cent of the propertied population, this middle group controlled 22 per cent of the taxable wealth in Boston in 1687. Half as numerous as the lowest group of property owners, these men possessed almost double the amount of taxable assets. (Table I)

Merchants with large investments in English and West Indian trade and individuals engaged in the ancillary industries of shipbuilding and distilling made up the top quarter of the taxable population in 1687. With taxable estates ranging from twenty to 170 pounds, this commercial group controlled 66 per cent of the town's wealth. But economic development had been too rapid, too uneven and incomplete, to allow the emergence of a well-defined merchant class endowed with a common outlook and clearly distinguished from the rest of the society. Only eighty-five of these men, one third of the wealthiest group in the community, owned dwellings valued at as much as twenty pounds. The majority held landed property valued at ten pounds, only a few pounds greater than that of the middle group of property holders. (See Table III.) The merchants had not shared equally in the accumulated fund of capital and experience which had accrued after fifty years of maritime

---

* The lower 50 per cent of the property owners is treated as a whole as Tables I and II and Chart A, below, indicate that the proportion of wealth held by this section of the population is approximately the same in 1687 and 1771.

activity. Profits had flowed to those whose daring initiative and initial resources had begun the exploitation of the lucrative colonial market. By 1687, the upper 15 per cent of the property owners held 52 per cent of the taxable assets of the town, while the fifty individuals who composed the highest 5 per cent of the taxable population accounted for more than 25 per cent of the wealth. (Table I)

By the end of the seventeenth century widespread involvement in commerce had effected a shift in the locus of social and political respectability in Boston and distinguished it from the surrounding communities. Five of the nine selectmen chosen by the town in 1687 were sea captains. This was more than deference to those accustomed to command. With total estates of £83, £29, £33, £33, and £24, Captains Elisha Hutchinson, John Fairweather, Theophilus Frary, Timothy Prout, and Daniel Turell were among the wealthiest 20 per cent of the population. Still, achievement in trade was not the only index of respectability. Henry Eames, George Cable, Isaac Goose, and Elnathan Lyon, the men appointed by the town to inspect the condition of the streets and roads, had the greater part of their wealth, £105 of £130, invested in land and livestock. And the presence of Deacon Henry Allen among the selectmen provided a tangible indication of the continuing influence of the church.

These legacies of an isolated religious society and a stable agricultural economy disappeared in the wake of the rapid growth which continued unabated until the middle of the eighteenth century. In the fifty years after 1690, the population of the town increased from 6,000 to 16,000. The farms of the south end vanished and the central business district became crowded. In the populous north end, buildings which had once housed seven people suddenly began to hold nine or ten. Accompanying this physical expansion of Boston was a diversification of economic endeavor. By 1742, the town led all the colonial cities in the production of export furniture and shoes, although master craftsmen continued to carry on most industry on a small scale geared to local needs. Prosperity and expansion continued to be rooted, not in the productive capacity or geographic position of the town, but in the ability of the Boston merchants to compete successfully in the highly competitive mercantile world.

After 1750, the economic health of the Massachusetts seaport

TABLE I

Distribution of assessed taxable wealth in Boston in 1687*

TOTAL VALUE OF TAXABLE WEALTH	NUMBER OF TAX- PAYERS IN EACH WEALTH BRACKET	TOTAL WEALTH IN EACH WEALTH BRACKET	CUMU- LATIVE TOTAL OF WEALTH	CUMU- LATIVE TOTAL OF TAXPAYERS	CUMULATIVE PERCENTAGE OF TAXPAYERS	CUMULATIVE PERCENTAGE OF WEALTH
£ 1	0	£ 0	£ 0	0	0.0%	0.0%
2	152	304	304	152	14.6	1.8
3	51	153	457	203	19.5	2.7
4	169	676	1,133	372	35.9	6.8
5	33	165	1,298	405	39.0	7.8
6	97	582	1,880	502	48.5	11.3
7	19	133	2,013	521	50.2	12.1
8	43	344	2,357	564	54.4	14.2
9	22	198	2,555	586	56.6	15.4
10	45	450	3,005	631	60.9	18.1
11	17	187	3,192	648	62.5	19.2
12	30	360	3,552	678	65.4	21.4
13	13	169	3,721	691	66.6	22.4
14	12	168	3,889	703	67.9	23.4
15	22	330	4,219	725	69.9	25.4
16	21	336	4,555	746	72.0	27.5
17	1	17	4,572	747	72.0	27.6
18	18	324	4,896	765	73.8	29.5
19	1	19	4,915	766	73.9	29.6
20	30	600	5,515	796	76.8	33.2
21–25	41	972	6,487	837	80.7	39.0
26–30	48	1,367	7,854	885	85.4	47.3
31–35	29	971	8,825	914	88.2	53.1
36–40	21	819	9,644	935	90.2	58.1
41–45	19	828	10,472	954	92.1	63.1
46–50	16	781	11,253	970	93.6	67.8
51–60	16	897	12,150	986	95.1	73.2
61–70	19	1,245	13,395	1,005	97.0	80.7
71–80	7	509	13,904	1,012	97.8	83.8
81–90	3	253	14,157	1,015	97.9	85.3
91–100	7	670	14,827	1,022	98.6	89.3
100–	14	1,764	16,591	1,036	100.0	100.0

* Money values are those of 1687. Many of the assessments fall at regular five pound intervals and must be considered as an estimate of the economic position

was jeopardized as New York and Philadelphia merchants, exploiting the rich productive lands at their backs and capitalizing upon their prime geographic position in the West Indian and southern coasting trade, diverted a significant portion of European trade from the New England traders. Without increasing returns from the lucrative "carrying" trade, Boston merchants could no longer subsidize the work of the shopkeepers, craftsmen, and laborers who supplied and maintained the commercial fleet. By 1760, the population of Boston had dropped to 15,000 persons, a level it did not exceed until after the Revolution.

The essential continuity of maritime enterprise in Boston from the late seventeenth to the mid-eighteenth century concealed the emergence of a new type of social system. After a certain point increases in the scale and extent of commercial endeavor produced a new, and more fluid, social order. The development of the economic system subjected the family, the basic social unit, to severe pressures. The fundamental link between one generation and another, the ability of the father to train his offspring for their life's work, was endangered by a process of change which rendered obsolete many of the skills and assumptions of the older, land-oriented generation and opened the prospect of success in new fields and new places. The well-known departure of Benjamin Franklin from his indenture to his brother was but one bright piece in the shifting mosaic of colonial life.

The traditional family unit had lost much of its cohesiveness by the third quarter of the eighteenth century. The Boston tax lists for 1771 indicate that dependents of property owners accounted for only 10 per cent of the adult male population as opposed to 16 per cent eighty-five years earlier. Increasingly children left their homes at an earlier age to seek their own way in the world.

A second factor in the trend away from dependency status was the decline in the availability of indentured servants during the eighteenth century. Fewer than 250 of 2,380 persons entering Boston from 1764 to 1768 were classified as indentured servants. These were scarcely enough to replace those whose indentures expired. More and more, the labor force had to be recruited from the ranks

---

of the individual. No attempt was made to compensate for systematic overvaluation or undervaluation inasmuch as the analysis measures relative wealth. The utility of a relative presentation of wealth (or income) is that it can be compared to another relative distribution without regard to absolute monetary values.

TABLE II

Distribution of assessed taxable wealth in Boston in 1771*

TOTAL VALUE OF TAXABLE WEALTH	NUMBER OF TAX-PAYERS IN EACH WEALTH BRACKET	TOTAL WEALTH IN EACH WEALTH BRACKET	CUMU-LATIVE TOTAL OF WEALTH	CUMU-LATIVE TOTAL OF TAX-PAYERS	CUMULATIVE PERCENTAGE OF TAXPAYERS	CUMULATIVE PERCENTAGE OF WEALTH
£ 3–30	78	£1,562	£1,562	78	5.0%	0.3%
31–40	86	2,996	4,558	164	10.6	0.9
41–50	112	5,378	9,936	276	17.9	2.2
51–60	74	4,398	14,334	350	22.6	3.5
61–70	33	3,122	17,456	383	24.7	3.8
71–80	165	12,864	30,320	548	35.4	6.5
81–90	24	2,048	32,368	572	36.9	7.0
91–100	142	13,684	46,052	714	46.1	10.0
101–110	14	494	46,546	728	47.1	10.1
111–120	149	17,844	64,390	877	56.7	13.9
121–130	20	2,570	66,960	897	58.0	14.5
131–140	26	4,600	71,560	923	59.7	15.5
141–150	20	2,698	74,258	943	60.9	16.1
151–160	88	14,048	88,306	1,031	66.6	19.1
161–170	11	1,846	90,152	1,042	67.4	19.6
171–180	18	3,128	93,280	1,060	68.6	20.3
181–190	10	1,888	95,168	1,070	69.2	20.7
191–200	47	9,368	104,536	1,117	72.2	22.7
201–300	126	31,097	135,633	1,243	80.4	29.4
301–400	60	21,799	157,432	1,303	84.2	34.1
401–500	58	24,947	182,379	1,361	88.0	39.6
501–600	14	7,841	190,220	1,375	88.9	41.3
601–700	24	15,531	205,751	1,399	90.4	44.6
701–800	26	19,518	225,269	1,425	92.2	48.9
801–900	20	17,020	242,289	1,445	93.4	52.6
901–1,000	16	15,328	257,617	1,461	95.4	55.9
1,001–1,500	41	48,364	305,963	1,502	97.1	66.4
1,501–5,000	37	85,326	391,289	1,539	99.5	84.9
5,001–	7	69,204	460,493	1,546	100.0	100.0

* The extant tax list is not complete. In ward 3, there are two pages and 69 polls missing; in ward 7, one page and 24 polls; in ward 12, an unknown number

of "unattached" workers who bartered their services for wages in a market economy.*

This laboring force consisted of the nondependent, propertyless workers of the community, now twice as numerous relative to the rest of the population as they had been a century before. In 1687, 14 per cent of the total number of adult males were without taxable property; by the eve of the Revolution, the propertyless accounted for 29 per cent. The social consequences of this increase were manifold. For every wage earner who competed in the economy as an autonomous entity at the end of the seventeenth century, there were four in 1771; for every man who slept in the back of a shop, in a tavern, or in a rented room in 1687, there were four in the later period. The population of Boston had doubled, but the number of propertyless men had increased fourfold.

The adult males without property, however, did not form a single unified class, a monolithic body of landless proletarians. Rather, the bottom of society consisted of a congeries of social and occupational groups with a highly transient maritime element at one end of the spectrum and a more stable and respected artisan segment at the other. Although they held no taxable property, hard-working and reputable craftsmen who had established a permanent residence in Boston participated in the town meeting and were elected to unpaid minor offices. In March 1771, for instance, John Dyer was selected by the people of the town as "Fence Viewer" for the following year. Yet according to the tax and valuation lists compiled less than six months later, Dyer was without taxable property. At the same town meeting, four carpenters, Joseph Ballard, Joseph Edmunds, Benjamin Page, and Joseph Butler, none of whom was listed as an owner of taxable property on the valua-

---

of pages and 225 polls. Only the total number of polls (224) is known for ward II. The missing entries amount to 558, or 19.3 per cent of the total number of polls on the tax list. Internal evidence (the totals for all wards are known) suggests the absent material is completely random. Nevertheless, it should be remembered that this table represents an 80 per cent sample.

The value of shipping investments and of "servants for life" was not included in the computation of the table as it was impossible to determine the assessor's valuation.

* For most of the 18th century, Negro slaves compensated for the lack of white servants. From 150 in 1690, the number of Negroes rose to 1,100 in a population of 13,000 in 1730. In that year, they made up 8.4 per cent of the population; in 1742, 8.4 per cent; in 1752, 9.7 per cent; but only 5.5 per cent in 1765.

tion lists, were chosen as "Measurers of Boards." That propertyless men should be selected for public office indicates that the concept of a "stake in society," which provided the theoretical underpinning for membership in the community of colonial Boston, was interpreted in the widest possible sense. Yet it was this very conception of the social order which was becoming anachronistic under the pressure of economic development. For how could the growing number of propertyless men be integrated into a social order based in the first instance on the principle that only those having a tangible interest in the town or a definite family link to the society would be truly interested in the welfare of the community?

Changes no less significant had taken place within the ranks of the propertied groups. By the third quarter of the eighteenth century, lines of economic division and marks of social status were crystalizing as Boston approached economic maturity. Present to some degree in all aspects of town life, these distinctions were very apparent in dwelling arrangements. In 1687, 85 per cent of Boston real estate holdings had been assessed within a narrow range of two to ten pounds; by the seventh decade of the eighteenth century, the same spectrum ran from twelve to two hundred pounds. (Table III) Gradations in housing were finer in 1771 and had social connotations which were hardly conceivable in the more primitive and more egalitarian society of the seventeenth century. This sense of distinctiveness was reinforced by geographic distribution. Affluent members of the community who had not transferred their residence to Roxbury, Cambridge, or Milton built in the spacious environs of the south and west ends. A strict segregation of the social groups was lacking; yet the milieu of the previous century, the interaction of merchant, trader, artisan, and laborer in a waterfront community, had all but disappeared.

The increasing differences between the social and economic groups within the New England seaport stemmed in part from the fact that craftsmen, laborers, and small shopkeepers had failed to maintain their relative position in the economic order. In the eighty-five years from 1687 to 1771, the share of the taxable wealth of the community controlled by the lower half of the propertied population declined from 12 to 10 per cent. (Table II) If these men lived better at the end of the century than at the beginning, it was not because the economic development of Boston had ef-

TABLE III

Real estate ownership in Boston in 1687 and 1771*

1687			1771		
Assessed Total Value of Real Estate	Number of Owners	Cumulative Total of Owners	Assessed Annual Worth of Real Estate	Number of Owners	Cumulative Total of Owners
£ 1	0	0	£ 1	0	0
2	168	168	2	1	1
3	75	243	3	9	10
4	203	446	4	49	59
5	85	531	5	22	81
6	167	698	6	79	160
7	3	701	7	0	160
8	54	755	8	115	275
9	2	757	9	3	278
10	107	864	10	91	369
11	0	864	11	4	373
12	24	888	12	43	416
13	0	888	13	163	579
14	3	891	14	10	589
15	25	916	15	3	592
16	8	924	16	148	740
17	0	924	17	6	746
18	7	931	18	7	753
19	1	932	19	5	758
20	46	978	20	236	994
21–30	25	1,003	21–25	41	1,035
31–40	11	1,014	26–30	163	1,198
41–50	2	1,016	31–35	93	1,291
			36–40	92	1,383
			41–45	5	1,388
			46–50	42	1,430
			51–60	32	1,462
			61–70	10	1,472
			71–80	9	1,481
			81–90	3	1,484
			91–100	3	1,487

* The assessed annual worth of real estate in the 1771 valuation must be multiplied by six to give the total property value.

fected a redistribution of wealth in favor of the laboring classes but because the long period of commercial prosperity had raised the purchasing power of every social group.

The decline in the economic distinctiveness of the middle group of property holders, the third quarter of the taxable population in the distribution of wealth, is even more significant. In 1771, these well-to-do artisans, shopkeepers, and traders (rising land values had eliminated the farmers and economic maturity the versatile merchant-sea captain) owned only 12½ per cent of the taxable wealth, a very substantial decrease from the 21 per cent held in 1687. These men lived considerably better than their counterparts in the seventeenth century; many owned homes and possessed furnishings rarely matched by the most elegant dwellings of the earlier period. But in relation to the other parts of the social order, their economic position had deteriorated drastically. This smaller middle group had been assessed for taxable estates twice as large as the bottom 50 per cent in 1687; by 1771 the assets of the two groups were equal.

On the other hand, the wealthiest 25 per cent of the taxable population by 1771 controlled 78 per cent of the assessed wealth of Boston. This represented a gain of 12 per cent from the end of the seventeenth century. An equally important shift had taken place within this elite portion of the population. In 1687, the richest 15 per cent of the taxpayers held 52 per cent of the taxable property, while the top 5 per cent owned 26.8 per cent. Eighty-five years later, the percentages were 65.9 and 44.1. (Tables I and II and Chart A)

Certain long-term economic developments accounted for the disappearance of a distinct middle group of property owners and the accumulation of wealth among a limited portion of the population. The scarcity of capital in a relatively underdeveloped economic system, one in which barter transactions were often necessary because of the lack of currency, required that the savings of all members of the society be tapped in the interest of economic expansion. The prospect of rapid commercial success and the high return on capital invested in mercantile activity attracted the small investor. During the first decade of the eighteenth century, nearly one of every three adult males in Boston was involved directly in trade, owning at least part of a vessel. In 1698 alone, 261 people held shares in a seagoing vessel. Trade had become "not so much a way of life as a way of making money; not a social condition but an economic activity." This widespread ownership of mercantile wealth resulted in the creation of a distinct economic "middle class" by the last decades of the seventeenth century.

A reflection of a discrete stage of economic growth, the involvement of disparate occupational and social groups in commerce was fleeting and transitory. It lasted only as long as the economy of the New England seaport remained underdeveloped, without large amounts of available capital. The increase in the wealth and resources of the town during the first half of the eighteenth century prompted a growing specialization of economic function; it was no longer necessary to rely on the investments of the less affluent members of the community for an expansion of commerce. This change was slow, almost imperceptible; but by 1771 the result was obvious. In that year, less than 5 per cent of the taxable population of Boston held shares in shipping of ten tons or more, even though the tonnage owned by the town was almost double that of 1698. Few men had investments of less than fifty tons; the average owner held 112 tons. By way of contrast, the average holding at the end of the seventeenth century had been about twenty-five tons. Moreover, on the eve of the Revolution ownership of shipping was concentrated among the wealthiest men of the community. Ninety per cent of the tonnage of Boston in 1771 was in the hands of those whose other assets placed them in the top quarter of the population.* With the increase in the wealth of the town had come a great increase in the number of propertyless men and a bifocalization of the property owners into (1) a large amorphous body of shopkeepers, artisans, and laborers with holdings primarily in real estate and (2) a smaller, somewhat more closely defined segment of the population with extensive commercial investments as well as elegant residences and personal possessions.

A similar trend was evident in other phases of town life. In the

---

* Only 2.3 per cent of the 8,898 tons of shipping for which the owners are known was held by individuals in the bottom half of the distribution of wealth (estates of £100 or less in Table II); 5.9 per cent more by those with estates valued from £100 to £200; and an additional 19 per cent by persons with wealth of £200 to £500. 73 per cent of Boston's shipping was held by the wealthiest 12 per cent of the propertied population, those with estates in excess of £500. See Table II.

transitional decades of the late seventeenth and early eighteenth century, the fluidity inherent in the primitive commercial system had produced a certain vagueness in the connotations of social and economic status. Over 10 per cent of the adult males in Boston designated themselves as "merchants" on the shipping registers of the period from 1698 to 1714, indicating not only the decline in the distinctiveness of a title traditionally limited to a carefully defined part of the community but also the feeling that any man could easily ascend the mercantile ladder. Economic opportunity was so evident, so promising, that the social demarcations of the more stable maritime communities of England seemed incongruous. By the sixth decade of the eighteenth century, however, rank and order were supplanting the earlier chaos as successful families tightened their control of trade. The founding in 1763 of a "Merchants Club" with 146 members was a dramatic indication that occupations and titles were regaining some of their traditional distinctiveness and meaning.

An economic profile of the 146 men who composed this self-constituted elite is revealing. Of those whose names appeared on the tax and valuation lists of 1771, only five had estates which placed them in the bottom three quarters of the distribution of wealth. Twenty-one were assessed for taxable property in excess of £1,500 and were thus in the top 1 per cent of the economic scale. The taxable assets of the rest averaged £650, an amount which put them among the wealthiest 15 per cent of the population.

That 146 men, 6½ per cent of the adult male population, were considered eligible for membership in a formal society of merchants indicates, however, that mercantile activity was not dominated by a narrow oligarchy. The range of wealth among the members of the top quarter of the propertied population was so great and the difference of social background so large as to preclude the creation of a monolithic class or guild with shared interests and beliefs.

Yet the influence of this segment of society was pervasive. By the third quarter of the eighteenth century, an integrated economic and political hierarchy based on mercantile wealth had emerged in Boston to replace the lack of social stratification of the early part of the century and the archaic distinctions of power and prestige of the religious community of the seventeenth century. All of the important offices of the town government, those with functions vital to the existence and prosperity of the town, were lodged firmly in the hands of a broad elite, entry into which was conditioned by commercial achievement and family background. The representatives to the General Court and the selectmen were the leaders of the town in economic endeavor as well as in political acumen. John Hancock's taxable wealth totaled £18,000; James Otis was assessed at £2,040, while Colonel Joseph Jackson had property valued at £1,288. Other levels of the administrative system were reserved for those whose business skills or reputation provided the necessary qualifications. Samuel Abbot, John Barrett, Benjamin Dolbeare, John Gore, William Phillips, William White, and William Whitewell, Overseers of the Poor in 1771, had taxable estates of £815, £5,520, £850, £1,747, £5,771, £1,953, and £1,502 respectively. All were among the wealthiest 7 per cent of the property owners; and Barrett and Phillips were two of the most respected merchants of the town. John Scollay, a distiller with an estate of £320, and Captain Benjamin Waldo, a shipmaster assessed at £500, who were among those chosen as "Firewards" in 1771, might in an earlier period have been dominant in town affairs; by the seventh decade of the century, in a mature economic environment, the merchant prince had replaced the man of action at the apex of the social order.

Gradations continued to the bottom of the scale. Different social and occupational levels of the population were tapped as the dignity and responsibility of the position demanded. It was not by accident that the estates of the town assessors, Jonathan Brown, Moses Deshon, and John Kneeland, were £208, £200, and £342. Or that those of the "Cullers of Staves," Henry Lucas, Thomas Knox, and Caleb Hayden, totaled £120, £144 and £156. The assumption of a graded social, economic, and political scale neatly calibrated so as to indicate the relation of each individual to the whole was the basic principle upon which the functioning of town meeting "democracy" depended. William Crafts, with a taxable estate of £80, was elected "Fence Viewer." Half this amount qualified William Barrett to be "Measurer of Coal Baskets," while Henry Allen and John Bulfinch, "Measurers of Boards," were assessed at £80 and £48. The design was nearly perfect, the correlation between town office and social and economic position almost exact.

As in 1687, the distribution of political power and influence in

CHART A

Lorenz curves showing the distribution of wealth in Boston in 1687 and 1771 (Drawn from data in Tables I and II.)

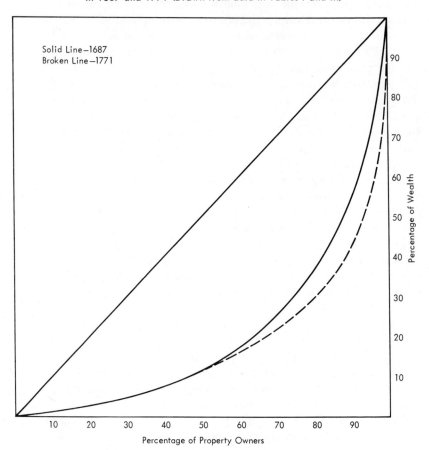

Solid Line—1687
Broken Line—1771

Percentage of Wealth

Percentage of Property Owners

Boston conformed to the standards and gradations of a wider, more inclusive hierarchy of status, one which purported to include the entire social order within the bounds of its authority. But the lines of force which had emerged on the eve of the American Revolution radiated from different economic and social groups than those of eighty-five years before, and now failed to encompass a significant portion of the population. The weakening of the "extended" family unit and the appearance of a large body of autonomous wage earners, "proletarians" in condition if not in consciousness, had introduced elements of mobility and diversity into the bottom part of society. Equally significant had been the growing inequality of the distribution of wealth among the propertied segment of the community, notably the greater exclusiveness and predominance of a mercantile "elite." Society had become more stratified and unequal. Influential groups, increasingly different from the small property owners who constituted the center portion of the community, had arisen at either end of the spectrum. Creations of the century-long development of a maritime economy in an urban setting, these "merchant princes" and "proletarians" stood out as the salient characteristics of a new social order.

18. | KENNETH LOCKRIDGE
| *"Land, Population, and the Evolution of*
| *New England Society, 1630–1790"*

Drawing upon the work of a number of local historians and upon his own research, Kenneth Lockridge has suggested some broad patterns of social and economic change in colonial New England. Reprinted with omission of most notes by permission of the author. From *Past and Present*, #39 (1968), 62–80.

I

Was early America an overcrowded society? Though the idea seems absurd on the face of it, there is evidence in its favour.

American society began with a few men set down in the midst of a vast and fruitful wilderness. From this beginning until late in the nineteenth century there was no time at which the country was without a frontier in the literal sense of the word. Whatever it was or whatever it has meant to those seeking the origins of the American character, the frontier has had one meaning upon which all men, colonial speculators, genteel visitors from abroad and modern historians alike, could agree. That meaning is room. Land was always available. If some did not take it up or if others found themselves holding bad land, still others, millions and generations of others who might never have had the opportunity had they lived in another country, did take up acres of good land and throve on those acres.

Yet at first Americans moved only slowly out into the wilderness. For most of the two hundred years preceding 1800 they clustered near the eastern coastline. Particularly in the later eighteenth century, even as Daniel Boone and Ethan Allen led settlers into what were to become the states of Kentucky and Vermont, a variety of circumstances held most would-be settlers back of the Appalachian mountains. Behind the mountains, this side of the war zones of the interior, there had developed by the end of the eighteenth century a society in some respects old, stable, concentrated.

Some historians have been led to reflect on the precocious maturity of late colonial and early national society to weigh the possibility that the society might have become less than comfortable for some of its inhabitants.* But the prevailing tendency has been to treat early American society as a relatively fixed conception, trimmed at either end by periods of "settlement" and "early nationhood", a conception in which the powerful influence of the frontier and the widespread existence of opportunity are not seriously questioned. Certainly no historian has yet come to grips with the quantitative problems posed by the maturation and relative containment of early American society. What does it signify that, by 1790, Americans were not entirely a new or a restless people, or that some counties in Virginia or Maryland and some towns in New England could trace their histories back through a century and a half? How much had the conditions of life changed with time? Was it everywhere, always, necessarily, the America of room and opportunity?

Land and time must be the touchstones of any enquiry into the social evolution of early America: land because the economy was overwhelmingly agricultural and because land has been both the symbol and the essence of American opportunity; time because there was so much of it, so much time in which evolution might have taken place. How much land was available to the typical farmer and how were this and other characteristics of the society changing with time? As a beginning, these questions will be asked

---

* Professors Peter Coleman, Jackson T. Main, Darrett Rutman, Philip Greven, Jr., and Van Beck Hall have rendered invaluable assistance in the preparation of this paper. Any errors are, of course, the author's responsibility.

of early New England at large and in particular of the agricultural towns of eastern Massachusetts in the years 1630–1790.

II

The only authoritative work on agriculture in colonial New England is a *History of Agriculture in the Northern United States, 1620–1860* (Washington, D.C., 1925) by P. W. Bidwell and J. I. Falconer. In discussing the average area of landholdings in early seventeenth century New England they offer a figure of 25 to 50 acres. But, as the authors freely admit, the evidence from which this figure is drawn is extremely weak. Nearly every one of the several hundred cases upon which they base their estimate is rendered valueless by the circumstances under which it was recorded.* But, if casting doubt on the 25–50 acre figure of Bidwell and Falconer is a simple matter, putting a new estimate in its place is not so simple. The best source of information on landholdings in these years should be the public records of land grants made by the various towns. These would show how much land the typical early settler could expect to receive in his lifetime.** The trouble with using New England town records as a source is that few are precise in recording the number and area of dividends granted. In spite of this difficulty, enough bits and pieces of evidence exist to replace Bidwell and Falconer's several hundred suspect cases with several hundred other, better examples. Drawn chiefly from the records of older communities in eastern Massachusetts, these cases show that the usual early settler received a good deal more than 25 to 50 acres.

* Two major flaws may be noted. In the cases drawn from the towns of Dorchester, Hartford and New Haven, the acreage-per-individual is merely that granted in a single public division of town land. As is well known and as will become evident below, a settler in most early towns could expect roughly three to ten such divisions to be made during his lifetime. Secondly, the figures for several towns on Long Island are only for taxable land. In the Long Island towns the figures "do not include pasture land which was largely held in common" and which was a major component of a man's land-rights. Had this been included, the average acreage would have been "much larger". This circumstance may also have prevailed near Boston; in any event Muddy River was an area assigned to Boston's poor—hardly a fair test-area!

** He might sell these lands as fast as they were granted him but on the other hand he might buy more land privately. Neither action, given a fairly self-contained local land market, would affect the average area of landholdings per man.

A thorough investigation has been made of the system of land allotment in Dedham, Massachusetts. Complete records of land acquisitions both public and private can be compiled for thirty-two of the first fifty men to settle in the town. They averaged no less than 210 acres apiece in grants and purchases during lifetimes which ended between 1650 and 1690. From the record of public land divisions alone (of which there were from ten to thirteen between the founding of Dedham in 1636 and the year 1660) it is clear that *any* man in town by 1640 and still alive in 1660 could have expected town grants of between 100 and 200 acres. Some men who died before 1660 and missed the large divisions of the 1650s received less than this, but others who lived long and prominent lives were granted public lands up to a total of 400 acres. Since the divisions continued into the first decade of the eighteenth century, the second generation likewise drew large totals of land. Altogether, there were not fewer than 200 individuals each of whom lived for more than three decades as an adult in the town between 1636 and 1690. The typical man among them received an average of 150 acres from the common lands of Dedham.

The records of neighbouring Watertown include land records which gave a complete survey of landholdings in the 1630s. For the 160 men listed at this time the average landholding was 126 acres. This average may exclude a few unlisted men who held no land, but it also excludes whatever lands those who were listed held in other towns or were granted in the several subsequent general divisions. Specifically, it does not take cognizance of the fact that the men who held only tiny "homelots" when this record was made were soon after granted farms of respectable acreage. With Dedham, Watertown gives from 300 to 400 cases averaging from 125 to 150 acres.

In six other towns of the immediate region there are indications that the seventeenth-century settlers found that America had plenty of land to offer. Medfield split off from Dedham in 1651; during the first two decades of its existence it made at least six general divisions of land. A man who lived in the town for these two decades would have received roughly 150 acres. The division of 1659 alone ranged from 50 to 150 acres per man. A recent study of Sudbury, Massachusetts implies that any men who lived in that town from its founding in 1638 until 1658 must have been granted approximately

150 acres apiece. The original proprietors of Milford, near Dedham in south-eastern Massachusetts, resolved in 1662 "that the divisions of land . . . shall be by these ensuing rules: that to one hundred pounds estate be granted one hundred and fifty acres of land". Since an estate of twice one hundred pounds was average, the forty original proprietor-settlers must have planned on very large individual holdings. The fifty-five founders of Billerica, north of Cambridge, started off with 115 acres each. A survey of the sixty men living in one section of Concord, Massachusetts in 1665 revealed that each of them held on the average 250 acres. In nearby Andover, "four successive divisions of town land [between 1646 and 1662], together with additional divisions of meadow and swampland, provided each of the inhabitants with at least one hundred acres of land for farming, and as much as six hundred acres". With the information from Dedham and Watertown, these references make it seem that an estimate of 150 acres for the typical early inhabitant of an eastern Massachusetts town is a reasonable figure. Scattered evidence from early communities elsewhere in New England re-enforces this assumption.

In 1786 the Revolution was over. America was now an independent nation. Dedham had been founded exactly a century and a half before; Watertown was older still; Milford, Medfield and the other towns not quite so old. By 1786 Dedham was a town of some 2,000 souls; Watertown had grown more slowly but contained nearly 1,000 inhabitants; there were more than 775 persons in Medfield, close to 1,500 in Billerica, nearly 2,000 in Concord and more than 2,000 in Sudbury. These were no longer tiny villages, but were now towns of a respectable population for an agricultural society. In 1786 the Commonwealth of Massachusetts enacted a law which required every community in the state to complete a detailed questionnaire on the basis of which taxes were to be assessed. Among other items to be filled in were the number of male polls (males over sixteen) and the acreage of every type of land within the town. This last is of the utmost importance. Included under it were "tillage", "English upland and mowing", "fresh meadow", "saltmarsh", "pasture", "woodlands", "other unimproved land", and "unimprovable land". No type of land was left out. By dividing the number of adult males in a given town (polls minus a quarter yields a rough estimate of the number of males over twenty-one) into the total acreage of the town, one may arrive at the average number of acres per man.*

In what had been the "Puritan Village" of Sudbury, there were now 56 acres for each man, and in Medfield and Dedham 44 and 38 acres respectively. Even though town lands and worn lands are indiscriminately included, this represents a shrinkage to less than one-third of the landholdings of the first generation. The shrinkage was greater in Watertown, where the average had fallen to a mere 17 acres per man—less than one-seventh of what it had been in the 1630s! But whether one-third or one-seventh, the change was substantial in each of these old towns. The same might be said of all the towns of the area, almost without exception. The truth is that for the whole of Suffolk County the land area per adult male now averaged no more than 43 acres. If the average rose to 71 acres in Chelsea, it fell to 22 acres next door in Roxbury; if to the south in Wrentham the imaginary "typical" man had 70 acres, to the east in Hingham he had but 32 acres.**

* The discussion which follows is based upon uncatalogued documents in the Archives of the State of Massachusetts. They are in microfilm in volume clxiii. The resultant figures do not include lands held in other towns, but what evidence exists argues that it was not usual for a man to hold more than trifling amounts of land in towns other than his own. Further, the results make no distinction between good and worn land. Since over a century of rather unsophisticated New World farming must have produced worn land in many towns, an acre in 1786 was likely to have been less productive than an acre in 1636. The Suffolk inventories also bear out this assertion. Finally, residual public (town) lands seem to be included in the total, though these were not in the possession of individual farmers. Subsequent computer analysis of the 1786 lists by Professor Van Beck Hall of the University of Pittsburgh indicates that the estimates derived here are in every respect conservative and that the *arable* land per adult male in the older areas of Massachusetts probably fell below five acres.

** The narrowness of the range from top to bottom is significant. The average of 43 acres for Suffolk County was not produced by a few impossibly crowded towns pulling down the average of a more comfortable, well-endowed majority. The figures for each town begin with Roxbury's 22 acres and rise through averages of 25, 32, 32, 36, 38, 42, 44, 44, 47, 51, 52, 60, 68 and 70 acres to the peak of 71. As the years passed many of the inventories of estates on file in the Suffolk County Courthouse became quite specific as to landholdings. A sample of 300 of these for the years 1765–75 confirms the average land-holding figure derived from the assessment lists of 1786. The average rural estate included 65 acres of land. There are good reasons why this earlier figure is a little above the 43 acres average of 1786. For one thing, these are acreages at death. A man is likely to have held more land at the end of his life than he held on the average throughout that life. There is a second way in which they reflect success. Though there are inventories for men who held no land whatsoever (and 17 per cent of the 300

If time and the growth that time brought were essential factors in the decrease in the average area of landholdings, the oldest towns in the county should have had the lowest average acreage per man. This was exactly the situation. Twelve towns of Suffolk County were founded between 1630 and 1673. In 1786, their adult males would have had but 37 acres apiece had all the land in these towns been parcelled out equally. The seven newer towns founded between 1705 and 1739 contained in 1786 some 55 acres for every adult male residing within their bounds—an average holding significantly above that found in the older towns, if still substantially below the average of the first generation of New England farmers. Moreover, there is evidence that pressure on the land supply was most severe in the older towns. "Woodlands" and "unimproved" lands totalled 25 acres per man in the towns begun since 1705 but only 13 acres in those begun before 1673. The older towns had half as much uncultivated land per capita because the need for farm land had become most intense in these towns and was pushing men to put poor land under the plough.

More sharply diminished landholdings and a greater cultivation of marginal lands in the older towns are two indications of a mounting pressure on the land supply. A third index is the level of land prices. If there was a disproportionate demand for land, land prices, and probably food prices as well, should have risen more than the prices of most other commodities through the colonial period. A perusal of hundreds of inventories of estates for all of the rural towns of Suffolk County in the years 1660–1760 reveals that land values easily doubled and often tripled over the century throughout the region. By contrast, there was a remarkable long-term stability in items of personal estate, such as furniture, tools,

---

had no land at death, confirming the indications of the assessment lists that the suffrage could not possibly have been above 90 per cent), inventories for servants and paupers who had virtually no real or personal estate are extremely rare—almost nonexistent. Evidence will be presented below to show that such persons must have existed. Their exclusion from the sample of inventories naturally raises the average landholdings attributed to those who were included. With these adjustments made, it may be seen that the inventories describe much the same situation with regard to landholdings as was described in the town assessment lists of 1786. And, as would be expected, the inventories of estates from the older towns tend to include less land than those based on estates in towns more recently established.

and even clothing. Though a systematic enquiry might refine this contrast, it seems to have been a general phenomenon.

A similar decline in average landholdings may have prevailed elsewhere in New England, and may elsewhere have reached the point at which many towns were becoming "crowded", with waste land turned to crops and the cost of land soaring. A striking study of one particular Connecticut town follows the fortunes of local families through three generations, from 1740 to 1800. Family lands were divided and divided again to accommodate the increasing numbers of young men in the families, young men who did not seem to want to try their fortunes elsewhere. Ultimately, in Kent, Connecticut, "economic opportunity, which had been exceptionally bright from 1740 to 1777, was darkened . . . by the pressure of population . . . against a limited supply of land". Speaking of the whole of late eighteenth century Connecticut, Albert Laverne Olson observed, "Contemporaries were well aware of the decline of Connecticut agriculture and the exhaustion of its soil". It was plain to several of these observers that the population, which had grown fourfold from 1715 to 1756, had become too great for the countryside to support. Land values were rising sharply and marginal lands were being turned into farmland.

The "why" of the process, whether in eastern Massachusetts or in Connecticut, is fairly obvious. In Suffolk County as in Kent, Connecticut the pressure of population against a limited supply of land was the critical mechanism. Boston and a few suburbs aside, Suffolk County was a predominantly agricultural area. Farmers, "yeoman" or "husbandman" or "gentleman" farmers were the solid main stock of inhabitants. Land was the essence of life throughout the region; a sufficiency of land was a vital concern of the great majority of men. Yet, despite the simultaneous settlement of scores of towns to the west, the estimates of the population of eastern Massachusetts reveal the same inexorable growth which was characteristic of Connecticut. Up until 1765, and for most towns even after, an increase of from one to five per cent a year was a normal condition of life. Accompanying this growth, again as in Connecticut, was a pattern of inheritance in which partible descent dominated. Virtually no men left their lands intact to any one son. A double share of the whole estate for the eldest son with equal shares going to all other children (sons and daughters alike) was the standard set by the law for cases of intestacy. Even the minority of men who left wills followed this standard with very few deviations. Since emigration was not sufficient to relieve the situation, the consequence was a process of division and re-division of landholdings.

The process was a product of the fundamental conditions of existence in New England, and its operation could be perceived long before its effects became serious. As early as 1721, "Amicus Patriae" observed that "many of our old towns are too full of inhabitants for husbandry; many of them living upon small shares of land, and generally all are husbandmen. . . . And also many of our people are slow in marrying for want of settlements: . . .". Had "Amicus Patriae" returned in 1790, he might well have redoubled his lamentations.

There is a paradox involved in considering that thousands of farmers in late eighteenth-century New England held on the average little over 40 acres of land apiece. It is the paradox of a land full of opportunity and with room to spare which in practice was coming to support an agricultural society reminiscent of that in the old, more limited nations of Europe. Nor is this just so much verbiage. The English yeoman of the previous century had farmed lands ranging in area from 25 to 200 acres. In terms of land, many "yeomen" or "husbandmen" in this section of late eighteenth-century America were not perceptibly better off as a result of the long-ago emigration of their great-great-grandfathers. In terms of the future, in terms of the sons of these American farmers and of the amount of land which each son could hope to inherit, America was no longer the land of opportunity.

III

Further evidence drawn from eastern Massachusetts brings to light the possibility that the process which was causing the decrease in average landholdings might have been accompanied by, and perhaps have been leading to, alterations in the structure of the society.

A study of the distribution of estates from the agricultural villages of Suffolk County has been undertaken to see if the pattern in which wealth was distributed in the society could have been changing with time. For the several years on either side of 1660, 300 inventories have been distributed according to their size in £100 increments and the same has been done for 310 inventories from the years adjoining 1765. A process of economic polarization was under way. In 1660 there were only 13 of 300 men whose estates surpassed £900 and only three of these were worth more than £1,500. By 1765 there were 53 out of 310 men worth more than £900 and 19 of them had estates which ranged above £1,500, averaging £2,200. The average estate in 1660 was worth £315; the average in 1765 was £525. This difference came about not because of any long-term inflation or because of any true increase in the individual wealth of most men (land prices went up, but landholdings fell); it is the huge estates of the fifty-four rich men which caused nearly all of the increased size of the "average" estate in the sample of 1765! If there were more very rich men, there were also more distinctly poor individuals among those sampled in 1765. In 1660, fifty-seven men had left estates worth less than £100. In 1765, in spite of the greater aggregate wealth represented in this later sample, seventy-two men had estates in the lowest category. Moreover, the distance between the poor and the rest of society was growing. In 1660 the better-off 80 per cent of the sample had an average wealth 7.6 times as great as the average wealth of the lowest 20 per cent. By 1765 the bulk of society had estates which averaged 13.75 times the size of the estates of the poorest one-fifth. Not only were the rich becoming more numerous and relatively more rich, but the poor were becoming more numerous and relatively poorer.

Before 1700, it had been rare for an inhabitant of a Suffolk County town to call himself "gentleman" or "Esquire" when the time came for him to write his will. This, too, changed as America approached the revolution and in one more small way this change hints at an evolving society. For by the 1750s no less than 12.5 per cent of some 150 men from the farming towns had appropriated these titles of distinction. This becomes more impressive when one considers that the corresponding figure for the great metropolis of Boston was only 13.5 per cent. Perhaps some sort of landed gentry was arising here in the hallowed home of the New England yeoman!

An American pauper class may also have been developing at the same time and for the same reasons. In Dedham the number of vagabonds warned out of town increased sixfold in the first three decades of the eighteenth century, reaching the point where three strangers had to be moved along in the typical year. There was a parallel increase in Watertown. In Rehoboth, the warnings-out increased steadily from one a year (1724–33) to 3.8 (1734–43) to 4.5 (1744–53) to 6.25 (1754–7—where the record ends). In all three towns in the previous century it had been an unusual year which had seen the selectmen have to bestir themselves to ask anyone to move along. By the middle 1700s the wandering poor had become a part of the landscape in this part of New England.

If the town of Dedham has been cited from time to time as an example, it is because this is the only town in the immediate area for which an intensive analysis has been made. Though that analysis has been carried in detail only to 1736, it has uncovered more bits and pieces of evidence indicating social change. Almost every development thus far suggested may be seen in microcosm in Dedham. To run through these quickly. The population grew steadily and few sons emigrated. "Worn land" appears in the inventories of Dedham estates after 1700. In the tax assessment surveys of the 1760s, 70s, and 80s a rich "loaner class" appears in the town, men with large amounts out at interest, men for whom very few seventeenth-century counterparts can be found to have existed. Not only do the numbers of vagabonds warned out increase but the numbers of indigenous poor also rise sharply after 1700. After 1710 the collective and very English term "the poor" comes into use in this town; contributions are taken under this heading almost yearly. As in the 610 Suffolk inventories, so in Dedham the pyramid of wealth derived from tax and proprietors' lists changes in such a way as to put a greater percentage of men in the lower brackets. The numbers of men with no taxable land increase from less than 5 per cent around 1700 to 12 per cent by 1736. Not fully developed in 1736, projected over another half-century these trends must have had a powerful effect on the nature of life in Dedham. Similar trends most certainly had a great effect on the society of Kent, Connecticut.

In all of this there is (as there is in the study of Kent) an assumption of some degree of cause-and-effect relationship between the process which was causing a shrinkage in landholdings and these indications of social polarization—the two together going to make up what has been labelled an "overcrowded" society. Various linkages are possible. The most obvious would run as follows. In the intensifying competition for land, some men would lose out through ill luck or a lack of business sense. Since competition would be pushing land prices up, a loser would find recovery ever more difficult, a family with little land would have a hard time acquiring more. By the same token those men and families who somehow had acquired large amounts of land would prosper as its value rose with rising demand. In such a process, the pressure would be greater at the lower end of the spectrum. There the continuing division by inheritance would reduce ever greater numbers of young men to dependence upon other sources of income, sources from which to supplement the insufficient profits from their small plots of land, sources which might or might not be available.

IV

Clearly there were evolutionary patterns present within the society of early New England, patterns which reflect most significantly on the direction in which that society was heading. To repeat the hypothesis, the trends which existed in New England were essentially those first isolated in Kent by Charles Grant:

Economic opportunity, bright in 1751, had turned relatively dark by 1796 . . . society, predominantly middle class in 1751, included a growing class of propertyless men by 1796 . . . increased poverty stemmed from the pressure of a population swollen by a fantastic birthrate against a limited amount of land.

A finite supply of land and a growing population, a population notably reluctant to emigrate, were combining to fragment and reduce landholdings, bringing marginal lands increasingly into cultivation and raising land prices. Ultimately, the collision of land and population may have been polarizing the structure of society, creating an agricultural "proletariat" and perhaps even a corresponding rural "gentry". As it was in Kent, so, our evidence has suggested, it could have been throughout much of eastern Massachusetts and implicitly throughout much of New England.

What might such a process mean for our understanding of the history of early America? Charles Grant saw one of the major implications of the process which had turned his "frontier town" of Kent into a crowded and poverty-stricken backwater within fifty years. Since 1955 Robert E. Brown has been insisting that colonial society can best be characterized as a "middle-class democracy". He depicts a prosperous, satisfied society in which room and opportunity were available to nearly all, a society in which land and wealth were distributed widely and in which the suffrage was accordingly broad (since the suffrage was tied to a property qualification). The era of the American Revolution, in Brown's view, involved little internal social antagonism. The colonists simply defended their "middle-class democracy", by throwing off British rule and writing the Federal Constitution.* Brown musters impressive evidence to support his analysis of the society, yet his critics and other analysts of the society have found scattered evidence to the contrary, evidence which argues for poverty, for a relative lack of opportunity, for a narrower suffrage than he claims prevailed, and for bitter social conflicts in the Revolutionary era. The real issue, as Grant perceived, may not be "who is right?" but "from what period of time does each side draw its evidence?" Thus:

If Kent were established as typical, then Brown's "middle-class democracy" would be characteristic of the early stages of a new settlement . . . On the other hand, Brown's prosperity would disappear, and the depressed conditions described by a Nettels or an Adams would creep in [together with a reduction in the numbers of men qualified to vote] at a later date. Such conditions . . . would emerge mainly from the pressure of population on a limited supply of land.

In short, as the century wears on Brown's thesis loses validity. In so far as the level of the suffrage is one (and to Brown the chief) element in political democracy, the overcrowding which was becoming a part of the social evolution of so many New England towns must have contributed to a reduction in democratic expression in the society by the time of the American Revolution or shortly after. As the numbers of landless or near-landless men rose, the numbers of men qualified to participate in the political process fell. The men of the Suffolk County town of Dorchester demonstrated their awareness of the political dimensions of the social change which was taking place when, in objecting to the suffrage qualifications written

---

* Robert E. Brown, *Middle-Class Democracy and the Revolution in Massachusetts* (Ithaca, 1955); Robert E. and B. Katherine Brown, *Virginia 1705–1786: Democracy or Aristocracy* (East Lansing, 1964).

into the Massachusetts Constitution of 1780, they observed that even a low property qualification "infringes upon the Rights and Liberties of a number of useful and Respectable members of Society; which number we believe is daily increasing and possibly may increase in such proportion that one half the people of this Commonwealth will have no choice in any branch of the General Court".

But the most important issue is not whether social changes were reducing the level of the suffrage in early America. Even when Charles Grant's book on Kent, Connecticut appeared in 1961, most historians were a bit weary of the battle over Brown's definition of political "democracy". Most were and are more occupied with political democracy as a matter of social attitudes and political traditions than as the difference between a suffrage of 90 per cent and one of 60 per cent.* What is of greatest consequence is not that the society was becoming less "democratic" in the sense of a narrowing suffrage, but that it was becoming less "middle-class". Brown treated eighteenth-century colonial society as relatively static, but the evolutionary hypothesis derived from Kent and from eastern Massachusetts shows the flaw in this conception and points to a society moving from decades of rosy "middle-class" existence toward years of economic polarization and potential class conflict.

Further, the evolutionary patterns which threatened to erode the "middle-class" society described by Brown may have shaped the thinking of many of America's Revolutionary leaders. Recent work suggests that a number of American clergymen and politicians of the later eighteenth century were dissatisfied with the condition of their society. That society was certainly not as stratified, oppressive and corrupt as the society of England had become, but it seemed to some men that it was moving in that direction. The fear of a gradual "Europeanization" of American society, a fear given ground by the tendencies outlined here, probably lent a special energy to their

---

* It might, however, be noted that the reduction in the suffrage caused by "overcrowding" might have been as great as the difference between a suffrage of 90 per cent and one of 60 per cent. The tax surveys of 1786 reveal that at least 20 per cent of the men in the towns of Suffolk County had not enough real or personal property to qualify as voters. See also Grant, *Kent*, p. 140 for evidence of a similar decline. It is only fair to add that Brown himself has broadened his definition of "democracy" and increased the subtlety of his argument.

Revolutionary rhetoric. Thus, the leaders of the Revolution adopted Enlightenment ideas with such speed and fervor not merely because these ideas described the egalitarian, "middle-class" society which was the distinctive feature of life in the American colonies, but also because independence and the reforms engendered by Enlightenment ideas would guarantee that happy society against the changes which even then were bringing it closer to the Old World model. The radical ideas of European intellectuals would restore and protect, as well as "complete, formalize, systematize and symbolize", the unique American social order which was the pride of the Revolutionary generation.

If the evolutionary hypothesis advanced here poses problems for one controversialist, it resurrects another. Frederick Jackson Turner was convinced that the frontier—and by this he meant above all the expansive frontier of the nineteenth century—had a great rôle in shaping an energetic, egalitarian and optimistic American character. His speculations have lent energy to several generations of undergraduate lecture courses, but they have most often served as targets for historians who have been more cautious if usually less interesting. Most of these critics have attacked Turner on the basis that conditions on the frontier either were not what he said they were or did not have the effect on men that he claimed they did, or both. A question which might better be asked is: Where would we have been without Turner's frontier? The trend to an overcrowded society sketched in the previous pages throws a new light on this question. Without the emigration that followed 1790, New England society would have become ever more crowded at a rapid rate. If already by 1790 many towns were experiencing an excessive demand for land and the attendant consequences of that demand, what would conditions have been twenty or thirty years later? The most important point to make about the mass exodus to the frontier of the nineteenth century may be that it rescued America as the land of mobility and opportunity at a time when it was beginning to lack both and was beginning to undergo major social changes as a result.*

* The hypothesis likewise reflects on the background of the exodus of 1790–1830. If conditions were tending in the directions depicted, it may be that the waves of New Englanders heading west after 1790 were more "pushed" west by the difficulties of life in Old New England than "pulled" west by the attraction of better land.

V

Regardless of one's view of the evidence and speculations presented here, it should be clear that historians' understanding of the evolution of early American society is not at all adequate.

For example, a decline in landholdings, even if it was general, need not have meant an overcrowded society. There are at least four interrelated propositions whose validity would render a substantial decline in landholdings meaningless in terms of "negative" social and economic effects. The validity of several of these propositions would open the possibility that any decline in landholdings could actually have been accompanied by an improvement in productivity and in the overall social and economic situation—the evidence offered above notwithstanding. First, agricultural methods might have improved to a substantial degree and, in company with the more favourable man-land ratio which could have resulted from a decrease in the land-area per man, this improvement would have meant that 40-odd acres in 1786 were far more productive than 150-odd acres *circa* 1660. Second, better transportation coupled with the growth of urban areas might have so improved the market situation that a given quantity of agricultural produce in 1786 was worth more than that same quantity *circa* 1660. Third, non-farm occupations (presumably crafts and manufacturing) might have increased in the period under consideration, offering lucrative alternatives to men who chose to or had to leave the land.* Finally, 40-odd acres, even though it included "worn" or waste lands, might still have been ample with which to support a large family. The point which must be made is that there is available virtually no evidence in favour of any of these propositions—probably because they are not valid, but also and most significantly because no one has cared to try to find the evidence. What evidence does exist argues that propositions one, two, and probably three are not valid. The only enquiry into the question of subsistence sets the total landholdings required for the support of a farm family at between 40 and 89

---

* Such large-scale commercialization of the lives of men who were formerly independent subsistence farmers would, however, have been in itself a major social change, one which would have created internal tensions and hostilities and alarm on the part of Revolutionary ideologues of the Jefferson school.

acres, indicating that Suffolk County had reached a critical point by 1786.

Papers calling for "further study" have become one of the clichés of the historical profession. Yet the unavoidable conclusion is that the impact of this paper must reside not so much in its evidence and speculations as in a long list of specific questions. Was the decline in landholdings general? Was it always accompanied by the use of marginal lands and by a relative rise in the price of land? How much of the land farmed in the late eighteenth century was "worn" land? Was there an improvement in agricultural techniques and in the man-land ratio? Was there an improvement in access to markets? Did non-farm occupations offer alternate sources of income? Why did sons not leave the crowded towns, towns like Kent, Connecticut and Watertown, Massachusetts, to take advantage of the room which the frontier seemed to offer? Was it fear of Indians or the traditional inertia of rural society or something not yet considered?* Was 40 acres enough to support a large family, and exactly how large were families in this period? Was the distribution of wealth in society changing with time? How reliable are inventories of estates in determining this? Are tax lists better sources for this purpose? Did the numbers of vagabonds and paupers increase with time? Was the increase, if any, greater than the mere rise in population would account for? Did the appropriation of titles of social distinction increase similarly? Who appropriated these titles and why? How did all these factors come together in the history of a single town? The studies of Kent, Connecticut and Dedham, Massachusetts are the only long-term local case histories presently available. We need more of them.** Finally, what were the

---

* This is an essential question, since, as this enquiry shows, the real problem may have been not so much the lack of a viable frontier as the relative failure to take advantage of that frontier.

** At the Iowa University Conference on Early American History in March of 1967, Professor John M. Bumsted delivered a paper on "Religion, Finance, and Democracy in Massachusetts; the Town of Norton as a Case Study"; Norton, like Kent, Connecticut was a relatively new town which within three generations began to experience many of the characteristic difficulties of overcrowding; here, as elsewhere, there was a reluctance to emigrate. A recent and excellent study of Andover, Massachusetts (Philip Greven, Jr., "Family Structure in . . . Andover", "Four Generations: a Study of Family Structure, Inheritance, and Mobility in Andover, Massachusetts, 1630–1750" [Ph.D. dissertation, Harvard University, 1965]) confirms the trends depicted here, but also supports the possibility that

attitudes of thoughtful men of the time regarding the state of their society? Was there a universal awareness of change?

Until this work is begun, the irritating hypothesis that much of New England was becoming seriously "overcrowded" by 1790 will have to stand. Instead of being the land of opportunity, this part of America was rapidly becoming more and more an old world society; old world in the sense of the size of farms, old world in the sense of an increasingly wide and articulated social hierarchy, old world in that "the poor" were ever present and in increasing numbers. The word "becoming" is carefully selected. The fact of independence and the egalitarian ideas broadcast by the Revolution, together with the great exodus to the west after 1790, quickly made it ridiculous to speak of this or any part of America as an old world society. Yet this had been the tendency in much of New England for decades. Had it been allowed, by some miraculous suspension of subsequent events, to continue unchecked—who can say what might have been the result? This part of America might soon have come to resemble the Anglicized society dreamed of by some arch-Federalists more than the vigorous, expansive society which has since been a characteristic feature of our national history.

19. | James T. Lemon and Gary B. Nash
      | *"The Distribution of Wealth in Eighteenth-Century*
      | *America: A Century of Change in Chester County,*
      | *Pennsylvania, 1693–1802"*

Surveying recent literature in the field of social structure, James T. Lemon and Gary B. Nash have raised problems of methodology and interpretation, and have used an empirical study of Chester County, Pennsylvania to illustrate their points. From *Journal of Social History*, 2 (1968), 1–24. Reprinted with omission of most notes by permission of the authors and the *Journal of Social History*.

---

these trends may have called forth a contemporaneous response. Emigration increased during the third and fourth generations, while the use of partible inheritance declined. When and where such responses operated, they could have done much to mitigate the effects of the trend to overcrowding.

The stratification of society, according to social theory, is closely linked to the economic system, the political structure, and the prevailing set of values (ideology). But connections between these variables are not easy to make, especially because social stratification involves not only the division of material wealth, but also the distribution of political power and social prestige. Though related, each of these dimensions of stratification is discrete and each has its own dynamics of change. The most obvious and most readily quantified criterion of stratification is the distribution of wealth; thus historians and social scientists concerned with class structure have often focused on the division of wealth as measured by property or income taxes.

This method of analysis, however, is difficult and fraught with dangers. Recent social studies of colonial America, based on extant sources which are scant and sometimes obscure, illustrate this point. Considered together, they demonstrate the complexity of describing even the distribution of wealth, let alone the class structure. Moreover, they testify to the far from uniform approach to the problem of social stratification and the wide variation in the use of evidence. Not surprisingly, their conclusions about the structure of colonial society, and the changes it underwent in the seventeenth and eighteenth centuries, are mixed and often contradictory.

The structure of early American society is of current significance because the older notion that before the Revolution the colonies were becoming increasingly differentiated into classes and showed a corresponding tendency toward political elitism has been forcefully challenged of late by a number of historians who argue that the availability of cheap land and the broad opportunity for advancement led to both economic and political democracy, which were in their view causally related. Following logically from this is the contention that the American Revolution had little effect on eighteenth-century society unless it was to democratize further a nation which had already removed most of the roadblocks to economic, social, and political opportunity, at least for adult white males. In this article we will survey the approaches, techniques, and conclusions of four recent studies and present a case study of Chester County, Pennsylvania, which may demonstrate some of the pitfalls that await those who use quantitative data to analyze the inner workings of colonial society.

The Browns, husband and wife, are the most insistent proponents of the "revisionist" view of colonial society. In their studies of Virginia and Massachusetts in the eighteenth century they maintain that by the time of the Revolution colonial society had achieved (at least compared with contemporary European societies) what they have called "middle-class democracy." Assuming that they consider this the achievement and not the initial condition of immigrant society, it may be inferred that they believe pre-Revolutionary society was moving steadily toward a condition of greater social mobility, less pronounced stratification, and more evenly distributed wealth—a process which the Revolution only accelerated. Political democracy flowed as a matter of course from this attainment of "economic democracy."

Qualified support for the Browns' thesis is provided by Charles Grant's pioneering study of the town of Kent, Connecticut. Using tax lists spanning six decades, Grant presents evidence indicating that there was a narrow range of wealth in western Connecticut, a relative absence of stratification, and a tendency for the small farmer before the Revolution to move upward into the "lower middle" and "upper middle" ranks of society. But Grant concludes that between 1777 and 1796 this fluidity disappeared. The ranks of the poor swelled from 25 to 42 percent of the adult males, while the relative strength of the upper-middle and lower-middle classes diminished. Economic changes produced roughly parallel political changes.

In his *Social Structure of Revolutionary America,* the first full-scale attempt to analyze colonial class structure, Jackson T. Main agrees with the Browns and Grant that people were socially mobile and that the disparity between the top and bottom of the social structure, at least outside the provincial towns, was unimpressive. Main, however, reverses Grant's formulation of the direction in which colonial society was changing. His data indicates that both the gap between rich and poor and the share of the wealth controlled by the wealthiest 10 percent of colonial taxpayers increased steadily during the generation before 1776. On the other hand, "the effect of the Revolution was to reverse these trends, at least temporarily." Main explains the pre-Revolutionary drift toward "greater inequality, with more marked class distinctions," as the result of the increasingly commercial complexion of society. As frontier regions turned to subsistence farming and then to commercial farming, economic and social differentiation increased, as did the share of the wealth possessed by the upper stratum of society. Regional variations were common, but typically the upper 10 percent of adult white males controlled about one-third of the taxable wealth on the frontier, slightly more in subsistence farming areas, and about half in commercial farming regions. In the cities social stratification and economic inequality, Main suggests, were even more marked.

A less comprehensive but more precise analysis of social structure and wealth distribution has been presented by James A. Henretta, who has studied the town of Boston between 1687 and 1771. Using two tax lists separated by more than eight decades, Henretta attempts to show that rapid commercial development in Massachusetts left Boston society far more stratified while reallocating the communities resources—and political power—so as to consolidate greatly the strength of the merchant elite at the expense of the lower and middle elements. There is little in Henretta's analysis to suggest that Boston on the eve of the Revolution, with the upper 15 percent of society controlling 66 percent of the assessable wealth and 29 percent of the adult white males holding no taxable property, was a "middle-class democracy."

These four studies offer different and even irreconcilable conclusions about the changing stratification of colonial society. The Browns imply a weakening of hierarchical structure throughout the eighteenth century. Grant found increasingly less differentiation before the Revolution but a reversal of this trend after 1777. Main and Henretta see greater structuring before the Revolution, and Main suggests that the Revolutionary period reversed this drift. But common to all these schemata, as with the earlier so-called Beard-Becker view, is the presumption that changes in the structure of society and the structure of politics went hand in hand.

These varied conclusions are in part the result of certain problems of methodology and technique. The Browns, for all the statistics they marshal in support of their thesis, never attempt to analyse the distribution of wealth in either Massachusetts or Virginia. This, of course, allows them to define "economic democracy" exclusively in terms of "opportunity"—opportunity to acquire land, to rise materially or to participate in the political process. Neither do the Browns deal adequately with the question of change: that colonial society became more democratic is implied, but there is little evidence provided to indicate the dimensions or degree of change. Nor is any real attempt made to differentiate between rural and urban communities.

Grant is far more exact in defining what he means by economic democracy and employs tax lists over a period of six decades to portray a changing class profile in Kent. But his use of a fixed scale of absolute wealth over an extended period to define "lower," "lower middle," and "upper middle" classes is probably too arbitrary to tell us whether a redistribution of wealth actually occurred during the Revolutionary era or whether all segments of society were adversely affected by economic dislocation. Possession of a £49 estate in 1740, for example, may have entitled one to "upper middle" class status at that time; that it would still do so in 1796 is uncertain.*

Because it encompasses only the years between 1763 and 1788, Main's study provides us with little opportunity to observe social change over an extended period of time and leaves obscure the relative importance of the Revolution in altering the social structure. Rather than study the metamorphosis of particular communities over several generations, Main has examined different kinds of societies—his categories are frontier, subsistence farming, commercial farming, and urban—within a narrow span of time and has concluded from the differences he found that colonial society, as it became more commercially oriented, moved toward a condition of greater inequality. Virtually no data are presented to show what economic and social forces identified with the Revolutionary era changed the social structure of particular communities. Indeed it is not possible to appreciate the degree or significance of changes occurring during the Revolutionary period until the extent and characteristics of change occurring before the 1760's is known. Besides, the criteria used for distinguishing subsistence from commercial farming areas are not very clear. As will be noted below, it is doubtful that these are valid categories.

---

* Grant used £29 and below for "poor class," £30 to £48 for "lower middle class," and £49 and above for "upper middle class." The boundaries were determined by "correlating tax figures and corresponding property ownership in 1796."

Henretta's analysis of Boston, though the most sophisticated study of structural changes in colonial society, is somewhat handicapped by the availability of only two tax lists for the period. This requires Henretta to analyse the community at two widely separated dates. Without any intermediate data between 1687 and 1771, it is impossible to chart the pattern of change or to correlate the redistribution of wealth with other variables. Like Main, Henretta ties the increasing concentration of wealth to commercial development. But a simple statistical correlation between two variables does not necessarily establish a causal relationship between them, exclusive of other factors. Henretta's analysis stops short of the Revolution, so there is no possibility of carrying his conclusions into the last quarter of the eighteenth century.

For at least one area in colonial America—Chester County, Pennsylvania—it is possible to chart shifts in the relative distribution of wealth over the entire course of the eighteenth century and perhaps eventually to draw out wider implications of social change. Not only have the records of the first provincial tax levied in 1693 survived, but also a large number of yearly tax lists, both county and provincial, for the remainder of the century. Taken together, they offer one of the richest collections of data available for studying in microcosm the changing social and economic characteristics of colonial America.

Chester County, including its eastern fifth that became Delaware County in 1789, is located in southeastern Pennsylvania, adjacent to the Delaware River and bordered by the counties of Philadelphia, Montgomery, Berks, and Lancaster and the states of Maryland and Delaware (Fig. 1). No point in the county was more than twenty-five miles from the navigable Delaware and partially navigable Schuylkill rivers or Chesapeake Bay. The southwestern corner, although fifty-five miles from Philadelphia, was only about thirty miles from Wilmington and less than forty miles from Baltimore. In the eighteenth century most goods were conveyed by wagon, usually on the Philadelphia-Lancaster Road through the Chester Valley (part of which became the Lancaster Turnpike in 1792) or the Newport Road which connected the western part of the county and the Lancaster Plain with Wilmington and the Brandywine complex of flour mills. Despite reliance on relatively expensive road transport, no part of the county was remote from markets or transshipment points. Transport costs did not inhibit greatly the development of a degree of commercial agriculture.

Although overshadowed by Lancaster County after the Revolution, Chester County was a prosperous rural area, partly because of its accessibility to water and markets, but also because of a growing season (more than 170 days) long enough to grow successfully many crops and the high quality of the land—well-drained loamy soils, derived mostly from crystalline gneisses and schists, but also from limestone (especially in Chester Valley), shales and coastal sediments. Even though it possessed far less area of limestone plain than Lancaster County, the inherent productivity of its soils was nearly as high as in Lancaster County. Most of the county had slopes gentle enough to be cultivated. In the eighteenth century farmers produced a wide range of crops and livestock for their own consumption and for sale. Wheat, often converted to flour in local mills, was the most important product sold. Some farmers, especially those near the Delaware River, fattened livestock and produced cheese and butter for the Philadelphia market, for ship provisioning, and for export to other mainland colonies or overseas.

There are some serious difficulties in interpreting the unusually complete record of wealth assessment for Chester County—difficulties which are common to almost all colonial tax lists but which too frequently have been glossed over by economic and social historians. First, tax returns frequently give separate assessments for land, livestock, servants, slaves, and, late in the century, buildings, personal goods, and occupations.* But it is still not possible to determine taxpayers' *actual* estates from these assessments, first because not all forms of wealth were taxed, and second because

---

* Land was sometimes differentiated on the lists as "cleared," "sown," or "meadow." Among personal possessions taxed were plate and carriages. Laws defining the assessable categories of wealth were passed throughout the period. The tendency over the course of a century was to: (1) refine real property assessments by differentiating land according to its quality and use; (2) extend the tax to non-landed wealth such as plate, carriages, and income derived from trade, professions, salaries, and lucrative offices; and (3) increase the tax on single freemen. Between 1757 and 1779 assessments were laid on the "clear yearly value of estates" which was defined as the rent they bring or, if not rented, what they would bring in rentals in the estimation of the assessor. Before and after this period the value of estates was assessed. In 1782 certain professions were exempted.

tax assessors had a marked tendency to undervalue the estates of the more affluent property owners, especially, it seems, in the seven or eight decades before the Revolution.* This tendency to under-value the property of the wealthiest property owners may be the reason for the reduction of the average value of estates (Table I, line O), and it compresses the range from top to bottom. A meticu-lous and comprehensive collating of tax lists with inventories of estate, frequently filed in the probate records, would enable a more precise description of wealth. But even then, the task could never be completed because inventories of estate were often not made or filed, and land, though specified by acreage and location in wills, was rarely appraised in inventories. Nonetheless, land composed the largest part of assessable wealth in rural areas and steadily through-out the eighteenth century tax laws were revised to include cate-gories of wealth other than land.

A second problem in using tax lists for social analysis involves distinguishing categories of taxpayers. Nonresident owners of land in Chester County, owners of parcels in more than one township, tenant farmers, "inmates" (who were married artisans and laborers living in houses owned by others), and single freemen were not al-ways differentiated from owner-occupiers on the tax lists. Some townships in some years listed "non-resident" landowners sepa-rately. On the basis of these samples, it appears that residents of Philadelphia, of other counties, and of other townships in Chester County composed between 5 and 20 percent of the taxpayers in each of Chester's townships. From the scant evidence available it also appears (as one might expect) that the number of nonresident taxpayers in any given township was on the rise in the eighteenth century. The effect of their swelling numbers for our purposes, however, is partially offset by the decreasing value of the property they held relative to that of the resident taxpayers. Because owners of land in two or more townships and the nonresident landowners are counted in our calculations for each parcel of land they held, we are dealing with property holdings rather than with people. With the wealth of some substantial persons thus split up, not only are the number of persons inflated by about 10 percent (Table I, line Q), but the rich appear less prosperous than they actually

* The most important assets and debts not included in the tax lists were forms of money wealth such as book credit, notes, bonds, and mortgages.

were. By the same token, the lower ranks of the economic spectrum appear somewhat enlarged beyond their actual size.

Part of the distortion in the real distribution of wealth caused by the problem of nonresidents is offset by the inclusion in the tax lists of tenant farmers. In 1760 and 1782 tenant farmers represented about 10 percent of all taxpayers and 25 percent of all farmers. They are almost always overrated in the calculations because the tax lists rarely reflect the fact that landlords usually paid most of the tax on land occupied by tenants. Therefore, high assessments for tenant farmers *tend* to cancel out split and low assessments of nonresidents and Chester County residents holding land in more than one township. It is impossible, given the incompleteness of the evidence, to be precise about this offsetting factor, though we suspect that the degree of distortion remains about the same over the course of a century.

"Inmates" are less of a problem, at least after 1760 when they are specified on most lists. From 1760 to 1802 inmates composed between 17 and 23 percent of all taxpayers. Together with tenant farmers, they raised the total of non-landholders to between 25 and 35 percent. Lacking data on inmates before 1760, it is difficult to discern any long-term trend. Single freemen are excluded from the calculations because normally they paid a standardized head tax rather than a tax on land, occupations, and goods. There seems to have been a gradual increase of these young men over twenty-one years of age, many of whom were the sons of residents. Indentured and hired servants and slaves are not included, since they are numbered (sometimes) but not valued on the lists.

Despite the difficulties inherent in the data, it is clear from the seven tax lists used in this study (Table I) that a gradual concentration of wealth and a relative widening of the gap between rich and poor occurred in Chester County during the eighteenth century. At the time of the first provincial tax in 1693 Chester County was notable for its unusually even distribution of wealth. The lowest 30 percent of the taxpayers commanded almost as much of the community's taxable wealth as the next 30 percent, while the upper tenth of the population held less than one-fourth of the county's taxable assets. The narrow limits of the economic spectrum are not altogether surprising since the area was populated almost entirely by members of the Society of Friends who, over the three decades

TABLE I

Vertical distribution of assessed taxable wealth in Chester County, 1693–1802

LINE	PERCENT OF TAXPAYERS	1693	1715	1730	1748	1760	1782	1800–1802*
A	0–10	5.8	3.1	1.9	3.7	0.7	0.8	0.8
B	10–20	5.8	5.0	3.7	3.8	2.5	1.5	1.3
C	20–30	5.8	5.0	4.2	5.6	3.3	2.4	1.8
D	30–40	6.2	7.0	5.7	6.1	4.8	3.7	2.4
E	40–50	7.1	7.5	7.2	7.5	6.8	5.6	4.4
F	50–60	7.8	8.4	8.8	8.1	8.9	8.0	6.9
G	60–70	9.4	10.3	10.4	9.8	11.5	10.8	10.0
H	70–80	12.7	12.6	12.5	11.6	13.9	14.4	14.0
I	80–90	15.6	15.2	16.9	15.0	17.9	19.3	20.2
J	90–100	23.8	25.9	28.6	28.7	29.9	33.6	38.3
K	Number of taxpayers (excluding freemen)	257	670	1791	2998	4290	5291	7247
L	Total taxes paid	1080s.	2665s.	9376s.	7970s.	66340s.	£41,324	$20,197.63
M	Average tax paid	4.20s.	3.98s.	5.20s.	2.66s.	15.50s.	£7.8	$2.79 = 20.9s.
N	Rate of tax per £	1d.	2d.	3d.	2d.	18d.	5.3d.	3 mills/$1 = 1.6d.†
O	Adjusted average tax (all at 1d./£)	4.25	1.99	1.73	1.33	0.86‡	(29.9)	(13.1)
P	Maximum assessed estate (adjusted)	£300	£120	£200	£180	£100‡	£5298	$39,666
Q	Total taxpayers	289	759	1977	3465	5127	6204	9023
R	Number of innates					859	1427	1601
	Percent of total taxpayers					16.8	23.0	17.7
S	Number of freemen	37	87	186	467	837	913§	1776
	Percent of total taxpayers	11.1	11.5	9.4	13.5	16.3	14.7	19.7

* Includes Delaware County, 1802
† Delaware County: 6 mills/$1 converted to 3 mills
‡ Assessed on yearly value of estates
§ Two townships, 1781

preceding settlement, had been recruited from the lower-middle ranks of English society. What is more, of those in England who purchased land from William Penn at the outset of colonization, it was typically the small purchaser who pulled up roots and immigrated to Pennsylvania, while the larger purchaser remained at home, holding his land for speculative gains. Of the 450 purchasers of land in 1682, for example, 266 (59.1 percent) made purchases of less than 1,000 acres. But in 1689, when the colony's first rent roll was compiled, 92.2 percent of the 192 landowners in Chester County held less than 1,000 acres and almost half of them (49.5 percent) less than 250 acres. At the standard land price set by Penn this represented an investment no larger than £5.

In the first quarter-century after the provincial tax of 1693, the distribution of wealth underwent only minor changes, although southeastern Pennsylvania was developing rapidly into one of the most productive grain-producing areas of the middle colonies. The share of the taxable wealth commanded by the middle strata of society increased slightly, while an incipient trend toward greater inequality is evident in the limited consolidation of wealth by the upper 10 percent of the community—composed of the largest or most productive landowners, some millowners, and a few merchants in the Delaware River port of Chester—and a somewhat more significant decrease in the share of wealth held by the lowest 30 percent of society.

For almost a half-century after 1715, while the county was growing in population from about 4,000 to over 25,000, the drift toward greater differentiation of wealth continued, though the pace of change, as is clear from Tables I and II, was not rapid. Such evidence as is available suggests that throughout the country—and in the province at large—the standard of living was on the rise. The decade of the 1730's was especially kind to Pennsylvania farmers, for it was a period of generally favorable weather and excellent harvests. Exports from Philadelphia, which had averaged about 4,900 tons per year in the 1720's, rose above 10,000 tons in five years of the next decade and averaged approximately 9,600 tons per year throughout the 1730's. Between 1725 and 1760 the population of southeastern Pennsylvania quadrupled while imports per capita increased tenfold. There is little doubt that Chester County participated in this period of growth and prosperity.

So far as the distribution of wealth was concerned during this era, the most impressive changes by far occurred at the top and bottom of the social ladder. Possession of the community's wealth by the poorest tenth of the taxpayers fell from 3.1 percent to 0.7 percent. The upper tenth of the community increased its share of the assessed wealth from about 26 to 30 percent. This gradual drift toward a more differentiated society is seen more clearly in Table II which, by collapsing the data from Table I, charts the marked decrease in economic leverage of the lowest 30 percent of the community, a loss matched by considerable, if unspectacular, gains in the upper-middle and upper segments of the population. This trend might be taken as a limited confirmation of Main's conclusion that social and economic elaboration increased with a greater emphasis on commercial farming, though a causal connection between the two is still uncertain.

The era of the American Revolution, far from reversing this creeping movement toward a consolidation of wealth and a deterioration in the economic position of the lower elements, as Main asserts, only continued the trend and apparently accelerated it somewhat. Between 1760 and 1782, when the earlier growth of both imports and exports slackened and then slowed to a trickle, the bottom third of the community saw its share of the wealth drop from 6.3 to 4.7 percent, while the upper tenth continued its century-long advance. Of even greater interest, perhaps, is the pro-

TABLE II

Summary view of vertical distribution of assessed taxable wealth in Chester County, 1693–1802

PERCENT OF TAXPAYERS	1693	1715	1730	1748	1760	1782	1800–1802
Lowest 30	17.4	13.1	9.8	13.1	6.3	4.7	3.9
Lower-Middle 30	21.1	22.9	21.7	21.7	20.5	17.3	13.7
Upper-Middle 30	37.7	38.1	39.8	36.4	43.3	44.5	44.2
Upper 10	23.8	25.9	28.6	28.7	29.9	33.6	38.3
Number of taxpayers*	257	670	1791	2998	4290	5291	7247

* Single freemen are excluded from calculations.

nounced decline of economic strength in the lower-middle segment (Table II) whose members until 1760 had maintained their position relative to other levels of society. Not until the late 1780's did the growing demand in Europe for Pennsylvania wheat and flour bring a return of prosperity to the area and even then the economy was subject to severe fluctuations for the rest of the century. During this period, from the end of the war to 1802, the erosion of the relative position of the lower-middle level was even more marked than before the war. At the same time, the advance of the uppermost stratum of society had never been so rapid within the span of a single generation.

Even though it is clear that the distance between rich and poor in Chester County was opening, as defined by the shifting disposition of wealth, we cannot be sure what this signifies about changes in absolute wealth or implies about the standard of living, let alone class structure. We do not know whether the poor actually became poorer, as their relative position weakened, or, conversely, whether the "cake" expanded so that their incomes and possessions increased, even if more slowly than the rich. Undoubtedly there were impoverished persons: they were sometimes specified as "poor" on tax lists. But the use of arbitrary standards of wealth to define class, such as £29 and below for "poor" or £49 and above for "upper-middle," is not justified over a whole century. As seen in Table I, line P, the maximum assessment in Chester County apparently declined from £300 in 1693 to £180 in 1748, but it is certain from wills, inventories of estate, and other evidence that a modestly affluent group of farmers, forge and millowners, and small shopkeepers had emerged. Thus, even though the adjusted average tax fell between 1693 and 1760 (Table I, line O), it would be a mistake to conclude that Chester County on the whole was becoming poorer. It is possible that the rapid influx of relatively poor immigrants from Ireland and Germany after 1710 created a class of "new poor," whose meagre estates pulled down the value of the average assessment and allowed an apparent consolidation of economic power at the top. If this is true, the increase in per capita consumption of imports would signify only a rapid acquisition rate of luxury goods by the more substantial taxpayers. But numerous accounts of Pennsylvania society during the pre-Revolutionary period indicate a growing prosperity in the middle ranks as well. Export statistics, data on wheat and flax production, and price levels also suggest that men at all levels were improving their condition, though clearly not at the same pace. Another possible explanation for the downward trend in the average taxes and increasing differentiation is that more and more persons were engaged in occupations off the land. If land remained the chief criterion of wealth, then persons in other occupations were undertaxed. This is not clear; for what it is worth, the average tax paid in 1774 by residents of the town of Lancaster, none of whom were farmers, was almost identical to the average in Lancaster County as a whole, suggesting that assessors did account for other forms of "wealth."

It does seem possible that during and after the Revolution the lower ranks of society suffered a decline in the standard of living. The relative change in proportions of wealth provides a hint of this. The significant increase in single freemen from 1782 to 1802 also suggests shrinking opportunities for new jobs. There are suggestions that movement westward was unusually heavy in the early 1790's. Grant found the 1790's a decade of hardship for the lower-middle class in Kent, causing many people to migrate westward. But we cannot follow Grant in attributing the deterioration of the lower class simply to population pressure on land supply induced by the maturing of the third generation. For in most of Chester County the third generation had emerged by 1760 without any abrupt change in demographic trends. It would appear that the period during and immediately after the Revolution saw a drastic reduction of British credit, weaker external markets, and so, presumably, a more difficult time for persons in the lower half of the wealth structure who were least well equipped to weather a period of economic dislocation.

Though connections between the redistribution of wealth in the eighteenth century and broader aspects of economic and social change are extremely difficult to make, some light can be shed on these relationships by analyzing for a single year the distribution of wealth in each of the fifty-two townships of Chester County. For this purpose the year 1760 has been chosen because it precedes the era of economic disruption that began in the 1770's, but still represents a point in the eighteenth century when all of the county had been settled for more than one generation (some parts for three).

Ideally, one would like to compare the distribution of wealth among townships where subsistence farming predominated, where commercial farming was conspicuous, and where substantial town development had occurred. This would allow a precise test of Main's organizing thesis that agricultural commercialization (and ultimately urbanization) caused increasing social stratification. Unfortunately, it is almost impossible to establish spatial patterns of agricultural development. Eighteenth-century farm records and production figures are far too scarce to allow any measurement or dating of commercialization in a given area. The available evidence suggests, moreover, that in most parts of the county there was no clear-cut distinction between subsistence and commercial farming. Nearly every farmer produced surpluses for the commercial market almost from the outset, although in lean years many did little more than support themselves. Main suggests that in colonial America there were "clearly identifiable" types of society—"frontier," "subsistence farming," "commercial farming," and "urban"—each with its characteristic social structure which reflected its stage of economic development. But in Chester County farmers were producing wheat for consumption in Philadelphia and for export to the West Indies within two years of initial settlement. It is possible, of course, that because of its superior soil and accessibility to commercial markets Chester County simply bypassed the frontier and subsistence farming stages of development. But Main's distinctions between areas and stages in development may be too artificial to serve any analytical purpose, especially if variations *within* a commercial farming area such as Chester County are found to be greater than variations *between* "types" of agricultural society.

Though the townships of Chester County cannot be differentiated by the degree of economic development, it is possible to plot spatial patterns of wealth distribution and then to establish some correlations with other variables such as access to the commercial centers of Chester and Philadelphia or to the Delaware River, soil conditions, population density, and religious and ethnic composition of the inhabitants. Figures 1 and 2 indicate the spatial distribution of wealth by quantiles in each of the county's fifty-two

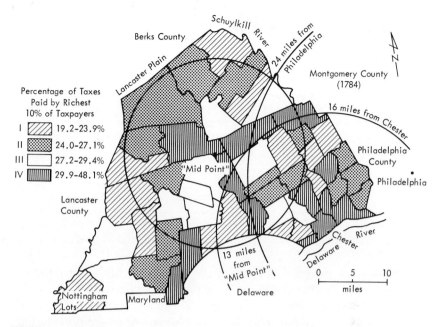

FIGURE 1

Percent of taxes paid by richest 10 percent of taxpayers in Chester County, 1760

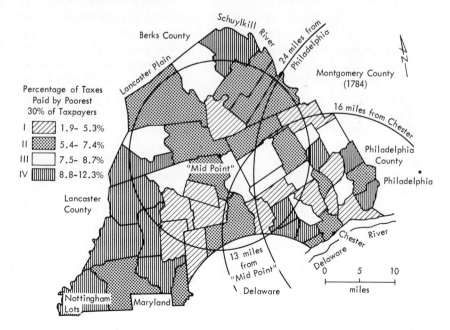

FIGURE 2

Percent of taxes paid by poorest 30 percent of taxpayers in Chester County, 1760

TABLE III

Share of taxable wealth held by poorest 30 percent in 13 townships (Fig. II) where upper 10 percent control a larger share of wealth than elsewhere (Category IV, Fig. I)

		QUANTILE		
	I *1.9–5.3* *(lowest)*	*II* *5.4–7.4* *(second lowest)*	*III* *7.5–8.7* *(second highest)*	*IV* *8.8–12.3* *(highest)*
Number of townships	7	4	2	0

townships, expressed in terms of the taxable wealth commanded by the upper 10 percent and lowest 30 percent of taxpayers.*

The most obvious fact that emerges from a comparative study of the townships is that there were wide variations in the distribution of wealth within the county. The taxable wealth held by the upper tenth varied from almost half (48.1 percent) to only a fifth (19.2 percent). Not unexpectedly, there is a strong correlation between the townships where the affluent were strongly entrenched and those in which the lower element had the least economic power. In the thirteen townships (top quantile, IV, Fig. 1) where the wealthiest tenth were most firmly in possession of the community's resources, the bottom-most 30 percent were usually in the most unenviable position (Table III). Where the upper tenth had the weakest grip, conversely, the lower elements were in a far stronger position.

In terms of distance from various points, Philadelphia, Chester and the "mid-point" of the county, no clear-cut change in stratification is apparent as one moves from the eastern, presumably more developed areas of the county, to the western, hypothetically less developed regions. To be sure, the thirteen townships where wealth was most concentrated at the top *tend* to be in the eastern half of the county, within twenty-four miles of Philadelphia or sixteen

---

* On Figures I and II circles have been drawn, using Philadelphia, Chester, and the approximate "mid-point" as foci, so as to include an equal number of townships within and beyond the lines. Where the lines cross townships, more than 50 percent had to be inside the circle to be included in the "within" group. Most of the area designated "Nottingham Lots" became a part of Maryland in 1764 but was taxed in Chester County until 1774.

miles of Chester, and the four townships where the upper 10 percent had the tightest hold on their community's wealth were near
the Delaware River. Only three of the thirteen townships with the
greatest concentration of wealth were wholly outside these perim-
eters. On the western and northern borders of the county wealth
was often more evenly distributed. And yet a number of townships
in the eastern half of the county were among those with the greatest
equality in allocation of wealth. Of the thirteen townships where
the wealthy were least entrenched, six were in the eastern half of
the county. Or, to look at the question differently, it can be seen
from Figure II that in the easternmost twenty-six townships, all
settled for more than a half-century by 1760 and all within easy
reach of Philadelphia and Chester, the upper stratum was completely mixed in the relative degree of control it exerted. In eight
townships the richest tenth of the taxpayers were in the top quantile of that category, but in six townships they were in the lowest
quantile (Table V).

Within the lower ranks of society a similarly mixed pattern is
found. In the most remote areas of the county the poor were somewhat more advantageously situated in relative terms. Those townships where the lowest 30 percent had the least economic power
were scattered in the eastern and central sections, giving some evidence that the cleavage between the top and bottom of society decreased as one moved away from the urban centers of Philadelphia
and Chester. But among the twenty-six easternmost townships the
lower ranks varied greatly from township to township in the posi-

TABLE IV

*Share of taxable wealth held by richest 10 percent in
13 townships (Fig. I) where lowest 30 percent control a
larger share of wealth than elsewhere (Category IV, Fig. II)*

	QUANTILE			
	I *19.2–23.9* *(lowest)*	*II* *24.0–27.1* *(second* *lowest)*	*III* *27.2–29.4* *(second* *highest)*	*IV* *29.9–48.1* *(highest)*
Number of townships	8	2	3	0

TABLE V

Percent of taxes paid by the richest 10 percent of taxpayers
(*Single freemen excluded*)

	QUANTILE			
	I 19.2–23.9	II 24–27.1	III 27.2–29.8	IV 29.9–48.1
Number of townships				
Within 24 miles of Philadelphia	6	6	6	8
Beyond 24 miles of Philadelphia	7	7	7	5
Within 16 miles of Chester	7	6	5	8
Beyond 16 miles of Chester	6	7	8	5

tion they held in their communities. In seven of these townships the lower 30 percent were in the bottom quantile of the poor. But in six townships they were in the highest quantile (Table VI). A similarly mixed pattern is apparent when using an area within thirteen miles of the "mid-point" in the county.

TABLE VI

Percent of taxes paid by poorest 30 percent of taxpayers
(*Single freemen excluded*)

	QUANTILE			
	I 1.9–5.3	II 5.4–7.4	III 7.5–8.7	IV 8.8–12.3
Number of townships				
Within 24 miles of Philadelphia	7	6	7	6
Beyond 24 miles of Philadelphia	6	7	6	7
Within 16 miles of Chester	7	6	7	6
Beyond 16 miles of Chester	6	7	6	7

An analysis of soil conditions and topographical features within the county provides some insight into variations in distribution of wealth. Soil and slope conditions throughout the county were favorable generally but were not uniform. The central and south-central area, including the Chester Valley, had the best soils, derived from limestone and crystalline gneisses and schists. The southwest and northern areas were characterized by somewhat steeper slopes, which probably reduced agricultural productivity. Pockets of poor serpentine soil existed in the southwest and east, though these were not widespread. Farmers in the eastern part of the county tilled inherently less fertile soils on the whole than in the central part, but this disadvantage was partially offset by easier access to water transportation and shorter distances to markets. Although precision in these matters is impossible, it is at least credible to point out that in the areas with the best soils, the distribution of wealth was generally less even than in areas where soils were not as good. There are exceptions to this, and soil conditions can, at best, be given only limited significance.

Population density did not correlate clearly with the distribution of wealth. One might expect greater differentiation where the people were more highly concentrated. In 1760 population densities fell off westward from the Delaware River; four townships near the river registered more than forty persons per square mile and in the northwest the most sparsely settled township had about thirteen. But through inspection of Figures I and II and from the discussion above it is apparent that distribution of wealth did not follow the same pattern.

Urbanization was slight in the county by 1760 and so it is difficult to draw conclusions on stratification from Chester (with fewer than 400 persons) and from two other smaller urban places (apart from hamlets). Besides, towns were not distinguished in township lists. On the basis of Chester township containing the town of Chester it would seem that urbanization might lead to greater differentiation, as others, including Main, have suggested for larger cities such as Philadelphia.

The national and religious backgrounds of the settlers may also have some limited importance; but again firm correlations are not warranted. German landowners of Lutheran and Reformed backgrounds predominated in the northern regions of the county, and

Scotch-Irish in the west and southwest, though many English Quakers farmed in that area also. In rough terms, these areas showed the most even wealth distribution. In the south and south-central areas, where many townships showed a high concentration of wealth in the upper stratum, English Quakers were strongly entrenched. In the east, where the distribution of wealth was extremely varied, English of both Quaker and Anglican persuasion and some Scotch-Irish were to be found. It does appear that Quakers were more materially successful than other groups. Those townships with large concentrations of Quakers yielded higher average taxes than elsewhere in the county. This may be explained partly by the Quakers' opportunity, as the first settlers in the area, to choose the most fertile sites. The greater emphasis upon discipline and mutual help displayed by the Quakers may also have been a factor in the greater average wealth and differentiation where they were located.

Perhaps the most important conclusion to be drawn from this blurred, inconsistent, and often confusing picture is that generalizations about social stratification or wealth distribution must be made with great caution. From the evidence presented it can be suggested, but not concluded, that wealth often (though not always) became more concentrated at the top of the social pyramid in areas accessible to water transportation and not distant from commercial centers, particularly if those areas were endowed with rich soils and inhabited by English and Irish Quakers whose presence dated back to the early period of settlement. In newer townships, often settled by non-Quakers and sometimes in areas with less productive soils, society was more likely to have a middling look.

Though the correlates of wealth redistribution, and, more broadly, of social change are not easily susceptible of analysis, perhaps we can suggest some limited hypotheses on the basis of the data presented, recognizing that Chester County may not have been representative of colonial society as a whole. First, since the economic orientation of Chester County underwent no basic changes in the eighteenth century and because a large proportion of the people were strongly moved toward individual achievement of material success (perhaps the best definition of "middle class"), a gradually increasing differentiation of wealth was to be expected.

Given the stable but expanding economy, the open society tended to favor the aggressive and able in their drive toward material self-aggrandizement. Hence, contrary to Grant's conclusions about Kent, Connecticut, differentiation may have continuously increased when opportunities were widely available. As Main points out, the gap between top and bottom was much greater in the cities than in rural areas, reflecting in part greater opportunity in the city for both the accumulation of significant wealth and upward and downward mobility. Following from this, it might be suggested that even if political democracy flourished in the eighteenth century, as Brown implies and Grant states, economic democracy in the form of greater material equality was not necessarily a corollary. That any symbiotic relationship existed between the two, as is assumed so often, is not readily apparent. To be sure, Pennsylvania functioned within a more democratic constitutional framework after 1776 and political participation increased; but neither of these developments, if Chester County can be taken as an example, stemmed from or led toward a more even distribution of the community's resources. Instead, the political and economic processes were moving in opposite directions. The rhetoric of the revolutionary era may have been strongly egalitarian in tone, stressing the rights of all white adult males to participate equally in the political process. But ironically this may have only strengthened the popular feeling that in economic affairs each man should be free to pursue his own ends, even if the result was a redistribution of wealth which favored the well-to-do at the expense of the poor. In this sense, the growth of political and cultural egalitarianism may have been accompanied by, and have indirectly sanctioned, the decline of economic equality. Third, during the era of the Revolution the trend toward greater differentiation, contrary to Main's thesis and most thinking on the subject, was not arrested or reversed but accelerated.

In sum, the experience of more than a century in Chester County seems to suggest that the comparatively open society, operating in a stable pre-industrial economic environment, encumbered with few governmental restraints, and subscribing to a liberal ideology confirmed by the political philosophy of the American Revolution, led to increasing social stratification, at least as measured by the distribution of wealth. Whether this meant more or less "economic democracy" is not easy to say. Only by correlating changes in the distribution of wealth with precise measurements of mobility and long-term economic trends would we be able to advance firm and broad conclusions concerning the transformation which eighteenth-century American society was undergoing.

5

---

unresolved problems
and new directions

It should be evident from the preceding articles that recent historians are attempting to arrive at a deeper understanding of the dynamics of colonial society by treating new sources and applying new concepts borrowed from related social sciences. The observant student will also understand by now that this new work has by no means solved all of the problems concerning internal change in eighteenth-century America. Perhaps more questions have been raised than answered; indeed, asking fresh questions may be the most important contribution of the new work thus far. Many of these unresolved questions and some of the problems concerning the use of data are raised in the preceding chapter, especially in the last two articles. The student of colonial history may want to refer back to these questions as he develops his thinking about the social anatomy of colonial America.

Thus the promise of the new studies in social structure, stressing quantification of previously untapped sources, has sometimes been greater than the actual delivery. But as more data is accumulated and additional micro-studies completed, it is anticipated that we ultimately will acquire the pieces of the jigsaw puzzle that will help form a far more complete and multi-dimensional picture of colonial society than we now possess. When that point is reached, colonial historians will have provided a firm basis for interpreting social change in the nineteenth and twentieth centuries.

The fullest understanding of social process in colonial America will come when social historians are able to integrate studies of social structure with analyses being conducted in related fields. It is essential to understand that studies of social structure, while valuable in themselves, do not realize their full potential until projected against and interleaved with studies of demography, social and geographic mobility, economic history, and historical geography. The achievement of this kind of complex interdisciplinary analysis will probably come first in community studies, which attempt to reconstruct the social and economic life of the entire population in a particular town or county, and then in regional studies built upon an aggregation of local micro-studies. An introduction to recent attempts at this kind of general social analysis on the local level is provided by J. M. Bumsted and J. T. Lemon, "New Approaches to Early American Studies: The Local Community in New England" (*Histoire Sociale/ Social History,* 1 [1968], 98–112).

Demographic studies, already well established in England and France, have only recently taken hold in America. In colonial history a number of historical demographers are gathering and analyzing data on a community level. Philip J. Greven, Jr., a leading exponent in the field, explains that the broad-scale attempt of this work is "to ascertain the complex, often elusive, but exceedingly important interrelationships between patterns of demographic phenomena such as birth rates, marriage ages, family sizes or lifespans, and the variations in land tenure, inheritance patterns, family structure, population mobility, and conditions of health prevalent within various social groups at different times" ("Historical Demography and Colonial America: A Review Article," *William and Mary Quarterly,* Third Series, 24 [1967], 438–54). Valuable demographic studies have been conducted by John Demos on Plymouth, Massachusetts and Bristol, Rhode Island; Philip Greven on Andover, Massachusetts; and Kenneth Lockridge on Dedham, Massachusetts (references are given in the following section, "Further Reading"). All of these studies focus on small New

England towns. We will need additional studies, however, particularly in the middle and southern colonies and in some of the colonial cities, before firm conclusions regarding demographic trends can be reached. But since the study of social structure begins with a study of the family—the smallest social unit in the society—students are well-advised to acquaint themselves with work in this important area.

Social and geographic mobility are also essential areas of concern. Studies of social structure frequently imply and sometimes state a good deal about vertical social mobility, as in Henretta's analysis of Boston. But very few detailed studies of movement up and down the social and economic ladder over extended periods of time in particular communities or areas are available, though Jackson T. Main has provided an overall assessment of mobility in *The Social Structure of Revolutionary America*. Some evidence and many tantalizing clues regarding patterns of geographic mobility are offered in the demographic studies by Demos, Greven and Lockridge, and by Charles C. Grant in his *Democracy in the Connecticut Frontier Town of Kent* (New York, 1961). Yet many critical questions remain unanswered. We have only half-formed notions of how family size, practices of land inheritance (primogeniture and partible inheritance), and long-term economic trends effected geographic mobility; and most of what we know pertains to New England. We have only a superficial, and perhaps mistaken, understanding of the relationship between changes in the distribution of wealth and patterns of vertical mobility. The relative drawing power that the city (as opposed to the frontier) held for ambitious young men of lower class origins, or the poor caught at the bottom of society, is largely unknown. Even the social recruitment of colonial elites, perhaps the least complex kind of social analysis to conduct, has not progressed far enough to allow firm generalizations.

The fields of historical geography and economic history also command the attention of the historian interested in social structure. An excellent introduction to historical geography and its uses for the colonial historian is H. Roy Merrens' article, "Historical Geography and Early American History" (*William and Mary Quarterly,* Third Series, 22 [1965], 529–48). Merrens suggests that strong connections may exist between the variables of soil and weather conditions, technological innovations, ecological developments, and social change in given areas. Work underway in colonial economic history is particularly important since it relates to the crucial question of commercialization. Recent quantitative analyses, as illustrated by William I. Davisson's "Essex County Wealth Trends: Wealth and Economic Growth in Seventeenth-Century Massachusetts" and "Essex County Price Trends: Money and Markets in Seventeenth-Century Massachusetts (*Essex Institute Historical Collections,* 103 [1967], 1–52, 144–85, 291–342), suggests that early American agricultural communities moved from subsistence to commercial farming much earlier than historians have suspected. Before we can generalize confidently we will need to know far more about the changing structure of capital investment in the colonies, the development of new agricultural markets outside the mainland, price trends, and growth of urban centers. All of this is of prime importance because the degree of commercialization, as Main has suggested in his analysis of social classes in the Revolutionary era, may be one of the critical determinants of social structure.

Cross-disciplinary studies of colonial society will attain even greater usefulness when they compel historians to deal comparatively with social change, both on an inter-regional basis within the colonies and on a transatlantic basis between the colonies and the mother country. Already social historians are developing a comparative perspective because quantitative studies have made it evident that regional differences, of varying degrees of significance and involving almost every aspect of social change from landholding patterns to birth rates to the distribution of wealth, are to be found within the American colonies. Similarly, new studies on both sides of the Atlantic have challenged some earlier assumptions about the degree to which emigrating English society was transformed in early America. For example, looking at the studies of rural society in seventeenth- and eighteenth-century England and America, historical demographers seem ready to conclude that there was less geographic mobility and more community stability in the New World than in the Old. Comparative studies may show eventually that the economic leverage wielded by the upper stratum of the population, or its access to higher education, or its entry into the professions was not sufficiently different in England and her colonies by the second half of the eighteenth century to justify the frequent claim that America was an egalitarian paradise. On the other hand, comparative data may ultimately indicate that access into the middle ranges of society and the incidence of poverty were significantly different in the two societies. Whatever the results of comparative research, the essential point is that quantitative studies of English society will provide a basis for assessing social change in colonial America, just as the new research in colonial history will supply essential comparative data for an appreciation of the evolution that transformed America into an industrialized and urbanized society in the nineteenth century.

Students of social structure should be aware of one final pitfall. All quantitative studies, regardless of the sophistication of research techniques or the completeness of the data, must be enlivened by a sensitivity for the social milieu of the area and period under study. Statistics, tables, and graphs can by themselves tell us a great deal about the colonial past. But they achieve their full significance and meaning only when integrated into larger interpretive frameworks built upon an understanding of the values, motivations, and ideology of individuals in a community, province, or region. A classic example of this need to set quantitative analysis in social context is the question of suffrage in colonial Massachusetts. In 1955, Robert E. Brown, a leader in the movement to reinterpret American colonial history by employing new sources and new methods of research, produced impressive new data to show that landholding and the right to vote were far more extensive in colonial Massachusetts than historians previously had believed. For more than a decade thereafter, historians expended enormous time and energy arguing over Brown's book, *Middle-Class Democracy and the Revolution in Massachusetts, 1691–1780* (Ithaca, 1955). For the most part, however, the arguments concerned Brown's sampling techniques and statistical manipulations of the evidence. Only recently has the ethos of the small Massachusetts town—the social context of voting rights and political participation—been closely scrutinized so as to give vital meaning to Brown's statistics. A recent article by Michael Zuckerman, "The Social Context of Democracy in Massachusetts" (*William and Mary Quarterly*, Third Series, 25 [1968], 523–44), should be considered carefully, since it illustrates the importance of integrating quantitative and qualitative data.

Thus, much remains to be done in reinterpreting the structure of early American society and in measuring, quantitatively and qualitatively, the changes it endured during the first century and a half of its existence. A generation of historians coming of age after the Second World War has offered the challenge of a new cross-disciplinary methodology and has begun to apply it with limited results. For historians working in the next few decades remains the task of refining the methodology, employing it on a much broader scale, and synthesizing the piecemeal work now in progress and yet to be done.

6

suggestions for further reading

A number of general surveys dealing with interdisciplinary approaches to social history are available to the student who wants a broad background for his studies of social structure. Among them are J. Jean Hecht, "Social History," and Peter Laslett, "History and the Social Sciences," *International Encyclopedia of the Social Sciences* (17 vols.; New York, 1967), VI, 455–62 and 434–40. Mario S. DePillis has surveyed work in American social history in "Trends in American Social History and the Possibilities of Behavioral Approaches," *Journal of Social History*, I (1967–68), 37–60.

The English and European background is indispensable for social analysis of colonial America. Peter Laslett's *The World We Have Lost* (New York, 1965) provides a general introduction to the seventeenth century. Lawrence Stone's *The Crisis of the Aristocracy* (Oxford, 1964) is a brilliant example of quantitative research set in social context. A number of local studies of Tudor and Stuart English communities will provide the student of American history with a rich perspective, among them Tom Atkinson, *Elizabethan Winchester* (London, 1963); James W. F. Hill, *Tudor and Stuart Lincoln* (Cambridge, 1956); Peter Laslett and John Harrison, "Clayworth and Cogenhoe," in H. E. Bell and R. L. Ollard, eds., *Historical Essays, 1660–1750, presented to David Ogg* (London, 1963); Wallace T. MacCaffrey, *Exeter, 1540–1640; The Growth of an English Town* (Cambridge, Mass., 1958); and William G. Hoskins, *The Midland Peasant; The Economic and Social History of a Leicestershire Village* (London, 1957). Other English studies of importance include W. M. Williams, *Gosforth: The Sociology of an English Village* (Glencoe, Ill., 1956), and *A West Country Village— Ashworthy. Family, kinship and land* (London, 1963); Lawrence Stone, "Social Mobility in England, 1500–1700," *Past and Present*, #33 (1966), 16–55; E. L. Jones, "Agriculture and Economic Growth in England, 1660–1750," and A. H. John, "Agricultural Productivity and Economic Growth in England, 1700–1760" *Journal of Economic History*, 25 (1965), 1–18 and 19–34; G. E. Mingay, *English Landed Society in the Eighteenth Century* (Toronto, 1963); J. Jean Hecht, *Continental and Colonial Servants in Eighteenth-Century England* (Northampton, Mass., 1954); and Hecht, *The Domestic Servant Class in Eighteenth-Century England* (London, 1956). Some of the best work on European social stratification in the seventeenth and eighteenth centuries is reprinted with a critical introduction in Bernard and Elinor G. Barber, *European Social Class: Stability and Change* (New York, 1965).

The best consideration of social stratification, set in historical context, is Bernard Barber, *Social Stratification: A Comparative Analysis of Structure and Process* (New York, 1957). Also valuable are Reinhard Bendix and S. M. Lipset, *Class, Status and Power: A Reader in Social Stratification* (2nd edit.; New York, 1966); and Joseph J. Spengler, "Changes in Income Distribution and Social Stratification: A Note," *American Journal of Sociology*, 59 (1953–54), 247–59. For conceptual treatments of social mobility, students should turn to P. A. Sorokin, *Social and Cultural Mobility* (New York, 1959); S. M. Miller, "Comparative Social Mobility," *Current Sociology*, 9 (1960), 1–61; and Richard Curtis, "Conceptual Problems in Social Mobility," *Sociology and Social Research*, 45 (1961), 387–95. Also helpful is Stephan Thernstrom, "Notes on the Historical Study of Social Mobility," *Comparative Studies in Society and History*, 10 (1968), 162–72.

Empirical studies of social stratification and social mobility range from treatments of colonial society as a whole to studies of individual provinces and single communities. Jackson T. Main's *The Social Structure of Revolutionary America* (Princeton, 1965) is the only treatment of all the colonies but it considers only the period from 1763 to 1788. An interpretive essay on the subject is Robert E. Brown, "Economic Democracy Before the Constitution," *American Quarterly,* 7 (1955), 257–74. Provincial studies, which usually take political behavior as their focus but use analyses of social structure and social mobility as explanatory aids, include Bernard Bailyn, *The New England Merchants in the Seventeenth Century* (Cambridge, Mass., 1955); Robert E. Brown, *Middle-Class Democracy and the Revolution in Massachusetts, 1691–1780* (Ithaca, 1955); Gary B. Nash, *Quakers and Politics; Pennsylvania, 1681–1726* (Princeton, 1968); Thomas J. Wertenbaker, *Patrician and Plebian in Virginia, Or, The Origins and Development of the Social Classes of the Old Dominion* (Charlottesville, 1910); Wertenbaker, *The Planters of Colonial Virginia* (Princeton, 1922); Bernard Bailyn, "Politics and Social Structure in Virginia," in James M. Smith, ed., *Seventeenth-Century America: Essays in Colonial History* (Chapel Hill, 1959); and Robert E. and B. Katherine Brown, *Virginia, 1705–1786: Democracy or Aristocracy?* (East Lansing, 1964).

Community studies include John Demos, *A Little Commonwealth; Family Life in Plymouth Colony* (New York, 1970); Charles S. Grant, *Democracy in the Connecticut Frontier Town of Kent* (New York, 1961); Kenneth Lockridge, *The Evolution of a New England Town: The First Hundred Years* (New York, 1969); Sumner Chilton Powell, *Puritan Village; The Formation of a New England Town* (Middletown, Conn., 1963); Darrett B. Rutman, *Winthrop's Boston: Portrait of a Puritan Town, 1630–1649* (Chapel Hill, 1965); Rutman, *Husbandmen of Plymouth: Farms and Villages in the Old Colony, 1620–1692* (Boston, 1967); and John J. Waters, "Hingham, Massachusetts, 1631–1661: An East Anglian Oligarchy in the New World," *Journal of Social History,* 1 (1967–68), 351–70.

Studies which deal more explicitly with social structure and mobility in colonial America, using both quantitative and non–quantitative analysis, include Mildred Campbell, "Social Origins of Some Early Americans" in Smith, ed., *Seventeenth-Century*

America; Catherine Crary, "The Humble Immigrant and the American Dream: Some Case Histories, 1746–1776," *Mississippi Valley Historical Review,* 46 (1959), 46–66; Eugene Litwack, "Geographic Mobility and Extended Family Cohesion," *American Sociological Review,* 25 (1960), 385–94; Philip J. Greven, Jr., "Old Patterns in the New World: The Distribution of Land in Seventeenth-Century Andover," *Essex Institute Historical Collections,* 101 (1965), 133–48; Donald W. Koch, "Income Distribution and Political Structure in Seventeenth-Century Salem, Massachusetts," *Essex Institute Historical Collections,* 105 (1969), ———; Edward S. Perzel, "Landholding in Ipswich," *Essex Institute Historical Collections,* 104 (1968), 303–28; Eugene Doll, "Social and Economic Organization in Two Pennsylvania German Religious Communities," *American Journal of Sociology,* 57 (1951), 168–77; Willard F. Bliss, "The Rise of Tenancy in Virginia," *Virginia Magazine of History and Biography,* 58 (1950), 427–41; Sigmund Diamond, "From Organization to Society: Virginia in the Seventeenth Century," *American Journal of Sociology,* 63 (1958), 457–75; James High, "The Origins of Maryland's Middle-Class in the Colonial Aristocratic Pattern," *Maryland Historical Magazine,* 57 (1962), 334–45; Aubrey C. Land, "Economic Behavior in a Planting Society: The Eighteenth-Century Chesapeake," *Journal of Southern History,* 33 (1967), 469–85; William A. Reavis, "The Maryland Gentry and Social Mobility, 1637–1676," *William and Mary Quarterly,* Third Series, 14 (1957), 418–28; and V. J. Wyckoff, "The Sizes of Plantations in Seventeenth-Century Maryland," *Maryland Historical Magazine,* 32 (1937), 331–39. Two instructive examples of social structure in neighboring seventeenth-century colonies are Sigmund Diamond, "An Experiment in Feudalism: French Canada in the Seventeenth Century," *William and Mary Quarterly,* Third Series, 18 (1961), 3–34; and Richard S. Dunn, "The Barbados Census of 1680: Profile of the Richest Colony in English America," *William and Mary Quarterly,* Third Series, 26 (1969), 3–30.

Recent work in the historical demography of colonial America is discussed by Philip J. Greven, Jr., "Historical Demography and Colonial America," *William and Mary Quarterly,* Third Series, 24 (1967), 438–53, and more extensively in James H. Cassedy, *Demography in Early America: Beginnings of the Statistical Mind, 1600–1800* (Cambridge, 1969). Students should not miss E. A. Wrigley, ed., *An Introduction to English Historical Demography* (London, 1966) or John T. Krause, "Some Implications of Recent Work in Historical Demography," *Comparative Studies in Society and History,* 1 (1958–59), 164–88. Demographic studies of individual colonial communities are John Demos, "Notes on Life in Plymouth Colony," *William and Mary Quarterly,* Third Series, 22 (1965), 264–86 and "Families in Colonial Bristol, Rhode Island: An Exercise in Historical Demography," *William and Mary Quarterly,* Third Series, 25 (1968), 40–57; Philip J. Greven, Jr., "Family Structure in Seventeenth-Century Andover, Massachusetts," *William and Mary Quarterly,* Third Series, 23 (1966), 234–56; Kenneth Lockridge, "The Population of Dedham, Massachusetts, 1636–1736," *Economic History Review,* Second Series, 19 (1966), 318–44; J. Potter, "The Growth of Population in America, 1700–1860," in D. V. Glass and D. E. C. Eversley, eds., *Population in History: Essays in Historical Demography* (Chicago, 1965); Herbert Moller, "Sex Composition and Correlated Culture Patterns of Colonial America," *William and Mary Quarterly,* Third Series, 2 (1945), 113–53; and Herbert A. Whitney, "Estimating Precensus Populations: A Method Suggested and Applied to the Towns of Rhode Island and Plymouth Colonies in 1689," *Annals of the Association of American Geographers,* 55 (1965), 179–89.

A review of relevant scholarship in historical geography is H. Roy Merrens, "Historical Geography and Early American History," *William and Mary Quarterly,* Third Series, 22 (1965), 529–48. Other particularly valuable works in this area include Erich Isaac, "Kent Island, Part I, The Period of Settlement," and "Kent Island, Part II, Settlement and Land Holding under the Proprietary," *Maryland Historical Magazine,* 52 (1957), 93–119, 210–232; James T. Lemon, "Urbanization and the Development of Eighteenth-Century Southeastern Pennsylvania and Adjacent Delaware," *William and Mary Quarterly,* Third Series, 24 (1967), 501–42; H. Roy Merrens, *Colonial North Carolina in the Eighteenth Century: A Study in Historical Geography* (Chapel Hill, 1964); and F. Grave Morris, "Some Aspects of the Rural Settlement of New England in Colonial Times," in Laurence D. Stamp, *London Essays in Geography* (Cambridge, 1951).

Studies in colonial economic history which bear upon questions of social structure are Stuart Bruchey, *The Roots of American Eco-*

nomic Growth, 1607–1861 (New York, 1965); George R. Taylor, "American Economic Growth before 1840," *Journal of Economic History,* 24 (1964), 427–44; William I. Davisson, "Essex County Wealth Trends: Wealth and Economic Growth in Seventeenth-Century Massachusetts," and "Essex County Price Trends: Money and Markets in Seventeenth-Century Massachusetts," *Essex Institute Historical Collections,* 103 (1967), 1–52, 144–85, 291–342; James T. Lemon, "Household Consumption in Eighteenth-Century America and its Relationship to Productions and Trade: The Situation Among Farmers in Southeastern Pennsylvania," *Agricultural History,* 41 (1967), 59–70; Emory G. Evans, "Planter Indebtedness and the Coming of the Revolution in Virginia," *William and Mary Quarterly,* Third Series, 19 (1962), 511–33; Jacob M. Price, "The Economic Growth of the Chesapeake and the European Market, 1697–1775," *Journal of Economic History,* 24 (1964), 496–511; Samuel M. Rosenblatt, "The Significance of Credit in the Tobacco Consignment Trade: A Study of John Norton & Sons, 1768–1775," *William and Mary Quarterly,* Third Series, 19 (1962), 383–99; James Shepherd, "A Balance of Payments for the Thirteen Colonies, 1768–1772; A Summary," *Journal of Economic History,* 25 (1965), 691–95; and Robert P. Thomas, "A Quantitative Approach to the Study of the Effect of British Imperial Policy upon Colonial Welfare: Some Preliminary Findings," *Journal of Economic History,* 28 (1965), 615–38.

index

Abbot, Samuel, 147
Adams, James Truslow, 27–48, 50
Adams, John, 11, 12
Allen, Ethan, 150
Allen, Henry, 137, 147
American Husbandry, 23–25
American Population before the Federal Census of 1790 (Greene and Harrington), 73
Andros, Edmund, 91
Annals of Pennsylvania, from the Discovery of Delaware, 1609–1682 (Hazard, ed.), 58
Aristocratic titles, 90–91
Arnold, Benedict, 92

Bacon, Nathaniel, 10, 12
Ballard, Joseph, 141
Baltimore Iron Works, 129
Barber, Bernard, 49, 75–89
Barrett, John, 147
Barrett, William, 147
Beard, Charles A., 169
Becker, Carl, 21–22

Bellomont, Gov., 33
Bennett, Richard, 117–18, 129
Benton, J. H. Jr., 73
Berkeley, Gov., 12
Bidwell, P. W., 151
Blackwell, John, 58
Bode, Henry, 93
Boone, Daniel, 150
Bordley, Thomas, 131, 132
Boylston, Zabdiel, 32
Bradbury, Thomas, 93
Brenton, William, 92
Bridenbaugh, Carl, 11
Brown, Jonathan, 147
Brown, Katherine B., 8, 11, 168–70, 187
Brown, Robert E., 8, 11, 161–62, 168–70, 183, 187
Bruce, Philip A., 22
Bulfinch, John, 147
Bulkeley, Edward, 31
Bumsted, John M., 165n
Butler, Joseph, 141
Butler, William, 105

Byrd, William, 37, 127
Byrd, William, II, 118

Cable, George, 137
Cammock, Thomas, 93
Carroll, Charles, 34, 47, 118, 126
Carroll, Charles (Dr.), 132
Carter, Robert, 118
Census records, analysis of, 73–75
Champernowne, Francis, 93
Chauncey, Charles, 90
Chester, Leonard, 93
Chew, Samuel, 132
Church, role in ranking of, 5–6
Cities
    class structure in, 111–14, 133–49
    social stratification in, 185
Class-consciousness, 5
Class struggle, 77
Class structure, economic, 101–7
Cleeve, George, 93
Coddington, William, 99
Coggershall, John, 99
Colden, Cadwallader, 22–23, 32, 33
Cole, William, 96
*Collection of the New-York Historical
    Society,* 23
Commercial farm communities, 109–
    11
    subsistence farm communities and,
    180–82
Coode, John, 10
Cooke, Eben, 121
Cooke, Joseph, 93
Coote, Richard, 91, 94
Cornbury, Lord, 33
Cotton, Joseph, 2
Coursey, Henry, 124
Crafts, William, 147
Creditors, southern planters as, 128–
    29
Crèvecoeur, Michel-Guillaume Jean
    de, 25–27
Culpeper, John, 10
Cutts, Richard, 96

Dale, Thomas, 2
Danforth, Samuel, 93
Davis, Kingsley, 79–80
Davisson, William I., 192
Davy, John, 91
Dawes, Norman H., 89–100

*Democracy in the Connecticutt Fron-
    tier Town of Kent* (Grant), 191
Demographic studies, future, 190–91
Demos, John, 190, 191
Derby, Richard, 113
Deshon, Moses, 147
Dolbeare, Benjamin, 147
Douglas, William, 32
Dress codes for ranking, 6
Duane, James, 102
Dudley, Samuel, 93
Dulany, Daniel, the Elder, 132
Dunkin, John, 94
Dyer, John, 141

Eames, Henry, 137
*Early Census Making in Massachu-
    setts, 1643–1765* (Benton), 73
Easton, Nicholas, 99
Economic history, 191–92
*Economic History of Virginia in the
    Seventeenth Century* (Bruce), 22
Edmunds, Joseph, 141
Education as dimension of social strat-
    ification, 84
Eliot, Jared, 32
Erving John, 134
Esquires, 91–92
Estates, inventory of, 65–73
Ethnic-group position, 85
Evans, Capt., 33

Fairweather, John, 137
Falconer, J. I., 151
Family position, 85
Fenwick, George, 91
Fitzhugh, William, 31
Fletcher, Benjamin, 33
Flint, Henry, 94
Fox, Dixon Ryan, 28
Frary, Theophilus, 137
Frontier, role of, 163

Gale, Ambrose, 100
Garrett, Amos, 132
Gassaway, Nicholas, 124
Gaudonnet, Dr., 32
Gentlemen, 92–94
Goodmen, 95–96
Gookin, Daniel, 90
Goose, Isaac, 137
Gore, John, 147

Grant, Charles, 105, 114, 117, 160–62, 168–69, 179, 187, 191
Greene, Evarts B., 73
Greene, Jon., 90
Greven, Philip, J. Jr., 165*n*, 190, 191

Hagar, Jonathan, 127
Hall, Van Beck, 154*n*
Hamilton, Alexander 3, 11, 31
Hancock, John, 147
Harrington, Virginia D., 73
Harrison, William, 93
Hawley, Joseph, 90
Hayden, Caleb, 147
Hazard, Samuel, 58
Henretta, James A., 133–49, 167, 171, 191
Henry, Patrick, 11
Historical geography, 191–92
History of Agriculture in the Northern United States, 1620–1860 (Bidwell and Falconer), 151
History of American Life (book series), 28
History of Political Parties in the Province of New York (Becker), 21, 27
Hooke, William, 93
Humphrey, John, 90–91, 93
Humphrey, Susan, 90–91
Hutchinson, Edward, 92
Hutchinson, Elisha, 137
Hutchinson, Thomas, 12

Ideology, social science and, 77, 78, 80
Immigration, 17–18
Income as dimension of social stratification, 83–84
International Encyclopedia of Social Sciences, 75
Iron works, 129

Jackson, Joseph, 147
Jefferson, Thomas, 128
Jerauld, Dr., 32
Johnson, Arbella, 90
Johnson, Isaac, 90
Josselyn, Henry, 93
Journal of Economic History, 117
Journal of Social History, 166

Kneeland, John, 147

Knight, Sarah, 35, 39
Knowledge as dimension of social stratification, 84
Knox, Henry, 102
Knox, Thomas, 147

Land
  population density on, 149–66, 176, 185
  prices of, 102–3
Land, Aubrey C., 117–32
Land records, analysis of, 57–63
Lawyers, 130–31
Le Baron, Dr., 32
Leisler, Jacob, 10
Lemon, James T., 166–88, 190
Letters from an American Farmer (Crèvecoeur), 25–27
Leverett, John, 97
Lloyd, David, 31
Lloyd, Edward, 118
Local-community status as dimension of social stratification, 85
Lockridge, Kenneth, 149–66, 190, 191
Logan, James, 57
Louis XIV, King of France, 17
Lucas, Henry, 147
Lyon, Elnathan, 137

Macnemara, Thomas, 132
Madison, James, 3
Main, Jackson T., 100–117, 168–71, 177, 185, 187, 191, 192
Manufacturers, southern planters as, 129–30
Marx, Karl, 49, 76–79
Marxian theory as social stratification theory, 77–78
Maryland Reports, 130
Masters, 94–95
Mather, Cotton, 32, 94, 96
Maverick, Moses, 99–100
Merchants, southern planters as, 127–28
Merrens, H. Roy, 191–92
Middle-Class Democracy and the Revolution in Massachusetts, 1691–1780 (Brown), 193
Mills, John, 105
Mitchell, John, 32
Moore, Wilbert, 79–80
Morison, Samuel E., 97

Nash, Gary B., 166–88, 190
Neale, Francis, 93
Nowell, Increase, 99

Occupational prestige as dimension of social stratification, 82–83
Olson, Albert Laverne, 156
Otis, James, 11, 147
Overpopulation, 149–66

Page, Benjamin, 141
Parsons, Talcott, 79–80
Past and Present (magazine), 149
Penn, William, 5, 17, 57, 58, 176
Pennsylvania Magazine of History and Biography, 52, 63
Phillips, William, 147
Phips, William, 91
Pigneron, Dr., 32
Planters of Colonial Virginia, the (Wertenbaker), 22
Planters, southern, 117–30
  as creditors, 128–29
  as manufacturers, 129–30
  as merchants, 127–28
  as speculators, 126–27
Plastowe, Josias, 100
Porchier, Dr., 32
Power as dimension of social stratification, 82
Preble, Jeremiah, 112
Prestige symbols, titles as, 89–100
Principia Works, 129
Probate records, analysis of, 63–73, 108
Proust, Timothy, 137
Provincial Society, 1690–1763 (J. T. Adams), 27–48
Pye, Edward, 124n
Pynchon, John, 93
Pynchon, William, 93

Ranking, 3–7, 86–87
  dress codes for, 6
  role of church in, 5–6
  titles and, 6–7
Reddan, Thaddeus, 100
Rednape, Joseph, 99
Reed, John, 46
Religious purity, 84–85
Reverends, 97–98
Ritual purity, 84–85
Rust, Henry, 105

Saltonstall, Richard, 91
Saltonstall, Robert, 93
Schlesinger, Arthur, 28
Schuyler, Philip, 105
Scolley, John, 147
Seven Years' War, 11
Slaves, 17–18, 118–25, 141n
Smith, John, 2, 8
Social mobility, 191
  social stratification and, 88–89
Social roles, evolution of, 1–2
Social science, ideology and, 77, 78, 80
Social stratification
  dimensions of, 82–85
    education and knowledge, 84
    family and ethnic position, 85
    income or wealth, 83–84
    local-community status, 85
    occupational prestige, 82–83
    power, 82
    religious and ritual purity, 84–85
  social mobility and, 88–89
  structure of systems of, 87–88
  theories of, 75–82, 168–71
    Marxian, 76–77
    Multidimensional, 79–80
    Trinitarian or Weberian, 78–79
Social Stratification: A Comparative Analysis of Structure and Process (Barber), 75
Social Structure of Revolutionary America (Main), 100–101, 168, 191
Soil conditions, 185, 192
Speculators, 102–3, 104
  southern planters as, 126–27
Spotswood, Alexander, 47
Status inconsistency, 86–87
Stone, Lawrence, 3
Subsistence farm communities, 103–9
  commercial farm communities and, 180–82

Tasker, Benjamin, 132
Tax records, analysis of, 51–56, 104–5, 108–10, 172–88
Temple, Thomas, 91
Titles
  as prestige symbols, 89–100
  ranking and, 6–7
Topographic features, 185
Turell, Daniel, 137

Turner, Frederick Jackson, 163

Urban working class, 141–42

Veblen, Thorstein, 84
Virginia Company, 124
Virginia Reports, 130

Waldo, Benjamin, 147
Wealth as dimension of social stratification, 83–84
Weber, Max, 49, 78–79
Weberian theory as social stratification theory, 78–79
Welles, Thomas, 31, 91, 92
Wendall, Jacob, 102
Wertenbaker, Thomas J., 22
White, William, 147

Whitewell, William, 147
William and Mary Quarterly, 84, 133
Williams, David A., 11
Williams, Roger, 37
Wills, 63–64
Winthrop, Adam, 93
Winthrop, Deane, 93
Winthrop, John, Jr., 91
Winthrop, John, Sr., 5, 93, 96, 99
Wolcott, Roger, 31
Word, Gordon R., 12
Wyllys, George, 93
Wyllys, Samuel, 93

Yeomen, 95–96

Zuckerman, Michael, 193–94